JOHN
ROBE
THE PRICE OF SUCCESS

JOHN FRENCH'S first job was as house manager at the Royal Court Theatre in London. There he worked with Lindsay Anderson, Anthony Page and Bill Gaskill and actors like Paul Scofield, Rachel Roberts, Alan Bates, Diana Dors and Paul Eddington.

A job at a theatrical agency followed. The agency looked after, among others, Sean Connery, Alan Bates, Sheila Hancock, Malcolm McDowell, Robert Shaw and Michael Crawford as well as screenwriters and directors. After three years John founded his own agency and went on to represent Robert Shaw, Julie Walters, Pete Postlethwaite, Zena Walker, Stephanie Beacham and film director Mike Newell.

His own writing includes plays performed at the Soho Theatre, the King's Head, the Battersea Arts Centre and many fringe venues. He has subsequently written over thirty novels (for Little Brown, Headline and Virgin) under various pseudonyms which have sold well over a million copies.

In more recent years he has worked as script editor and writer on the *CSI: Crime Scene Investigation* TV series.

JOHN FRENCH

ROBERT SHAW:
THE PRICE OF SUCCESS

DEAN STREET PRESS

For David Williams, who also died too young and did not believe in heaven, and for my son Sam.

La date la plus importante, dans la vie
   d'un homme, est celle de la mort de son père

George Simenon

You see I have thrown contempt upon your gold,
Not that I want it not, for I do piteously;
In order I will come unto't, and make use on't,
But 'twas not held so precious to begin with . . .

Thomas Middleton/William Rowley
The Changeling

INTRODUCTION

by Richard Freyfuss

ROBERT WAS the largest personality I have ever encountered.

He told the best stories. Like watching Brando do Antony in the 50's with other stars-to-be from the 60's, and all turning to one another silently with a look that said, contrary to all the notices Brando had had flung at him, 'He's genius'.

One afternoon in the sleeping quarters of the Orca, the workboat that was our 'at sea' rest area/equipment holder/ kitchen, as we were waiting through another interminable amount of time for a sailboat to get out of our shot which could sometimes take an hour, Robert, who was in another bunk, jumped up and said 'I know, I'll play the ghost to your Hamlet if you play the Fool to my Lear!'

'You got it!' I answered, 'but not for ten years.'

"Why?" he asked, and I said 'Because you'd blow me out of the water any time sooner, and you know it.'

And he laughed, and laughed, and agreed.

One thing I'm sure of is that he'd lived, we'd have done it together long before this.

He was Big, Brilliant, Boisterous, a work of Art unto himself, like a cross between Beethoven's thunder and Loki's jokes. He terrified me and I loved him. I was his Gunga Din, sometimes to be flayed, sometimes singled out for praise.

He was the most competitive human being ever. Richard Zanuck held up shooting all day once because Robert kept beating Dick at ping pong, and Richard was the producer who let the cost of the day's shoot slide away rather than let Robert beat him.

The day he decided to shoot the story of the SS Indianapolis REALLY drunk, became the longest day of my life, because he couldn't do it; I was in the shot with him, listening. Everyone felt sorry for him; we were all aware that he was aware which made him drink more; finally Steven Spielberg simply waited for Robert to get to the end of a sentence, and called 'Great! Wrap'. That was ten long hours.

That night at 3am, he called Steven Spielberg and said 'How badly did I humiliate myself?'

'Not fatally' Steven replied, and the next day he did the entire monologue in one take.

Brilliantly.

One day I saw him crossing his name off a piece of paper and asked him what it was about. He explained that the play *The Man in the Glass Booth* that he had written had been turned into a film, and the meaning of the play had been distorted, so he was taking his name off it.

I asked what it was about, and two minutes later we were sitting in the hold of the Orca and he was explaining it was the story of a man who was either an Eichmann that the Israelis had kidnapped and brought home for trial, or he was an insane Jew pretending to be a Nazi. I think he read all of the play to me, and then he read all of the finale, a long and terrifying speech that began 'Let me speak to you of love; let me speak to you of the Führer.' Then it concluded with Robert saying his character's final lines right into my eyes: 'Children of Israel – Children of Israel, if he had chosen You, you also would have followed where he led.'

I had been entranced by all of him, the intellect, the courage of what we now call 'the political incorrectness'; the voice, (my God, give me that voice), the art of his prose, and I awoke from that only to realize that the entire crew had been filling the portholes, listening, including Steven, as hypnotized as I. Maybe three hours, thousands of dollars; worth every penny.

He was astonishing in his acting: I thought his Claudius the best and told him and he was childlike with pleasure. No matter that this book says he wasted himself, so did all the others I worshipped that Robert thought were ahead of him: Burton, O'Toole, Harris ...

I complimented him on his Henry VIII in *A Man For All Seasons* for which he had won an Oscar nomination; he cackled like Quint and then he told me that he'd played the part in one day.

In the morning, first, the landing of the king, off the river boat; then the leaving of the king onto the riverboat; then dancing with Vanessa Redgrave; and then the long and enormously dramatic scene with Paul Scofield. Take a look. One day. That's what he said.

On the day I heard he'd died I drove to Steven's house, and found him wordlessly playing the piano; I think I might have tried to speak but he was only sitting and playing, head down. For a long time. I left and drove my Mercedes aimlessly.

I was cheated out of playing his Fool. I miss him, more than even then I knew, because recently I was on an Irish talk show and was introduced to his great grand-daughter, who had never met him, and I burst into uncontrollable tears; I think because a part of me still grieves at what I could have learned, and how spectacular a companion he was.

'Imperious Caesar dead and turned to clay ...'

January, 2015.

Contents

Acknowledgements

The author would like to thank the following for their assistance and patience and memory in the preparation of this book: Mrs G. Tromans, Henry Fowler, Larry Ellis, Diana Sullivan, Robert Hardy, Peter Barkworth, John Gielgud, Philip Broadley, Alex Davion, Alec Guinness, Noel Coleman, Philip Saville, Bob Parrish, Gordon Ryley, Nancy Ryley, Joyce Doggert, Archie Bevan, Edna O'Brien, Lesley Linder, Tom Maschler, Zsuzsi Roboz, Jill Balcon, Leo Lehmann, Ralph Michael, Lew Grade, Sydney Cole and many others, and with special thanks to Ilona Graetz.

The staff of the British Theatre Museum, the Press Association library, and the Directors Guild of America have been most helpful and I would like to offer special thanks to the staff of the British Film Institute Catalogue.

I would like to offer thanks, perhaps most of all, to Nick Hern, who did not laugh at the preposterous idea that an agent might be able to write, and whose attention to detail on the manuscript was both necessary and welcome.

Preface

As a biographer I have been faced with what is a rare, if not unique problem. For the last five years of his life I was Robert Shaw's agent and for three years before that, worked for his then agent as an assistant. In preparing this book, therefore, I was faced with a dilemma. I first met Robert Shaw in Richard Hatton's offices in Curzon Street after his return from appearing in the musical of *Elmer Gantry* on Broadway in 1970. Properly therefore, in the telling of the story, an 'I' should enter the narrative at the half-way point in the book. As this, to my mind, would have been intrusive in the story of someone else's life, there seemed to be only one solution and that was to treat John French like any of the other characters who appear in the book, and use the third person. The introduction of an 'I' would have changed biography into a sort of hybrid autobiography. Hopefully this device will not appear too arch to the reader.

Immediately after Shaw's death, some of the more sensational aspects of this book might well have appealed to the tabloid press. His sudden death was, after all, a good story. I felt, however, that then was not the time to publish. Not only would the more prurient events be taken out of context but such treatment would do nothing to explain and characterise a quite extraordinary man. The main purpose of this book, for me at least, is to explain to those who knew Robert Shaw what had gone wrong in his life and to try, for those who didn't, to bring alive a man whose vivacity, charisma and sheer personality were unique, while documenting how this personality and its undue weight of talent came to such an untimely and unfulfilled end.

April 1993.

Chapter One

It was rumoured in Westhoughton, Lancashire, where Robert Shaw
was born, that his parents had married to prevent scandal and to
legitimise their son. It was not true, but it said a lot about the way the
small town viewed the couple – as racy outsiders. They were certainly
outsiders. Dr Thomas Shaw and Doreen Avery were married in
Truro on 22 April 1926, and their first child Robert Archibald Shaw
was born on 9 August 1927. Thomas Shaw was from the Midlands
where his father had also been a doctor, but the family originated in
Cornwall so it seemed natural for him to gravitate there after he
qualified in 1924. Doreen Avery's father, John Avery, had trained in
the Cornish tin mines as a mining engineer before taking employment
in the iron ore mines of Pigg's Park, Swaziland where Doreen was
born – she was fond of telling people she was the only living 'white
Swazi'. When Doreen decided she wanted to train to become a nurse
(with the intention of returning to Africa once qualified) she, too,
came back to Cornwall and to Truro near to where her sister lived. It
was these circumstances that brought the couple together at the Royal
Cornish Infirmary where they met in 1925.

Doreen was undoubtedly a beautiful young woman. She was tall,
slim and elegant, her straight back reflecting a forthright attitude to
life. Her features suited the large brimmed hats of the period. She had
no intention of being cowed by social convention and openly smoked
in public. She was a conquest that the flamboyant and dashing Dr
Thomas Shaw – a figure straight out of romantic fiction – was keen to
make. It was difficult for any woman to say no to Dr Shaw. He was
athletic, tall and dark and handsome with an immense charm and
apparent love of life that made his company intoxicating. Behind this
charisma, however, and at first well hidden, lurked a complex
character; behind the hail-fellow-well-met with which he greeted the
world was a personality that was to make it increasingly difficult for
him to come to terms with life.

Doreen, after his assiduous courtship, abandoned her plans to
return to Africa, and they were married. Dr Shaw applied to buy
various practices as a General Practitioner and eventually settled on

Westhoughton where a Dr W. D. Hatton had died a few weeks earlier. It might appear that the pastoral and maritime bliss of Truro was a long way from the Northern grime and dark Satanic mills of Westhoughton on the outskirts of Bolton, but, in fact, Westhoughton in 1926 was not a town of Lowryesque factory chimneys belching sulphur into the air. It was pleasantly surrounded by open countryside and sheep farms. It had its cotton mills, like everywhere within the hinterland of the port of Liverpool and Manchester Ship Canal, and it had its coal pits, but they did not dominate the town as they did the more densely populated areas of Lancashire. Nonetheless, West-houghton had suffered one of the worst industrial accidents of the period when the local Pretoria Pit collapsed in 1910 and 344 men and boys (before regulation of child employment) were killed.

As Oakleagh, Dr Hatton's house and surgery was badly in need of redecoration, and in order to keep the practice going while builders were brought in, the Shaws moved into a small terraced property round the corner at 51 King Street. It was the sort of two-up two-down with a back addition and walled yard which had been built all over England to house the workers of the Victorian industrial revolution. At the back of King Street, however, was not another row of houses, but an allotment, a low-growing magnolia tree and open fields.

It was in this house that Robert Shaw was born.

As soon as the builders had finished, the Shaws took up residence in Oakleagh, a large rectangular Victorian house with extensive gardens. With the help of a resident maid and a charwoman they lived comfortably enough and between 1927 and 1932 Doreen gave birth to three more children, Elizabeth, Joanna and finally another boy, Alexander (hereafter called Sandy). Oakleagh in Bolton Road was opposite the local infants' school, the White Horse Infant School, and the pub, the Rose and Crown, a large country-style hostelry not at all like the traditional cramped, corner of a terrace premises of Northern myth and television legend.

Oakleagh had a large front garden and Joyce Ryley, who lived across the road, remembered that sometimes in the summer, the school-teacher would take their class, including Robert, into the garden to have lessons in the sun. The Ryleys had once lived in Oakleagh themselves. Nancy Ryley, Joyce's mother, had been brought up in the house until her father had been killed in a riding accident and their reduced financial circumstances forced them to move into the smaller cottage over the road.

Dr Shaw, she recalls, was a handsome man and a good doctor. His charm made it easy for him to make his patients feel at ease and well cared-for. 'A cold,' he used to say, 'is four days coming, four days with you, and four days going.' When he called on Nancy Ryley's mother, whom he attended regularly into her old age, he always liked to make sure she had a good 'nip' to make her feel better. But the latter was a medicine he was much too fond of himself. Even to Nancy Ryley's untutored eye there was no doubt that Dr Shaw was an alcoholic. He always carried a hip flask – 'for medicinal purposes' – and his visits to the Rose and Crown were many and various. Despite having a good practice he was borrowing money frequently, in an effort to hide from Doreen how much he was spending on drink, and often sat in the pub until he was forced to go home.

On the other hand he had been an athlete and was still a keen rugby player. He played rugby for Bolton Old Boys, as a guest player, and was a keen golfer. Practising his swing on the front lawn of Oakleagh sometimes led to golf balls breaking neighbours' windows, though the good doctor's charm always managed to defuse any acrimony.

Doreen Shaw was less outgoing. Nancy Ryley felt she was a typical Southerner keeping herself to herself, aloof, and not liking the Northern traditional neighbourliness, nosiness and ever-open back doors. But clearly Doreen had her own agenda, coping with her husband's drinking as it got progressively worse, trying to save their marriage and bring up their increasing family. Equally clearly, as pregnancy followed pregnancy, however angry she might be at her husband's behaviour, his persuasive charm overcame any misgivings she might have had as to the wisdom of bringing children into such an unstable marriage.

Robert Shaw was, according to another school friend, a 'wild boy'. Oakleagh had a bay window on the ground floor with a flat narrow ledge on the top accessible by opening the sash window above it on the first floor. At the bottom of Bolton Road was a weaving mill and as the mill-girls came home up the road in their wooden clogs they would be entertained by the sight of the young Shaw wearing his father's top-hat, with his father's walking-stick tucked under his arm, dancing on the narrow ledge. If one of his sisters tried to join him Robert would push them back inside, concerned for their safety but not his own, before continuing the show. Nancy Ryley had said to his father at the time, 'I don't know what's to be done with the boy. He's a born actor.'

In a BBC *Omnibus* on Robert Shaw broadcast in 1970 he was asked about his childhood. A frisson of pain crossed his face at the question, followed by a long pause as he decided how much to reveal. His father, he said finally, he remembered drunk and sober. Sober he was 'flamboyant', drunk he was 'troubled'. He used to come into his son's

3

room, after an evening's drinking and weep hopelessly on his son's bed.

Dr Shaw's alcoholism got no better with the passage of time. It was clear to his wife that something had to be done if his reputation as a doctor and their marriage were to survive. Whatever demon was driving the doctor to drink had to be exorcised; the problem was in identifying its cause. He argued that he needed a new start, somewhere away from the pressures of medicine in an industrial environment, somewhere different, where he could change the whole pattern of his life and thus remove the need to drink. Doreen was far from convinced by this argument but seeing no alternative she agreed. They started looking for a new home.

In 1933 Dr Shaw bought a small practice in Stromness in the Orkney Islands, one of only two in the town, and the family moved into a characteristic stone house overlooking the sea. The climatic difference between Stromness and Westhoughton was marked and clearly made a lasting impression on the young Shaw, as he was to describe it so graphically in his first novel, *The Hiding Place*:

> The clouds hung over his head like the fitted sails of a great armada, swelling and swelling, dropping and dropping, till they almost touched the ground. His mother shouted him into the kitchen closing the doors and windows fast shut. The little boy did not want to come inside, for he had never seen such stillness – the air so dense that the grass was sweating.

The social climate was different too for the young Shaw. In Lancashire he had been very much a part of school life, but at the Stromness Academy he was an outsider with a strange accent. He was a 'ferry-louper'. His developing athletic prowess was snubbed and he was not picked for the school football team. Nor did his father's troubles diminish, the nocturnal visits continued, his father only able to communicate his perception of the world through shuddering and pitiful tears as he knelt by his son's bed, his face buried in the blankets.

The pattern of life established in Westhoughton soon re-asserted itself in Stromness. Dr Shaw was widely respected as a doctor but his drunkenness, in a community that was well versed in drinking, soon became a matter of public concern. With only two thousand inhabitants gossip spread quickly: the practice suffered accordingly.

At home it did not take long for Doreen to realise that hopes of a change were to be short-lived. A series of rows followed. Her husband's pledge to her that he would cut down on his drinking had proved worthless. If anything his consumption had increased. He had

4

a responsibility to his wife and his children yet he was treating them as if they did not exist, as if he simply didn't care. If things didn't improve, Doreen was going to leave, taking the children with her. Things did not. In fact they got so bad that at one stage Doreen moved the children and herself into the local pastor's house in an effort to convince her husband that she was serious. Finally her sister, who had seen Dr Shaw's condition for herself on a visit to Westhoughton, was consulted, and it was decided that Doreen should take the children to live in Cornwall where her sister had a farm. Three years after moving to Stromness she took her family South.

Installed in Treworyan Farm, near Ladock, in Cornwall with her sister and husband, the Cock family, things were very different for the Shaw children. Robert was enrolled at Ladock Church School which his cousins attended. With four adults and seven children, the farmhouse was very crowded. The building did have internal sanitation, but it was decided that the children should use the earth closets dug at the bottom of the garden. This was adjacent to where the pigs were kept, and the children were so convinced that the pigs would burrow through and happily eat their tender white backsides, that they would go to the toilet in twos, no matter what function was to be performed. This may have been the origin of Robert's total lack of inhibition when it came to scatological functions – he was quite likely to invite a friend into the bathroom with him for a talk, while he took a shit.

But Dr Shaw had not given up on his attempts to reform. In 1937 he wrote to Doreen again to tell her he had a job in Keinton Mandeville in Somerset and begging her to join him there with the children. This time, he promised, it would be a new start. He would take his drinking problem seriously, he would take control of his life. Doreen saw no option but to give him another chance, and the family moved into a large family house, which happened to have been the birthplace of Henry Irving a century earlier.

Dr Shaw had not lost his ability to charm his wife, and in 1938 she gave birth to a fifth child, another daughter, Wendy. But his resolution did not last long. He was trapped, torn between his need to drink and his desire to keep his family together. He wanted children, he wanted his wife to have babies, but found it increasingly difficult to cope with them. Robert remembers being bundled into his father's car with his brother and sisters and driven off at breakneck speed through the countryside while his father talked incessantly of things he did not understand. At the Somerset cliffs the doctor would stop, driving the car as near to the edge as he could get. 'Shall I drive us over? Shall I? Shall I?' he'd ask his eldest son. 'End it all? Ah?' It was not a joke, and, according to Robert, it happened on more than one occasion.

That same year, 1938, despite all his elaborate promises to induce Doreen to come back to him, Dr Shaw did 'end it all'. He told his wife, not for the first time, that he was determined to kill himself. She did not believe him, as she had not on all the previous occasions. He went into his surgery and took poison. Robert was 11 years old.

Naturally enough his memory of his father's death was confused. In one version he was at home and heard his father announce his intentions. His mother begged him not to do it in front of the children. In another he was at school, and the Headmaster of Truro School came to call him out of class. The Headmaster had been willing to drive him back to Somerset immediately but Robert had, as he recalled, said he would prefer to remain in class. In fact Robert did not enrol at Truro School until the following year. By the '70s the story was refined still further and Robert recalled his father coming to his bedroom crying – a reprise of early events – and telling him he was going to kill himself 'because I can bear the world no longer'. Gradually Robert had assumed the central role in the story, placing himself alone with his father's despair. A still later version had his father drowning himself; a confusion no doubt with a real incident in Stromness when his father rescued two children from the sea. As Robert got older his feelings towards his father intensified, and they were feelings he found harder and harder to cope with.

From Somerset the family moved back to Cornwall. Using the bulk of her late husband's estate Doreen bought a large house on the main road in Tresillian not too far from Ladock and her sister's farm. The house, covered with Virginia creeper, had a large garden backing on to a water reservoir. At first Shaw returned to the local Ladock Church School but in 1939 his mother, using income from the rest of the estate, and from a lump sum bequeathed by her father on his death, as well as other sums of money made available by the Avery family, decided to send him to the fee-paying Truro School, first as a day boy and eventually as a boarder, for which he was granted a scholarship (which eased the financial pressures on his family).

For Shaw after 1939 and his enrolment at Truro School life was, at last, more settled. He lived in the same house and went to the same school. His athleticism developed and normal childhood pursuits were much in evidence, but there was, to anyone who knew him then, a certain amount of brooding and unpredictability that was unchild-like. 'He was a loner,' Elwyn Thomas, a school friend, would remember.

However, it was from this age that Shaw developed the character-istic that most of his later friends remember best – his competitiveness. Shaw wanted to win. He didn't just like winning, it was essential to him. 'Victory,' he told *T V Times*, 'is utterly consoling to me . . . the nicest way to put it is that I have a colossal curiosity about myself. So when I unearth an aptitude, I want to perfect it into a skill to be proud of.' Equally he hated losing. Both his adult life and his childhood are littered with anecdotes about his competitive instincts and his desire to win. At Truro School he was Junior Victor Ludorum in 1943 and overall Victor Ludorum in 1945. In both years sprinting was the basis of his success.

He did not like defeat. Returning to Treworyan Farm one summer, to help with the harvest, he boasted to one of the farm workers of his prowess in running. Though the man was 20 years his elder he took up the challenge, stripped off his jacket and agreed a circuit along a country road. Though Shaw led from the start gradually the man caught up and, though Shaw was still ahead of him at the finishing line, it was a very close thing. The fact that he had nearly been beaten by a man of 35 produced a look of astonishment on his face that the friends who had been watching would never forget.

At rugby, one of the abiding loves of his life, Shaw was a late developer. He was not picked for the First XV at Truro until he was 17. But from that moment he was an exceptional player, his speed as a sprinter making him a devastating wing-three-quarter. He was good enough to play for Camborne Town, for whom he scored a spectacular try that he would recall as one of the singular achievements of his life. He would always talk about it with unbounded enthusiasm, remembering as he got older more and more detail, embellishing every aspect of the story until the number of hand-offs and dummies he delivered and sold respectively were of epic proportions. The match was between Redruth and Camborne on Boxing Day 1947. Shaw's last account, to the *Evening Standard* in 1977, tells the story:

We were playing up the slope. In those days Redruth was very fashionable, and Camborne was a mixture of Camborne miners and the Camborne School of Miners, from which many Cornishmen have gone round the world. E. K. Scott was the English captain [E. K. Scott played for England but was never captain], and he was playing with Redruth. They had a very fast wing with red hair who was called Grey. They had not been beaten for two years until we'd played them the week before and we had won. Therefore, Redruth were after our blood. It was the local derby.

E. K. Scott cross-kicked. It went a little too far, came behind the dead ball line, and I caught it before it bounced. I had played against the Redruth wing at school, and I knew I could run around him, either inside or outside. I passed him, and Scott was coming across.

I was only seventeen but I had great wisdom about games. I knew that if I handed-off Scott real hard, it would take him about five seconds to recover, and I hit him with my left hand as hard as I could, and he went down, flat!

The stand-off was called Arnold Pascoe, and he came across covering. I knew him because we'd been to the same school. . . We were not mugs. Never beaten in three years. Anyway, Pascoe came across, and to him it was a perfunctory tackle. I didn't even bother to hand him off. I just hit him with my shoulder. He went down flat on his back. The one person I was worried about was the Redruth full back, who was an old miner of about 43 or 44 who had played for England and hit you like a tank. He could break three ribs with a single tackle, so I wasn't going to take a single chance with him. I kicked over his head, and the ref was right up with the play. He couldn't tackle me, I caught it on the bounce, and scored right between the posts.

However much this was an exaggeration of the truth the try was memorable enough to be recorded in the Camborne Centenary Programme of the 1946–47 season:

It was during the season that Robert Shaw who later became internationally famous in the literary and theatrical worlds made his debut while studying at Truro . . . Shaw was a fast and dangerous wing and in Camborne's match at Redruth on Boxing Day 1947 was considered the most outstanding three-quarter. After one Redruth attack he seized on a badly directed kick to his own line and after racing about half the length of the field kicked ahead and re-captured the ball to race over for a spectacular try.

Shaw was capable of working extremely hard. If he was not good at something he worked on it until he was proficient. It was this trait, obviously attractive to his teachers, combined with his athleticism, which no English public school is slow to overlook, that made him a candidate for Head Boy. In this position Shaw gained a certain amount of power, and power that he enjoyed. As he told an interviewer, 'I didn't like school before I was made Head Boy but the power made it palatable.' But in this position he attracted criticism. Colin Nunn, a fellow prefect, remembers Shaw's performance in this 'role' as erratic. On the one hand he was tough, not afraid to shop offenders to the masters; Nunn, himself, being a victim of punishment after Shaw reported him for attending a V.E. night dance without permission and for smoking. On the other hand he would mooch around apparently oblivious to anyone and anything, totally absorbed in a world of his own making, allowing transgressions to pass until suddenly he would snap out of it and immediately criticise a boy for some misdemeanour or other. His lack of consistency was, Nunn felt, a function of his self-absorption.

Shaw was – according to Elwyn Thomas, another school friend of the period – a philosopher, and it was difficult to get close to him. He had no close friends, no best friend. He was moody and suffered from a definite pattern of highs preceded by lows. He cultivated an unapproachfulness. There were undoubtedly depths in Shaw that the other boys saw quite clearly, without being aware of their precise nature.

There was, however, no doubt about his ability as an actor. John Kendall Carpenter, who went on to captain England at rugby, as well as becoming Headmaster of Wellington School and head of the organisation for the Rugby World Cup in 1991, saw Shaw's talent clearly. Being younger than Shaw, Kendall Carpenter was often cast in the female roles opposite him. He remembers the 16-year-old Shaw as Mark Antony in 1943. 'It was a great success. He had a professional command of language. His voice was abrasive but with real power.' In later roles Shaw was even praised for his performances as Peter Pan.

But, for Kendall Carpenter, Shaw's finest performance and his most 'alarming', was in Patrick Hamilton's *The Duke of Darkness* playing Gribaud (the part created by Michael Redgrave in 1942), who, in the third act descends into madness:

> Who am I? Why do you excite yourself sir? I am nothing. I am a thing. I am a table. I am a chair. No. I am a table. That is me. Can you not see that I am a table? Eat your food off me, sir, or you will be hungry.

Shaw was so effective in the part that he positively scared the boys in the audience. Kendall Carpenter felt the madness offered Shaw a freedom to explore areas he was already well aware of. It has long been a truism of psychology that acting is regarded as a therapy for a range of problems and especially as a means of coming to terms with trauma, and Shaw certainly had a well of emotional crises in which to delve.

Whether as a result of his success on the school stage or the feeling of command and pleasure that exercising an obvious talent gave him, by 1944 Shaw's mind was set on becoming an actor, and, he would always add, a writer.

His early abilities as a writer are less well documented mostly due to the exigencies of war and the lack of paper for school magazines. Shaw had started to write in Stromness and his father had encouraged him, particularly impressed by one story he wrote about the survivors of a shipwreck floating in a life-raft being forced, after eating all their supplies, to eat the cook. The fact that it was the cook, the provider of food, who suffered this fate, was crucially important to the impact of the story. Shaw wrote consistently through his boyhood, was praised for essays, and frequently stated his intention to write professionally. But acting was his primary ambition. He was encouraged in it by the master in charge of drama, Cyril Wilkes. Wilkes was the typical left-wing tweed-jacketed, natural teacher encountered by lucky pupils in many English schools. He possessed the ability to inspire and enthuse the right pupil with an attitude towards learning and literature that would last a lifetime: the sort of teacher who creates the impression that learning is a two-way street and that he has as much to learn from his pupils, as his pupils have from him. To the young and impressionable Shaw, in need of a father figure, Wilkes's talent in this regard was particularly beguiling.

But the world was at war, and there were other priorities. In common with many of his contemporaries Shaw desperately wanted to get into the war and win it for the allies. Elwyn Thomas and he discussed their future at length: the first order of business was to join the army and destroy the German War Machine, by this time already beginning to crumble. Only after this small task was accomplished would there be time to think of a career.

And the war was all too real. One morning Shaw and his brother were in their bedroom when they saw a Messerschmidt zeroing in on their house on the main road. The two boys stood at the window fascinated as the plane, unopposed by local anti-aircraft fire, headed towards the house. As it got close enough the pilot fired the guns in both wings before zooming off into the distance. Shaw swore that he could see the pilot's face as he flew by, framed by his helmet and goggles.

Shaw's experience of girls at this point was about on a par with his experience of warfare. He was very close to his sister Joanna (in fact so close his sister Elizabeth would describe their relationship as 'unhealthy') but, as for the rest of womankind, he appeared unimpressed. Florence Christie, a daughter of a friend of Doreen Shaw's, visited the house at Tresillian regularly. Shaw, she states, was 'not romantically inclined'. As he was handsome, in her view, with black curly hair and penetrating blue eyes, girls were keen enough on him, but the interest was not reciprocated. Moreover, there was no shortage of girls as Truro School was housing evacuees from two London girls' schools. But the plethora of choice left Shaw unmoved. It was another trait that was to continue into later life: Shaw was never a womaniser.

The question of Shaw's future career was raised in the family. The British Medical Council ran a scholarship to Epsom College for the sons – not, at that time, for the daughters – of deceased doctors, and, of course, Shaw qualified. Fortunately for him his brother Sandy showed an early interest in matters medical, and any pressure for the eldest son to follow the family business and take up doctoring quickly evaporated when Sandy made his intentions clear.

But Doreen Shaw was ambitious for her children educationally and there was still the question of university. An aunt had left Shaw £400 in trust but had stipulated that it could only be used for entrance to the Royal Academy of Dramatic Art (RADA) if he failed to get into Cambridge. Shaw had already passed Cambridge common entrance at Truro so it looked as though his aunt's money would be applied to a Cambridge degree and not to furthering his acting ambitions. But he had a get-out. Part of the matriculation for an English degree was a special Latin examination. Shaw strode into the exam-room, sat at a desk, took out his pen, did a quick and inaccurate sketch of the invigilator and spent the rest of the allotted time staring at the walls. Thus a university degree was despatched from his life with hardly a thought and, subsequently, no regret.

Before Shaw could think of RADA, and though the war was quite obviously drawing to a close, he was still keen to join the Army. But, despite Shaw's obvious physical fitness and athletic ability, he failed his Army medical. In his lower back two vertebrae were partly fused. He had always suffered – and would always suffer – from a nagging back pain, and this was the cause. It did not stop him sprinting, or scoring memorable tries, but it did put an end to dreams of a glorious military career. It also explained the extraordinary loping gait he affected throughout his life, one shoulder up, one dipping down, rolling on the balls of his feet with his body swaying to one side as he moved forward.

The medical shattered another dream for Shaw. Playing and competing, as he was, with current and future England rugby players, Shaw had imagined, not at all fondly, that he would one day be in the running for an England rugby shirt. With a definitive medical problem, however, there was no way that the Rugby Football Union would ever consider him for the English side.

It was a hard knock, which he brushed off with his usual ability to sublimate rather than face pain; but not being able to win, not being able to impose his will on the world, was, for him, the most difficult thing to come to terms with.

By this time it was the summer of 1945 and Shaw was 18. Even if he was accepted for RADA he could not begin until September 1946. His mother, living on investment income and working as a part-time nurse, with four children still in private education, was in no position to support a healthy strapping lad, so he applied for a job as a junior teacher at a private preparatory school in Saltburn, Yorkshire, where he lived in digs, taught English and games, prepared himself for his RADA audition and realised he was not cut out to be a teacher.

Getting into RADA would be difficult. In the intake of 1946 there would be men returning from the services who had had their education interrupted by the war, and were entitled, by right, to claim the places at educational establishments that they had gained before the call-up. This reduced the number of available places significantly and competition, for RADA in particular, was fierce.

Bearing in mind the success he had achieved with Mark Antony at school it was an obvious choice for an audition piece (a Shakespearean role was compulsory). For his 'modern speech' he selected Professor Higgins as a contrast.

As is often the case when provincial talent is tested against nationwide field, what was regarded locally as first class can come to be seen as only mediocre. Shaw's audition for RADA was not a success. He was accepted, but only just.

At the age of 19 in September 1946 Shaw took up his place. He had been the Chairman of Toc H at Truro School and through that organisation was given a place in their Fitzroy Square hostel. Toc H itself was a charity bent on bringing together people of different backgrounds and providing practical help in the community. At that time it was a large organisation with hostels all over Britain. The accommodation was free but the quid pro quo was to engage in voluntary work in the area. At that time Fitzroy Square Toc H was involved with a project in the slums of Whitechapel where German bombs had made an already chronic situation a great deal worse. Shaw spent weekends cleaning and painting renovated housing, his first experience of living conditions among the poor.

Cyril Wilkes had imparted his left-wing leanings to Shaw, and it was an attitude that would stay with him all his life. Though his mother had made him conscious of his social standing and did not like him playing with the 'common' children, Shaw never took her snobbery to heart.

In the '60s Shaw returned to Ladock Church School, where, after all, he had spent only a short time, to open their centenary fête. He returned to Truro School too, when Elwyn Thomas, by then chairman of the Old Boys, invited him down. On both occasions he was full of charm and chat, generous in his praise, accurate in his memory of faces, reminiscing freely, genuinely interested in the fortunes of his contemporaries. His affection for this period of his life was obvious for all to see. He took his first wife, Jennifer, to Cornwall in the '50s and to the Orkneys and repeated these trips in the '60s with Mary Ure. As his life became more complex his desire to recall the past did not diminish. In fact the past became almost too real.

It is axiomatic that an unhappy and traumatic childhood leaves deep scars; the past appears very much alive, very much part of the present. As Shaw got older his dreams – particularly his nightmares – and memories of his childhood became ever more vivid, ever more part of his present life. The looming figure of his father, and the image of his father's suicide, came to be with him part of the landscape of the day. As the pattern of successive highs and lows that had already been noticed at school become more insistent, as the lows got lower and the highs more difficult to attain under the depressive influence of alcohol, the hurts of his childhood festered and grew. On the positive side, they would inform his writing, giving it a depth and perception of mortality; on the negative, they were, in combination with 'the slings and arrows of outrageous fortune', to create a psychological profile that he found almost impossible to deal with.

Chapter Two

The RADA of 1946, in common with the rest of London, was austere. For those who didn't experience it directly, it is difficult to imagine the extent of the bomb damage that had laid waste huge areas of the city and the slowness with which life was returning to normal. With rationing and conscription still in force and England dependent on American Marshall Aid to retrieve the economy from the brink of disaster, austerity was the order of the day. On the other hand there was a feeling of tremendous hope and vitality, a desire to make sure another war never happened again and a realisation that, with the development and use of the atom bomb, this sentiment would never be an empty echo of the aftermath of the 1914–18 war.

The victory of Clement Attlee in the 1945 election gave the young socialists, among whom Robert Shaw counted himself a member, cause for real hope and enthusiasm. At last a social charter was to be enacted that would give genuine rights to the poor. Shaw, of course, did not yet have the vote (the voting age was then 21) but talked excitedly of the opportunities that lay ahead for the Labour Government. Though he had lived in what he subsequently described as 'genteel poverty', his 'poverty' had little in common with the deprivation he would see on the streets of London and on his forays into Whitechapel. In every sense Shaw was middle-class. He had gone to a public school and lived in a large 'posh' house. But this did not mean he was not deeply affected by the poverty he saw. Shaw would always describe himself as a socialist. He would argue the socialist corner on television chat shows, and his subsequent wealth would not change his attitude. Indeed one of the causes of his later unease was his desire to reconcile his socialist principles with his new wealth. But socialism for him was an expression of an attitude towards people as well as a political philosophy. Shaw regarded everyone as equal. He had no time for titles, rank or seniority, whether earned or inherited. To Shaw an Irish gardener was as interesting and worthy as a captain of industry or an important writer. They would be treated the same no matter what they had done, or how much they earned.

The administrative secretary at RADA made some attempt to

brighten the greyness of austerity by introducing a Rainbow Corner. By the main entrance she had set up a series of self-standing noticeboards detailing timetables of lessons and classes in bright primary colours. At this point RADA's only theatre was in the basement (the theatre in Malet Street was as yet a bombsite), and public shows were given at the St James's Theatre in the West End.

Shaw was, for the first time, a small fish in a big pond, and he found the adjustment hard to make. As Head Boy at Truro School he had been the natural centre of attraction, but now he was just another ambulatory student. His reaction was predictable, he was aggressive and uncooperative. He cast himself in the role of outsider. He despised the teaching methods and the organisation of RADA, describing it later as a concentration camp. It was a reaction conditioned by his inability to 'win'.

Movement classes, when the wearing of black tights was obligatory, were hardly likely to attract Shaw who was blessed with notoriously knobbly knees. The technique classes of Fabia Drake were more to his taste. Reading some dull piece of prose, and making it in turn charming, passionate, dramatic, was a game he could enjoy. Equally, delivering Hamlet's 'Speak the speech I pray you . . .' using only five gestures, was something very much to his taste. Other than this his contempt for the teaching was in direct proportion to the length of time it took RADA to recognise his talent. None of his parts in December 1946 or March 1947 were more than 'spear-carriers' (with or without spears) and by July he was still being cast in minor roles – Cameron and Dr Coutts in *A Sleeping Clergyman* and Macduff in *Macbeth*. Things improved slightly by December when he was cast as Don Pedro and Benedick in *Much Ado*. But the comments on his performances during the year were not encouraging. He was criticised extensively. A 'light nasal and high tone voice' was noted, along with the need to beware of 'voice mannerisms' and to 'see to his hair'. Comments like 'promising' and 'good attack' were hardly enough to appease his desire for success.

In a sense, of course, Shaw was not what has come to be called a RADA actor, especially not the RADA of 1947. He had a Cornish burr to his voice – which RADA worked hard to eliminate – and his back problem combined with his comparative shortness (he was 5ft 10in though he would never admit it) gave him an ungainly awkward appearance. Michael Denison he was not. In a world where the common topic of conversation was whether the acting styles of Gielgud or Olivier were to be preferred, the untutored energy and charisma of Shaw counted for little, initially. In terms of ability too, he had a great deal of competition. Among his contemporaries were many who would become successful actors: Laurence Harvey, John Neville, Edward Woodward and Barbara Jefford.

Another problem for Shaw was that the students at RADA divided into those who had been in the war and had been demobbed and those, like himself, who were too young and had come straight from school. Stories of wartime experiences made good listening in comparison to boyish pranks. And Shaw was never a good listener.

Peter Barkworth was also a fellow student and one who actively disliked Shaw's sullen and sneering behaviour. 'I thought he was arrogant and boastful and too like a peacock: he paraded himself in front of us and swaggered.' But Shaw's view of Barkworth was less hostile and at the end of class one day he suggested they go to the movies together. 'The idea of an evening with Robert was appalling,' Barkworth recalled, but he couldn't think of an excuse fast enough and off they went. It says much for the film *Les Enfants du Paradis* that, over coffee afterwards, their common enjoyment of the film turned to mutual respect and friendship.

Not long after, Strowan Robertson, a friend of Barkworth's at RADA, was vacating his flat and suggested that the new-found friends should take it over. He did not need to ask twice. The Basement Flat, 66 Regent's Park Road at the bottom of Primrose Hill cost the two young men 3 guineas a week.

For Shaw it was a positive step. Toc H was very much part of school life in Truro and not living with other actors had an isolating effect. Now he had a place of his own and could feel, through Barkworth, more connected.

Shaw was a good flatmate. The flat was spartan with little furniture, an old sofa and armchair, a dining table and chairs. The two went shopping together in Camden Market and would cook meals in the tiny kitchen. Shaw read a great deal and wrote a great deal, filling notebooks with poetry. He read Yeats and Eliot but singular praise was reserved for Auden whose attitudes heavily influence Shaw's literary efforts and his 'quest' for a stance in relation to life. Auden's basic belief that man is a religious animal – in the widest sense – and his attempt to reconcile this with socialism, his positioning of himself vis-à-vis life ('All I have is a voice') and his opposition to Fascism ('The best reason I have for opposing Fascism is that at school I lived in a Fascist state') were all themes that would occupy Shaw.

On Barkworth's birthday Shaw gave him a copy of Gertrude Stein's *Three Lives* in which he had inscribed a pastiche of an Auden poem:

> So I need not wish you
> Any sense of theatre

Two

Those who love illusion
Know it will go far
Never spend your shillings
On a silly picture,
What we never say and do
And who we never are.

You have known for hours
The simple revelation
'Why we're all like people
Acting in a play.'
And will utter, Peter
Man's unique temptation
Precisely centre-curtain
A technical cliché.

Remember if you're able
Only the author can
Change the lines and
Give you the lead
A silly sort of statement
Is wisest in the night, what
You cannot get away with
You have no need.

What else shall I wish you?
Shall I wish you marriage
Shall I wish you lovers,
money, happiness?
No! for Mr Auden
Recalls an ancient proverb
'Nothing' he says so
'Fails like success.'

I'm not such an idiot
As to claim the power
To peer into the future
To see how tall the lights
I'm prepared to guess you
Sleep best in the day-time
Work most every evening
And great long nights.

If I've ever known you
May you all your troubles
Carry in a suitcase

In a normal way.
Balance on the tightrope
Cleverly combining
Gusto and intelligence,
Night and day.

I can think of other things
But you understand me
I must learn my part
Bring these verses to a close.
Happy Birthday Peter
Live above your income
Travel for enjoyment
Follow your own nose.

Barkworth's enduring memory of Shaw is perhaps unexpected. On summer days they would go over to the steep banks of Primrose Hill and lie in the sun. Barkworth remembers Shaw lying on his stomach on the grass supporting himself on one elbow while he worked out a poem in an exercise book in front of his chin. To Shaw, he felt, this represented total contentment. It was true. Over and over again Shaw would speak of the pleasure of writing; a physical pleasure and a spiritual one – 'though one cannot always/ Remember exactly why one has been happy,/ There is no forgetting that one was.' ('Goodbye to the Mezzogiorno' by W.H. Auden, a poem he loved to read aloud.)

Another snapshot of Shaw at this period conforms better to expectation. Philip Broadley, another RADA student (later to become known as a television writer rather than as an actor), was living in a flat in which he had set up a three-quarter-size table-tennis table he had been given. Shaw got to know of this and out of the blue one night turned up at Broadley's front door asking for a game. Broadley was an experienced player and beat him. The table was riddled with woodworm and every time a hard point was scored wood dust showered on to the floor and bits would fly off the table. They played again. Broadley beat Shaw again. They played again with the same result. Shaw went home. The next night, equally unexpectedly, Shaw turned up. Could they have another game? He was beaten conclusively again. Over the next weeks Shaw visited Broadley over and over again. Gradually the beatings were less conclusive. Then Shaw won. It was the beginning of an important friendship in Shaw's life. It was amazing that the table-tennis table survived its inception.

These two images of Shaw, the quiet contented writer and the aggressive never-say-die competitor with the overweening desire to win, are echoes of the schoolboy: the moody self-absorbed loner as opposed to the Victor Ludorum winner and First XV rugby player. They were contradictions in personality that would run all the way through Robert Shaw's life: the quietness always connected to writing, the competitiveness becoming attached to his acting career. They were contradictions he was never able to resolve.

Whether by virtue of his friendships and domestic situation and integrating more into the society of RADA life – no longer protecting himself by playing the outsider – or whether because tutors had begun to appreciate what Shaw had to offer as an actor, his stock in the school was beginning to rise. In February 1948 he was cast as Addlesham in *This Woman Business* and was commended for being 'breezy and expressive'. In March his David Choirmaster in *The Witch* was done 'very well' and by the time of his final assessment in October 1948 the praise was almost fulsome:

> He has shown signs of brilliance in some of his performances, which are inclined to be uneven . . . He is the kind of personality who might become remarkable in the professional theatre.

The use of the word 'personality' rather than 'talent' says more about RADA than it does about Shaw.

Peter Barkworth was less encouraging. Two people, Shaw used to tell his friends, had advised him to give up acting and avoid the disappointment of failure. Cy Endfield (the director of *Zulu*) and Peter Barkworth.

In discussion with his mother and aunt, Shaw had decided to take the London University Diploma of Dramatic Art. Shaw's family had no experience of the life of an actor but imagined, rightly, that it could be extremely precarious. The Diploma was at least a qualification that would allow Shaw to teach and would therefore give him something to fall back on. Among the other students at the time only Peter Barkworth, by coincidence, took the Diploma. Both of them passed. Clifford Turner, who judged the spoken reading, felt Shaw had a 'declamatory style, but it's better to over-colour than be colourless.' 'Colourless' was never going to be a description that would fit Robert Shaw.

Nor were his opinions pallid. Before leaving RADA Peter Barkworth had got a job at the Intimate Theatre, Palmers Green, playing Young Woodley for director David Garth. Shaw came to see the play and did not hesitate to express his unwavering criticism, delivering an indictment not only of Barkworth and the play but of the whole system. Barkworth and the 'rest of the cast' were using 'a bucketful of clichés' to convey character. 'I suppose dogmatic methods are essential in this ghastly business of weekly rep.' The play was overall 'too acted'. Shaw, whatever else RADA had given him, had a well-established idea of what acting should be and what it should not be, by the time he left.

Behind Shaw's bluff hectoring exterior there was a fine mind. He knew what represented his best interest. When Philip Broadley tried to talk him out of the part of Hercules in the Sophocles play, because he thought the costume of hard leather armour, moulded to the chest, would make a very definite impact, Shaw politely but firmly refused. 'No boy, I think we'll stay as we are, boy.' ('Boy' was to remain his favoured and often-used diminutive.)

But it had greater, more altruistic depths. Shaw was interested in religion and metaphysics. He was concerned about religion because, like Camus and Auden, he believed man to be a deeply religious animal. Religion was an attempt to place man in a context of some greater order; an attempt that, owing to the widespread loss of faith, seemed to have failed. Socialism and humanism were, for him, statements of a religious belief. But he was vehemently opposed to organised religion and found the rituals of the church abhorrent to him. Unlike his hero Auden, Shaw would not embrace Christianity. He was braver, leaving specific instructions that he should not be given a Christian funeral.

With women the young Shaw was very much as he had been as a schoolboy. He regarded them with curiosity but generally speaking they were more interested in him than he in them. He had a succession of girlfriends, the most important of which were Barbara Jefford, who shared the Cornish heritage, and Sally Viner, a 'big bosomy girl' (who later, as Sally Oppenheimer, became Consumer Affairs Minister in Mrs Thatcher's government), but the friendships from RADA that remained with him his entire life were all male. Shaw could be himself with another man, except, as Philip Broadley pointed out, he would never show even a hint of vulnerability. But in the presence of a woman Shaw started to perform. It was either a witty, charming, disarming seductive performance or an attempt to shock by crudity or rudeness, depending on the result he wanted to achieve. Whichever role he played it indicated his uneasiness with women, at least in public. That is not to say Shaw wasn't good company to a woman, but he was ultimately a man's man. He liked men. He said he liked women too, but the truth was that he loved women, occasionally lusted for women but did not really understand them nor make a true friendship with one. He never created a major female character in any of his books or plays. The only apparent exception was to be Susan Thistlewood in *Cato Street*, but she was originally a male character whose name he changed to a woman's for various, and some would say dubious, reasons. His female characters are well-drawn, and sometimes, like Mrs Calvin in *The Flag*, moving, but they are all subsidiary to the men.

Clearly this uneasiness devolved from his relationship with his mother. Shaw was always fulsome in his praise of her and his respect for her. But Doreen Shaw had her own problems and her own life to cope with. She dealt with her husband's suicide with icy stoicism (and a degree of self-delusion: according to Shaw she always claimed it was, in fact, an accident). Thomas Shaw had manipulated her into having one child after another. No one was going to use her like that again. The wall of defences she built around herself was formidable. Everyone who met her subsequently described her in the same vein as 'tough', 'independent', 'self-contained'. She 'had her own memories and intended to keep them her own'.

In later years she never seemed to enjoy her son's success: it was as if, in withholding her praise and approval, she did not want to post a hostage to fortune. She anticipated the inevitable – that it would be for nothing. She never let her son feel that what he was doing was valuable or even acceptable. In her 60s she returned to Africa to teach, living her own life on her own terms. The rest was too painful. Shaw gave her money regularly but she never asked for it and never referred to it. In 1970 Shaw said in an interview that he would never say or 'write about my childhood until my mother is dead'. He said nothing about her that was not a description of her character. 'She was a puritan in the true sense of the word.' He did not live to write about his childhood. It was not any vestige of puritanism that shaped Shaw's attitude to drink; in the past he regarded it in much the same way as he regarded women. It was a subject of interest to him but a matter of no great passion. During his years at RADA no one has any recollection of Shaw drinking. With Broadley he hardly drank at all and with Barkworth it was just the odd glass of wine: 'Nobody could afford to drink.'

Shaw graduated from RADA in the summer of 1949 and was thrown on to the employment market in common with 200 other actors that year. He had no doubt about his ability as an actor and no doubt that he would succeed. But the opportunity to show what he could offer was not going to be easy to come by. He started writing letters to reps, reading *The Stage*, and going for any auditions he could get. A letter to Stratford Memorial Theatre, where another friend from RADA, Alex Davion, had already been working for a year, brought a chance to audition for what was probably the most prestigious theatre company in England at that time, not excluding the work being done at the Old Vic.

Anthony Quayle had taken over sole directorship of Stratford in 1948. His enthusiasm and charm, his ability to appeal to actors' moral rather than financial sense, his natural leadership qualities, and his quite enormous delight in what he was doing enabled Quayle to establish a theatre company that would dominate the rest of the 20th century. By the time Peter Hall took over in 1961 (changing the name of the troupe to The Royal Shakespeare Company) major actors did not need convincing that Stratford was no longer part of the 'provinces' in theatrical terms, and indeed several major actors had been nurtured in the theatre itself. In effect, Quayle took what was a provincial repertory company, with provincial funding, in a poorly designed and ugly building ('the jam factory' was Michael Redgrave's epithet) and thrust it on to the national and international stage. It became central to the theatre in England. He persuaded John Gielgud, Peggy Ashcroft, Jack Hawkins, Michael Redgrave, Margaret Leighton, Laurence Olivier and Ralph Richardson to work for little more than standard repertory salaries. He enlisted Tyrone Guthrie and Glen Byam Shaw, Peter Brook and Gielgud as his directors as well as himself. He brought on the talents of Laurence Harvey, Donald Pleasence, Robert Hardy and Richard Burton and for the first time – surprisingly, considering the publicity surrounding later efforts – conceived the idea of doing Shakespeare's History Plays as a full cycle in chronological order.

To Quayle can also be credited, if a point is stretched, the responsibility for setting up the English Stage Company at the Royal Court, since it was he who asked George Devine – who had been working with Michel Saint-Denis and Glen Byam Shaw at the Phoenix Theatre Company before the war – to look for a London base for the company in Stratford. George found the Royal Court but decided he wanted to start a company there for himself.

Robert Shaw was auditioned by Michael Langham, an associate director at Stratford, and was told on the spot that he would be given a contract for the 1949–50 season starting in September on a 'play as cast' contract: in other words, with no named parts. He would receive £6 per week rising to £9 if he were invited back for a second season. It was the start that Shaw had confidently expected. He was on his way. There was no question in his mind that he would make a significant impact on Stratford.

His first appearance on stage in the professional theatre was as Angus in Godfrey Tearle's *Macbeth*, directed by Anthony Quayle:

We are sent/To give thee from our royal master thanks,/ Only to herald thee into his sight/Not pay thee.

As Jupiter in *Cymbeline* his body was covered with gold paint which took several tubs of make-up remover to clean off, before he went home – often before the curtain call – a minor act of rebellion that would not have gone unnoticed. Suffolk in *Henry VIII* directed by Guthrie, was his third named part in the season, though he 'walked-on' in crowd scenes in all the productions. They were not the range of parts Shaw had imagined his talent would evoke.

Stratford was a big company and Shaw had his friend Alex Davion to ease him into the social scene. As with RADA, the company was divided between those who had served in the war and those who had missed it, though there was no sense of resentment among the former, no sense that the young had not done their duty.

Among those who had fought were Quayle himself and a young actor who had just been demobbed from the RAF, Robert Hardy. Hardy and Shaw became friends and both were confirmed for the next season starting in February 1950. Meantime Shaw toured Australia with the company in the same line of parts. It was his first trip abroad.

Back in Stratford, Hardy and Shaw rented a cottage in Wilmcote, a four-mile bike-ride into Stratford. Shaw, naturally enough, never wanted to dawdle on the ride in, but challenged Hardy to race. As with Peter Barkworth in Primrose Hill, a comfortable pattern of life was established. Shaw would share the household chores and specialised in cooking stews, while Hardy would produce the curries. Occasionally, when they could afford it, the meal would include a bottle of wine, but generally speaking the fare was not lavish. Hardy's mother, knowing things were tight, bought them a whole ham to cook. A dinner party was arranged to consume her largess but unfortunately neither man had any idea how long such a big piece of meat would take to cook. They left it in the oven so long it caught fire and so, in turn, did the oven and the kitchen. Hardy's mother was obliged to pay for the damages. She never bought them another ham.

Shaw would give Hardy endless advice on what to do with and how to handle his girlfriends: 'You see what you've got to do boy, is treat them . . .' He, for one, clearly followed his own advice as Hardy remembers a succession of Shaw's girlfriends, where he had none. But Shaw's amorous conquests – he had apparently discovered that women had one distinct advantage over men – and his energetic playfulness – like a young St Bernard dog always wanting to play but knocking everyone down in the process, one member of the company recalled – did not prevent him from sliding into depression. His moroseness was always accompanied by talk of his father.

The disappointment with which he greeted his line of parts in the second season was marked. He put it down to his own personality. He was too naive, he didn't understand, or was not prepared to play, the games that would get him on in the company, so he said. As usual, 'losing' did not improve his demeanour. As he later told a journalist, 'I hadn't got the gift of charm like Burton, so I felt my individuality was being stifled and I supposed I showed my resentment.' He did.

As the Messenger in *Julius Caesar*, however, he impressed Harold Hobson, who wrote that he was a young actor 'of considerable force'. (Hobson's liking for Shaw would follow him through his career in both his acting and his writing.) He played the Duke of Burgundy in Gielgud's *King Lear*, which Gielgud directed himself, but was cast only as a Page in *Much Ado*, which Gielgud was also directing. Fortunately for his temper, during rehearsals the actor playing Conrad was fired and Shaw was given his most substantial part so far, as the villainous servant.

Though Shaw was heavily discontented with the run of parts he was playing, he was undoubtedly making an impact on his fellow professionals. Few people who saw him in that season failed to remember him in what, after all, were very small parts. Zena Walker, for instance, a friend of Alex Davion's (who was later to play Juliet to Laurence Harvey's Romeo and Miranda to Ralph Richardson's Prospero at Stratford), remembers him in Peter Brook's production of *Measure for Measure*. As he knelt in front of Mistress Overdone, his hands clutching at her thighs he delivered the line:

'How now? Which of your hips has the most profound sciatica?' as though 'sciatica' was the direct result of sexual activity and was only to be cured by further lascivious massage.

Sybil Burton, Richard's wife, has an equally vivid memory of Shaw in a crowd scene at Stratford during the period. 'There was something about his presence that made it impossible for you to take your eyes off him. You could pick him out instantly in any crowd.'

It was Shaw's role in *Much Ado* that was to get him noticed professionally in the most helpful way. Alec Guinness saw his performance and came backstage afterwards to see him. Alex Davion, who shared a dressing room with Shaw, remembers the tentative knock at the door and Shaw's imperious cry of 'Enter!' Shaw sat with his feet up on the make-up table swinging to and fro on the back legs of an upright chair, as Alec Guinness shuffled in.

'Alec Guinness,' Guinness said shyly.

Shaw made no attempt to get up or take his feet off the table, or make any other form of obsequious gesture.

'I'd like you to be in my *Hamlet*,' he continued.

For a senior actor like Guinness to come round personally to make an offer to a young unknown actor was an unheard-of honour. Shaw was not impressed. He swung further back on his chair looking at Guinness only in the dressing room mirror.

'What part?'

'Er, I thought Rosencrantz.'

'How much?'

Whether through Guinness's astonishment at being treated so cavalierly or his regard for Shaw's self-possession, it was evident that Guinness became taken with Shaw. When the producer came to negotiate the salary, it was clear that he had been told by Guinness that Shaw was a must. Again Shaw behaved not at all like a grateful young actor only too glad to get his first part in the West End but more as if they should be grateful to him. 'What we do,' Shaw suggested 'is you write what you want to pay and I'll write what I think I'm worth and we'll split the difference.' Given Guinness's insistence, the producer had little choice and Shaw got the unheard-of salary of £20 a week.

Hamlet started rehearsing in London in April with Guinness directing himself. It was a disastrous production. The designer Marianon Andreu was so busy with other commitments he was unable to attend any production meetings with the result that the doorways in the sets he had designed were not big enough to accommodate the actors in full costume. When it opened on 17 May 1951 at the New Theatre the lighting board jammed on the first lighting cue and the rest of the play was performed with the stark overhead 'working lights' and no lighting changes of any sort, a particular problem in a play featuring a ghost. Shaw made Rosencrantz a villainous figure, playing the part with a black eye-patch.

Hamlet closed after discouraging reviews and Shaw was out of work again. From the poems he had written at RADA his writing had graduated to verse plays, in common with many aspiring writers of the period (John Osborne admits to writing two). In the early '50s verse drama was regarded as the way forward. Not only was it successful – Christopher Fry's *A Phoenix Too Frequent* with Paul Schofield and *The Lady's Not For Burning* with John Gielgud had both scored significantly with the public – but it offered an opportunity to write a play that signified its serious intent by virtue of its form. There was a feeling that there was an audience who were more literate and who were prepared to go to the theatre for more than entertainment, a feeling confirmed by the numerous Shakespearean productions in the West End at the time, and later exploited by George Devine's policies at the Royal Court. With his passion for poetry, Shaw obviously felt that this in combination with his theatrical experience made verse drama a natural form for his writing talent. Between 1951 and the publication of his first novel, *The Hiding Place*, in 1959, he would admit to writing 15 verse plays, though he was prone to exaggeration. There were certainly a good few, however, and friends were frequently invited round to hear a reading of the latest effort. All felt they were interminable.

Guinness persisted in his regard for Shaw, and became something of a father figure. Shaw visited his house on several occasions. During these visits Shaw's mood was often sullen, when he was not affecting a sort of manic optimism in his ability to succeed. It was natural that with Guinness he should talk of his father and his father's suicide. He told the story of how he had informed the Headmaster he would rather stay in class than be driven home to his family, the distortions of the truth already evident.

Guinesses's next project was the film of *The Lavender Hill Mob* to be directed by Charles Crichton at Ealing Studios with Stanley Holloway – who had played the 1st Gravedigger in his *Hamlet*. Guinness rowed Shaw into the film in a small part of a chemist at a police exhibition. In the script the part amounted to five or six lines. In the finished film the lines were cut and it is possible only to catch the most fleeting of glimpses of Shaw dressed in a white lab coat as the technician who puts the gold Eiffel Tower into a solution of chemicals before Stanley Holloway snatches it away. He is appropriately anonymous and was uncredited. Audrey Hepburn made a similarly small appearance in the film.

On Shaw's 24th birthday, Guinness threw an extravagant party at the Anglo-Greek White Tower restaurant, by any standards an expensive establishment. Friends from RADA and Stratford were invited, including Robert Hardy and Barbara Jefford. Speculation on the reason for Guinness's lavish generosity to the young Shaw was rife. 'Didn't you know,' one friend volunteered, 'Alec's fallen in love with him.'

Later Guinness suggested a weekend in Brighton with himself and Russell Enoch, another actor from the production of *Hamlet*. Shaw happily agreed; it was, after all, an all-expenses-paid weekend away from his miserable digs. Later, he recalled, there was a frisson in the Old Ship Hotel when Guinness touched his hand for a second or two, but the 'love' remained only a friendship.

Shaw's first two years in the theatre had not been the stuff of which dreams, particularly his dreams, were made. It had been an unpromising beginning but he had not gone unnoticed and had impressed, if not exactly dazzled, some of the more robust directors at Stratford who were prepared to tolerate or ignore his carping and scorn.

Chapter Three

By the time Tony Guthrie called Shaw in October, with an invitation to join the Old Vic Company, his only professional work since finishing *Hamlet* in June had been the four days on *The Lavender Hill Mob*. Guthrie offered him the parts of Cassio in *Othello* and Lysander in *A Midsummer Night's Dream*. Having been out of work for so long, Shaw accepted at once despite the fact that he told friends the parts were hardly an improvement on what he had been playing at Stratford. In fact they were a distinct promotion.

Going to work at the Old Vic meant that in the space of three years as an actor, Shaw would have worked for the two major theatre companies in England, watching some of the finest acting of the era and, arguably, of the century. The post-war period saw an explosion of performances in the great Shakespeare roles. Perhaps enriched and deepened by the experience of war, perhaps merely frustrated by its exigencies, or just rested, whatever the reason, Redgrave, Gielgud, Richardson, Olivier and Ashcroft were giving performances at the Old Vic and Stratford that would be regarded as benchmarks among critics and fellow professionals.

Shaw was on stage with many of them but remained characteristically unimpressed. 'I was the spear-carrier, the one who came on with a two-line message for Gielgud, Burton or Redgrave. Some nights I wanted to throw a spear at them.' (Shaw was never on stage with Richard Burton.)

Shaw had fondly imagined that by now he would have taken the theatre by storm, that Guthrie and Glen Byam Shaw would be offering him the sort of parts Burton and John Neville were playing. That they were not was something he met with a sort of surly arrogance. But in the theatre of 1951, where actors wore suit and tie at all times and were expected to address their betters as 'sir', regardless of any knighthood, it was not an attitude that was particularly helpful to his career prospects.

Titania's three fairies in *A Midsummer Night's Dream* were played by Joan Plowright, Jill Balcon and a beautiful young blonde called Jennifer Bourke. Jennifer was the most attractive and most unobtainable of the Old Vic Company, and Shaw, his competitive instincts roused by the challenge, set out his stall for her.

Jennifer Bourke was a white Jamaican. Her mother had divorced her first husband to marry Henry Fowler, a brilliant educationalist. Fowler moved in government circles and Jennifer became friendly with the Governor of Jamaica's daughter, Cherry Huggins. Lady Huggins, as befits the Governor's wife, was a great giver of parties and at one such affair Jennifer had been introduced to Noël Coward. Coward took an immediate liking to the girl, and when she told him her ambition was to be an actress he did not lecture her as if she was one of Mrs Worthington's daughters. On the contrary he made a special trip into Kingston and arranged the use of the local theatre so he could audition her. On the basis of what he saw, he backed her application to the Old Vic Theatre School on whose board he sat. Michel Saint-Denis was not going to refuse The Master.

Jennifer's first impression of Shaw was not favourable. She had played cricket against him on a visit to Stratford the previous year, and he had bowled her out first ball with an overarm delivery when he should have been bowling underarm. But during the 1951/52 season Shaw made determined efforts to change her mind and by the time the company set off for a tour of South Africa and Rhodesia, as it then was, with Shaw adding to his roles Malcolm in Douglas Campbell's *Macbeth*, he had succeeded. There is no question that to Shaw Jennifer was a target, a notch on his belt. However, having achieved his objective with extravagant avowals of undying, total, cosmic and devoted love, sometimes whispered on stage, Shaw found, perhaps to his own surprise, that it was true. He was indeed in love with Jennifer and, what's more, fiercely jealous of any rivals.

Since Stratford, Shaw had had success with women by exploiting his charismatic personality and good looks, but his attitude to them had not changed. They were still a game, like squash, table tennis and rugby, something to be won; but, unlike sport, they were not a game he particularly enjoyed. And they were not a game to take seriously. Finding a woman with whom he could have a measure of companionship was a relief to Shaw, which is why he dashed into marriage at a comparatively early age. It was one less concern. He could concentrate on more important matters and on games that he did enjoy.

From South Africa the tour moved to Rhodesia. It was in Bulawayo in August 1952 that Robert Shaw and Jennifer Bourke were married. Shaw was just 22. No parents were at the wedding. The ceremony itself, with Patrick Wymark as best man, nearly had to be abandoned when Shaw was required to state his full name – Robert Archibald Shaw. Jennifer had no idea of his middle name and immediately

erupted into a fit of uncontrollable giggles. After her third attempt to
control herself failed, it was only the Registrar's stern admonishment
that they might prefer to come back another time, that finally enabled
her to carry on.

It is remarkable that, not only did Shaw want to get married so
young and settle into a domestic routine, he was also keen to start a
family immediately. Like his father, it seemed, Shaw's preoccupation
– one that would manifest itself with all his wives – was to have a child.
He succeeded in persuading Jennifer that this was an urgent priority
and an attractive proposition despite the obvious practical difficulties
that having a baby would involve. They had nowhere to live, no
income and, when the tour finished, no employment. To have
Jennifer staying at home to look after a baby would mean their chances
of getting employment would rest solely on Shaw, whereas had they
both been able to work, at least there was double the chance of some
income. None of this seemed to daunt Shaw, or Jennifer either for that
matter. Having a baby was an act of selfish irresponsibility or of blithe
optimism, or both. Shaw wanted a baby.

He was bailed out of his predicament by an act of kindness from a
woman he hardly knew. During the Old Vic season, Shaw had lived
in digs around the corner from the theatre, in a Victorian family
house. It was quite clear that Shaw could not bring his new wife, and
subsequently new-born baby, there so they moved into the tiny flat
Jennifer's parents had provided. But, with only two rooms, it was
quite unsuitable for a child.

At the first night party for *A Midsummer Night's Dream* Patrick
Wymark had introduced Shaw to Francesca Wilson. Perhaps because
of Shaw's extensive reading and ambitions to write, Francesca took to
him immediately and the feeling was clearly reciprocated. In her '60s,
having graduated from Oxford in English before Shaw was born, she
had travelled to Russia – in the style of the legendary eccentric
Englishwoman – where she had been so appalled at the poverty and
lack of basic hygiene that she had set up a school and clinic and stayed
for some years. At the outbreak of Civil War in Spain she had moved
to Malaga starting a field hospital for both sides, recruiting staff from
London and all over Europe. Returning to London she had gone about
befriending doctors, artistes and writers, inviting them to her large
penthouse flat for literary evenings, where work was read and food
and wine freely available. It was a Bloomsbury set manqué.

Clearly her range of experience was quite outside Shaw's compass.
For the first time in his adult life he listened, his imagination no doubt
set alight by her stories delivered in the voice of the English upper-
classes – an easy target for Joyce Grenfell parody. He was particularly

interested in her stories of Spain and the battle of Toledo where the Royalist military academy had been surrounded and extensively shelled by the communists. The commander of the school held out; however, using his pupils to fight before he himself was killed. But the senior cadet took over command and the siege continued. The communists had captured the cadet's father and got him to phone his son: but the idea misfired when the father told his son not to surrender and to 'die like a man'.

Francesca Wilson had the penthouse flat in a rare modern, i.e. post-war, block of flats in Swiss Cottage. The style alone – then called Contemporary – fascinated Shaw on his first visit, the 'bricks' made of opaque glass used in the foyer, the diamond-yellow enamelled metal that decorated the banisters, the long windows running the whole length of the room and the rounded edges of the building echoing Art Deco. Inside the penthouse the spacious rooms were crammed with memorabilia of Spain and Russia and Africa – where she had been during the war. And her collection of books, to his special delight, was monumental. The two ensuite bathrooms and the central heating were something Shaw had not seen before.

On their return from the African tour the Shaws were greeted by Francesca with an immediate offer of hospitality. They could stay at the penthouse while the baby was born until they got themselves 'sorted out'. In any event Francesca spent a great deal of time at her cottage in Walberswick in Suffolk, so an empty flat would be on her conscience. The Shaws happily agreed.

Shaw had landed on his feet. But with the end of the Old Vic season he was out of work again and so was Jennifer. At the beginning of September 1952 he auditioned for John Wyse who was directing *Caro Williams*, a new play by William Douglas Home being produced at the nearby Embassy Theatre (now used by a drama school). After a tense wait he was offered the part of George Lamb, William Lamb's brother. It was not a large part but it was his second West End role – the Embassy Theatre despite its geographical location was regarded as being in the 'West End' – and a step-up from spear-carrying. It opened on 22 October 1952, with Robert Harris as William Lamb and Daphne Arthur as Caro. It was not a success. Shaw was mentioned in the reviews in common with the other actors as being 'good' but was not singled out. The play closed in the first week of November.

Guthrie had promised Shaw work in the Stratford season of 1953 but Shaw was not optimistic about the prospects of a reasonable line of parts. He hoped fervently to be able to tell Stratford where they could put their spears but with the birth of Deborah in February 1953 he had no option but to accept the offer. He was cast as Gratiano in *The*

Merchant of Venice with Peggy Ashcroft as Portia and Redgrave as
Shylock, Dolabella in the Gielgud and Ashcroft *Antony and Cleopatra*,
Tranio in *The Taming of the Shrew* and Edmund in Redgrave's *Lear*. He
was noticed by Kenneth Tynan who wrote that Shaw 'delighted
himself and us by giving a fiery and determined performance . . .' as
Gratiano.

It was a pleasant summer living in the country with a new baby and
a new marriage. Peggy Ashcroft was as passionate about cricket as
Shaw was about sport in general (at school he had found cricket too
passive for his taste) and during the season organised a series of male
versus female matches, as she had in 1951 when Jennifer first met
Shaw. It was agreed that the men would bat left-handed (or right
depending on their bent) and bowl underarm but Shaw, put into bat,
insisted on smashing sixes around the ground. Finally he was caught
on the boundary by Angela Baddeley.

Shaw had made two new friends, Edmund Purdom and Donald
Pleasence. Purdom's rebellious spirit made him a natural ally for the
carping Shaw and the two complained bitterly about the inequities of
the system. Purdom complained rather too publicly, however, and
was fired mid-season. Shaw was thrown on to the friendship of
Pleasence who was a very different sort of personality. Pleasence was
far from rebellious. Shaw later remembered asking him at this time if
he would be prepared to give up the chance of making a fortune in
return for a regular and permanent weekly wage. Pleasence replied
that he certainly would, while Shaw scoffed and said he certainly
would not. It was fortunate for Pleasence that Shaw had been prepared
to gamble, considering the later financial arrangements between the
two men.

The production of *Antony and Cleopatra* was the biggest success of
the season and was completely sold out at every performance. It was
decided that it should be transferred to London. Shaw, as ever
discontented with the size of his part, asked Glen Byam Shaw, the
production's director, if there was the chance he could be promoted to
a slightly better part. No, Byam Shaw explained, the whole company
has agreed to come to London so everyone is cast as is. Shaw, with no
other work on offer, reluctantly accepted. He had little choice. It
opened on 4 November 1953 at the Prince's Theatre and ran until
January. Donald Pleasence was also in the cast.

At Christmas Jennifer became pregnant again. The decision to have
a second child seemed an even greater triumph of optimism over
adversity. They were still living in Francesca Wilson's penthouse and
it had been made clear to Shaw by Stratford that there was nothing for
him in the 1954 season, a decision on their part no doubt prompted by

Shaw's avowed dissatisfaction not only with the lines of parts he was getting but the way the theatre was run in general. With a second child on the way Shaw might have had to waive his pride. He was not given the opportunity.

Following the run at the Prince's Theatre, *Antony and Cleopatra* was taken on a short tour of The Hague, Amsterdam, Antwerp, Brussels and Paris. In Paris the company was invited to a dinner given for them by the Comédie Française. The largess of the French government to their theatre in comparison with English parsimony was only too obvious as the champagne flowed at a lavish banquet.

In February Shaw returned to his wife in Swiss Cottage with no job and no prospects, but at least they did manage to move out of Francesca Wilson's penthouse into a place of their own for the first time. A cousin of Jennifer's had offered them a flat around the corner at 61 Haverstock Hill, not far from Chalk Farm tube station, at a reduced rent.

The year 1954 was to be a disaster for Shaw. Having made himself unpopular with the massed ranks of managements at Stratford and the Old Vic, there was little work forthcoming on the theatre front. Dr Jeremiah Slattery, whom Shaw had met and befriended at one of Francesca Wilson's literary soirées and who had a large coterie of patients and friends among the theatrical and publishing fraternity, managed to rope Shaw into writing reviews for the minor literary journals that dotted the market at that time. But this hardly put bread on the table. Most of the income in 1954 was borrowed. Jennifer's family provided some money, and friends were prevailed on to provide more, but it was hard. To make matters worse the flat was cold, especially to Jennifer's Jamaican taste, and the bathroom primitive. By the time Penny was born in October 1954 things had gone from bad to worse, and Shaw was beginning to run out of people to tap for money.

Strangely it seemed a happy time for Shaw in comparison with what was to come later. Drink was not then a problem. Very simply he could not afford it. He could spend time with his baby daughters, and his wife was simply a delight, warm, affectionate, kind and extraordinarily beautiful. Philip Broadley thought her the perfect wife for Shaw, an earth mother with the looks of a beauty queen. Shaw could behave and do exactly as he wished. He had strong male friendships which he enjoyed. He had a remarkable and enduring sense of humour and an endless entertaining conversation which made him a good companion and guest. Nor had he for one moment lost his self-confidence and his belief in his ability.

He played squash, tennis and table tennis whenever and wherever he could. He was occasionally given a game of rugby for WASPS (not in the first team). His competitive spirit meant he would challenge anyone to anything and hope to win. Nor would he let his responsibility to his family dampen his zeal for the sport. Both Broadley and Alex Davion remember him swearing them to secrecy when he used money that should have gone to household expenses on buying the latest advance in squash rackets.

Behind the cheery smile and verbal exuberance Shaw was still inclined to brood. The brooding often found an outlet in his writing. During 1954 he had little to distract him from this endeavour and worked on several plays. Only two have survived, *Simon of Gidding*, which was never performed, and *Off the Mainland*, which was.

The story of Simon of Gidding, a sort of medieval English Joan of Arc, might be thought of as unlikely material for Shaw. Simon's vision of a kinder, more forgiving God was unlikely to be welcomed by an established church devoted to dispensing hellfire and brimstone as a means of oppressing the people. The sanction for such heresy, burning at the stake, is invoked immediately in Shaw's play, but unfortunately a stake cannot be found. Ever inventive, the priests proceed to tie Simon to a kitchen table and burn him with Holy Oil. But as the fire is about to be lit, *deus ex machina* snow begins to fall and a cuckoo is heard though it is August:

> We cannot light the fires. The Holy Oil will not burn . . . Simon, Simon. The snow has come. Oh Simon the snow has come . . . (*There is weeping and laughter and the snow falls and so does the CURTAIN*).

Simon, who seems to be having trouble remembering what his vision actually entailed, makes no attempt to save himself by rallying the people to his cause. The villagers, who at first are delighted by the news he brings from God, giving him various gifts – including carte blanche from a husband to have an affair with his wife – are soon cowed back to passivity by the authorities. What the effect of hearing a cuckoo in August is likely to be on them is not divulged.

Behind this improbable story there is an attempt at a serious theme – how to reconcile religious faith with the concept of the church as a political state. But *Simon of Gidding* is most remarkable for what it is not. Despite being written by an actor it is incredibly untheatrical and undramatic. There is a great deal of talk, but apart from the attempted auto-da-fé in the third act, very little happens and Shaw's exposition of ideas in the dialogue seems artificial.

Shaw's attempts to gain employment necessarily had extended

outside his profession and he finally got a job at H.J. Heinz's canning factory in Waxlow Road. Getting on the No 187 bus every morning, he worked five days a week for £7.50 packing cans of baked beans into boxes.

More seriously, Shaw decided it was time to find an agent for his talents. American-style agents – truly speaking, personal managers – were a comparatively new phenomenon in England. Before the war, in this country, agents had worked for the theatres not for actors, performing the role now taken by a modern casting director. There were some exceptions to this rule, where literary agents had started to look after the more senior actors, as Cecil Tennant did for Laurence Olivier, doing their deals and organising their engagements, but this was not, in a sense, a mainstream business.

In America between the wars, with the explosion of the film industry in Hollywood, things had been very different. As the power shifted from the major studios to the stars themselves, actors began employing personal managers to help them deal with the increasing complexities of their lives and their contracts. Usually these people were either lawyers or accountants but soon a specialised profession grew up around an urgent and developing need.

After the war an actor-turned-agent decided to come to England to try to start the same kind of business over here. Al Parker was a blunt, direct and tough American who immediately set up a startlingly successful personal management business with a stable of important film stars. Within a couple of years Christopher Mann, who had been a literary agent, also diversified into actors and two or three other companies started in what was virtually a new field.

Richard Hatton had been the comedian Vic Oliver's assistant, before which he had been an actor. Getting nowhere after returning to acting he thought of setting up a theatrical agency (the word 'theatrical' a hangover from pre-war days) and with the help of Basil Appleby and Lesley Linder and financial backing from friends and would-be clients; including Alan Wheatley and Herbert Lom's wife, they began Richard Hatton Ltd in 1953.

One of his first clients was a Chinese lady called Chin Yu who was playing the role of Bloody Mary in *South Pacific*, then the hit show in London. A young man in the chorus at the time was also looking for an agent. She introduced him to Richard who after their interview, when the young man did not wear a tie and appeared to be decidedly grubby, was not impressed. He was prevailed upon to take him on, however, and Sean Connery had his first agent, with whom he was to remain until Richard retired in 1972.

By the time Shaw was introduced to the agency by Donald

Pleasence in 1954 Hatton had developed his business and was particularly well connected in the film and burgeoning television world. One of his clients and investors was currently starring in ATV's *The Adventures of Robin Hood* – one of the biggest successes on television in 1954 – in which Alan Wheatley made a big impact as the villainous Sheriff of Nottingham. Apart from *The Lavender Hill Mob*, Shaw had not been near a film studio and had never worked on television in the five years since he had graduated from RADA. His acting friends made him all too aware of the financial rewards available, especially in films, something he would have been very grateful for in the impecunious times of 1954.*

Still, 1955 did not start much better for Shaw despite having an agent. It was May before he acted again, a break of some 15 months since the end of *Antony and Cleopatra* on tour. But his next part when it came was a step forward. Richard Hatton had suggested him for the part of the flight sergeant to Richard Todd's captain in what was to turn out to be the top film in England when it was released later in the year. *The Dam Busters* was directed by Michael Anderson with a screenplay by R.C. Sherriff. It was a four week engagement for Shaw and he was spaid £500. What is more it was a substantial part, though once again, a great deal of it was lost on the cutting room floor.

The Dam Busters was typical of a particular genre of British war films of the time, characterised by a patriotic attitude, a stiff upper lip and sentiment bordering on the jingoistic. Ten years after the war, the British film industry was still fighting it. Historical perspective had certainly not yet been achieved. The historical basis for *The Dam Busters* for instance – that Barnes Wallis' bouncing bombs smashed the Eder dams, thereby flooding and destroying the industrial heartland of Germany's war machine in the Ruhr valley and significantly shortening the war – has subsequently been shown to be quite erroneous.

But for Robert Shaw, his first speaking role in front of the cameras demonstrated an assurance and, more importantly, a genuine rapport with the camera. He had clearly learnt that screen-acting is very different from stage-acting; a close-up of a face in the cinema gives it a height of 30 feet. The slightest movement is acting enough, and even

* In Vanessa Redgrave's autobiography she states that she saw Robert Shaw in the part of Dunois in *St Joan* at the 'Q' Theatre with her mother Rachel Kempson in the title role. In fact the 'Q' Theatre did not mount a production of *St Joan* in 1954 nor at any time before it was knocked down. Nor was there any production of *St Joan* in London during the fifties or sixties, for that matter, which featured Rachel Kempson or Robert Shaw. Ms Kempson's own entry in *Who's Who in the Theatre* includes no reference to her ever having played *St Joan*.

that may be superfluous. The Russian director V.I. Pudovkin had done a series of experiments in the 1920s with close-ups of Mosjukhin, a well-known actor of the period, holding a blank expressionless gaze and then intercutting this shot with first an open coffin in which lay a dead woman, then a little girl playing with a funny toy bear, and then a plate of soup. Mosjukin's face did not change but the audience imagined it registered, in turn, shock, pleasure and hunger. RADA made few concessions to film or television technique during the '40s and '50s, but Shaw seemed to have an untutored ability to judge exactly how little was needed to convey complex emotions, despite spending much of his screen time behind the oxygen mask of a Lancaster bomber.

During the filming of *The Dam Busters*, Michael Redgrave, who was playing Barnes Wallis, mentioned to Shaw that his next project was Christopher Fry's adaptation of Giraudoux's *Tiger at the Gates* (*La Guerre de Troie n'aura pas lieu*) and there could well be a part in it for him. Richard Hatton arranged for him to be auditioned by Harold Clurman from the Group Theatre in New York. Shaw was offered the part of Topman. Clurman was a top-class director – Redgrave said he 'seemed by his very presence to extract the very best the cast is capable of' – and when the play opened at the Apollo Theatre on 2 June 1955 it was a success, with Diane Cilento's beauty as Helen widely admired. Shaw was not mentioned in the reviews. The play ran until September when Roger Stevens, the New York impresario, was to take it to Broadway.

Unfortunately, Shaw had inflated ideas of his worth. His 15-month lay-off had done nothing to destroy his confidence, boosted by *The Dam Busters*, and when Stevens offered him the same money as the other supporting actors, Shaw turned him down. Stevens would not want to go to the bother of rehearsing another actor into the part, Shaw argued. He was sure to up his offer. Shaw completely misjudged the situation. Stevens, an old-time Broadway producer, was not going to be dictated to by one of the supporting cast. He re-cast Topman without hesitation.

Luckily for Shaw his disappointment was short-lived. He got a part in another war film, this time as a soldier, in *Hill in Korea* (released in the USA as *Hell in Korea*) directed by Julian Amyes and starring Stanley Baker. The screenplay was by Ian Dalrymple and Anthony Squire, who also produced the film. Here, propaganda was very much part of the message, as the Korean war had only been over for two years and this story of a gallant British patrol fighting off the Chinese from a position on top of a hill was, though with a thread of anti-war sentiment, angled to show the stirring work of our gallant boys.

Shaw was engaged for eight weeks, six of which were on location in Portugal. He was paid £120 per week. Among the other squaddies fighting off the Chinese was an equally inexperienced Michael Caine.

Shaw's reaction to earning money was predictable. He spent it immediately. He bought a second-hand car, his first, and entertained friends. Some loans were repaid and others were not.

But the best news for Shaw in 1955 was that Andre Van Gyseghem had decided he wanted to direct Shaw's play *Off the Mainland* and had arranged a production at the Arts Theatre, the venue that was later to launch Harold Pinter's career with *The Caretaker* in 1960. Apart from the odd book review in London literary journals, and two episodes of the radio series *For the Children*, Shaw's writing talent had produced little income and received no recognition. Now his dreams of success as a writer looked as though they were about to come true. With the promise from Anthony Squire of a part in his next film in January, and the prospect of his first play being produced, 1956 looked like being an exciting year. It was to be much more so than he could have guessed.

Chapter Four

The year nonetheless started badly. The part Squire had promised Shaw in his next film, *Doublecross*, was so small that Shaw refused it. Squire was apologetic. The character he had in mind for Shaw was prominent in the first draft script but by the time revisions had been done it had virtually disappeared. So once again there were several months of unemployment to face.

In April, rehearsals for *Off the Mainland* began with Shaw himself playing Laszlo, Connie Wake as Francesca and Ralph Michael as the Commandant. The play opened on 30 May 1956 at The Arts in the same month that *Look Back in Anger* opened at the Royal Court.

At this distance it is difficult to know what Shaw was trying to achieve with the play. On the surface it is an attempt to modernise the story of Francesca de Rimini which is told in Dante's *Inferno*. She was married to the Lord of Rimini but her love for his younger brother, Paolo, was discovered and both were put to death. Leigh Hunt, the English poet, used the story for a poem written in 1812 and, at the turn of the 19th century there were at least three versions in the theatre. In Shaw's play it is the brothers who die leaving Francesca alive.

Shaw transposes the story of an island off the mainland of some unnamed Eastern bloc country where political prisoners are brought to be interrogated and tortured to reveal information – of what relevance to what situation is apparently not important as it is never stated. The effect of this unmitigated brutality on the torturers is seen to be as dehumanising as on those who are tortured. Colonel Rimini, Commandant of the island, contending not only with this burden but the fact that he has a fatal disease, is undergoing a period of mental instability inextricably linked to his inability to father children. When his young brother Laszlo arrives on the island – though it may seem an unlikely place for a holiday – and begins an affair with the Commandant's beautiful and much younger wife Francesca, impregnating her almost immediately, Rimini's reaction is unexpected. He claims Francesca's son for his own so he may at last enjoy the pleasures of fatherhood, planning to take his revenge in the more customary murderous manner only after the birth. Laszlo, tipped off to his brothers plans, tries to steal Francesca away, only to be surrounded by Rimini's troops. In a Western-style shoot-out both brothers are killed, leaving the pregnant Francesca as the sole survivor of the sorry affair.

It is a play of unremitting gloom, and of many gunshots, which may serve to keep the audience awake after the long speeches about the nature of man and the cruelty of life. There is Chekhovian symbolism – a young 'fisherboy', like the seagull a symbol of innocence and hope, shot down in his prime – and a Chekhovian doctor given to pronouncing Chekhovian thoughts: 'Only by an effort, and indeed a discipline greater than any society has yet seen necessary to impose, will material knowledge and power be gained without loss of spirit.' And: 'The entire civilised world will die of . . . boredom.' Only when Rimini realises he has a chance to claim Francesca's son as his own is there any light in the gloom; the child, not God nor religion nor political will, offering salvation:

> God leaves me cold, so does the devil
> It was not these who made me
> One day I shall my sin unravel
> Because my child will aid me.

[Shaw uses quotes from the Hungarian poet Attila Jozcef.]

Any relevance the play may have had to the particular events of 1956 that a modern reader may have missed were certainly not revealed by the critics. Most praised the first act and were severely disappointed by the second. *The Times*, for instance, found, 'the play . . . promises to develop a certain marked attraction but with the second act the author swerves into crude melodrama.' Milton Shulman was critical of 'talk in exclamation marks', the 'extravagant symbolism' that filled the play which, for him, 'only narrowly misses being ludicrous'. The play closed after running for its prescribed four weeks to poor houses.

Shaw was now as gloomy as his play. Any hope he may have had that the play was going to set him aside as a writer of note was dashed by the reviews. He read the notices over and over again, as he was to do with notices all his life, taking crumbs of comfort from the more positive comments. But staring through the lights every night into the more than half empty house reinforced the message of the reviews. As Connie Wake said later, 'It was simply a bad play.'

At this low ebb Shaw was saved from despair and further penury by the unlikely figure of Lew Grade who would later claim, quite correctly, to have given Shaw his first 'break'. Hannah Weinstein, a successful American producer, had made the television series, *The Adventures of Robin Hood*, for Lew Grade's ATV in 1954. Grade had pre-sold the original 39 episodes to CBS in America, a considerable coup as it constituted a full season of shows (American television executives calculated the year as 39 weeks not 52 as their research showed there was no audience for television in the summer). The series proved so popular that it finally run for 165 episodes and created a particular genre of 30-minute filmed costume drama that lasted well into the '60s with the likes of *Sword of Freedom*, *William Tell*, *Sir Francis Drake* and *Ivanhoe*. Curiously, though, the popularity of *Robin Hood* did not propel its star, Richard Greene, to further celebrity.

To follow up on her success Hannah Weinstein developed a pilot for a series on pirates with her script editor Ian Hunter, an American who had left Hollywood under the persecution of McCarthyism, as had many of the writers who worked on *Robin Hood*. The series, to be called *The Buccaneers*, was immediately commissioned by Lew Grade and pre-sold to CBS for American television.

There was an apocryphal story of how Shaw got the part of Dan Tempest in *The Buccaneers*. The story goes that the American-made pilot of the series had Alec Clunes playing Dan Tempest and Robert Shaw as one of his crew. At a showing of the pilot, the executive in charge disliked the casting of Clunes in the lead. 'Get me the one with balls' he (or she) shouted, referring to Shaw. But the story is patently untrue. Lew Grade and Sydney Cole, the 'line' producer (the producer responsible for the day-to-day running of the filming) both denied there ever having been a pilot. Pilots were common in American television but not in England. It is possible that the origin of the story comes from the film tests and that Hannah Weinstein was to remark that Shaw had 'balls' in comparison to Clunes; but Clunes was never considered for the leading part in the series.

It was seven months' work and Shaw was paid £200 per episode plus some expenses. To the struggling Shaw it was a fortune. The role was perfect for Shaw because it gave full play to his physical prowess and his strong screen presence. His athletic physique was frequently displayed during the course of an episode when his shirt would be discarded or torn in a sword fight. The series, unusually for television, was made in 35mm and later reduced to 16mm, so Shaw was working in front of full-size film cameras. The location work was done at Falmouth, with a schooner moored in the harbour, and the studio work at Twickenham.

On the first day of rehearsals Shaw proudly produced his authentic Cornish accent – previously hidden under the RADA-acquired gloss. But Hannah Weinstein took Shaw aside to explain, not all that politely, that the series was pre-sold to American television and she felt instinctively that he would make a bigger impact on the American public if they could actually understand what he was saying. 'See, I know 'cause I'm an American,' she told him, 'And I can't get one damn word.' Shaw was never one to argue artistic differences in the face of such an assessment of his career prospects and dropped the accent at once.

Alec Clunes played the subsidiary role of Woodes Rogers but in fact was playing Lancelot in another television series at the same time so his appearances were limited. Peter Proud, the production designer who had worked on Alfred Hitchcock's British pictures, designed 16th-century West Indies and the second unit director was John Schlesinger. The scripts were unremarkable and Shaw would soon take to the practice of making them up as he went along. No one objected as long as the sense was approximately correct.

As usual, Shaw's competitive instincts surfaced and table tennis at Twickenham Studios became a regular lunchtime pastime. In Fowey Harbour on a night shoot, he challenged Donald Houston to swim across the bay at three in the morning. Sometimes the competitive spirit even got in the way of filming. In one episode Noel Coleman, another friend from RADA days, was playing the villain, an expert swordsman. Shaw was required to lose their sword fight but got so carried away he forced Noel back, and whipped his sword away.

It did not take long before Shaw was telling his friends how awful the scripts were and how bored he was by the whole thing. He was doing it for the money, he would say, and it was a 'pretty depressing business'.

The series was first transmitted in England on 19 September 1956 at 7.05 p.m. on ITV, proclaimed in *TV Times* – above a half-page advertisement for Olivier cigarettes with Laurence Olivier smoking happily – as a new 'adventure series'. Shaw was featured in an article in which he declared his direct descent from Cornish pirates, the Averys! The 25-minute shows were an instant success. Robert Shaw had become, at least, a television star. 'Television,' he was fond of saying later, 'makes you a household face, films make you a household name.' It was true. In the street Shaw was recognised but few could actually put a name to the face, other than the character he played in the series.

Shaw's dreams of acting stardom were very different. He had, in common with most classically educated actors, dreamt of bestriding the stage at Stratford or the Old Vic, playing the great Shakespearean roles, precisely what Richard Burton was currently doing. Dan Tempest in a Lew Grade series with housewives in curlers asking for his autograph in Tesco's was not a dream come true. As a natural competitor he was quick to see rivalry. All his life he would regard

Burton as a rival though they rarely met, never worked together, and the feeling was not reciprocated.

Other than various features in *TV Times* and the odd newspaper feature article, British television was slow to promote itself and its leading actors in the '50s and '60s. There seemed to be a certain British reserve about the whole business of marketing in terms of television. It may be that the necessity to sell television programmes to an audience, when the BBC had a single channel monopoly, appeared superfluous, but the arrival of a second ITV channel did little to change things. *The Buccaneers* was not greeted by the sort of press that would accompany a highly popular series today.

Shaw provided a little do-it-yourself publicity however. Using a friend's houseboat to write he took his young daughters with him on some occasion when Jennifer had an appointment. Leaving them to play on deck he worked at his desk until Penny's cries alerted him. Debbie had fallen into the river. Diving in, he rescued her. Next day 'Brave Dan Tempest' was pictured in the *Daily Mail*, daughter in arms. Who called the photographer is another matter.

The Americans, however, had an entirely different approach to publicity and promotion and when the series was launched in the States in 1957 Shaw was flown in to encourage viewing figures. It was his first visit to New York.

By coincidence his old friend Philip Broadley was living in New York at the time trying to make it as an actor and was delighted to see Shaw, who took him to the launch party held by CBS. Scantily-clad girls sporting black eye-patches, wooden cutlasses and waving Jolly Rogers were draped around Dan Tempest for the benefit of photographers, against a background of a vast cardboard flat of a 16th-century galleon. In Macy's Thanksgiving Day Parade he was ushered into a Cadillac landau with Basil Rathbone and Roy Rogers. As they waved to the crowds, he remembered, Rogers, one of the wealthiest men in Hollywood, showed him his diamond-encrusted, and tax-deductible, Colt 45s, while Rathbone dispensed brandy from an oversized hip flask.

Shaw's reaction to comparative wealth was, again, to spend it. He bought a 1933 Rolls Royce and a set of golf clubs. He went on holiday to Truro where he showed off his wife, his car and his accomplishments, not necessarily in that order. The prodigal had returned, it would appear. It was to be typical of Shaw, telling friends how he resented the work while wallowing in the advantages it provided, and wanting everyone to see his success.

To Sydney Cole he expressed doubts about his career: it was not going where he wanted it to go; it had no focal point. Crucially after

The Buccaneers he would face several problems. He would be 'type-cast', directors only thinking of him for the same type of part, swaggering, athletic, boisterous heroes. There was also, markedly in the 50's a snobbery, where producers and directors of more serious ventures, particularly theatrical ventures, would not consider actors from the lesser media – and television was looked down upon in many quarters. And there was the problem of over-exposure, a feeling that an actor's face brings too many preconceptions to be suitable for a part requiring none. Had *The Buccaneers* continued, Shaw would have been confronted with the difficult decision facing all actors in a successful series, to continue in the part – thus exacerbating the problems once the series is over – or to face unemployment again. But after the first 39 episodes CBS did not take up their option for a further series and Lew Grade, never one to make programmes purely for the domestic market, especially relatively expensive ones like *The Buccaneers*, did not offer Shaw a new contract.

It was spring 1957 and Shaw was out of work for a year. His extravagance meant that things were once more very tight and the Rolls Royce was the first thing to go. Shaw immersed himself in writing. He continued to attend Francesca Wilson's literary soirées where, as well as Dr Slattery, he had met another man who was to become a friend, the writer Leo Lehmann. Shaw was continuing in his efforts to write plays and credited Lehmann with giving him the idea to turn to the novel. Whoever suggested it, the idea was like a light going on in a darkened room. Shaw took to it immediately, and, as with everything in his life, rushed to start.

Shaw struggled with play-writing. Strangely for an actor perhaps, he had never been able to find the right blend between drama and monologue, between lecturing the audience on the meaning of life and illustrating it dramatically. In the novel form this was never a problem for him; the message never strained the medium.

Taking Francesca Wilson's offer of one of her two cottages in Walberswick, the Shaw family descended on Suffolk where he started work on his first novel. The cottage was often lent to writers and Leo Lehmann had taken advantage of it on many occasions. Lehmann, who had written one of the first 'soaps' for the BBC, *The Common Room*, was also credited by Shaw with his literary education. 'Being Polish,' Shaw said, 'he knew nothing of English and because of it wrote better English than I could.' At the cottage he helped Shaw wrest with the unfamiliar problems of the narrative form. He remembered vividly the excitement when they all gathered round the radio to hear the news of the first Sputnik in space launched by the Russians. Shaw was greatly amused, apparently, by the immediate

American reaction that it was hardly an important event and they couldn't understand what all the fuss was about. The Sputnik was launched on 4 October 1957. It weighted 180 lbs and circled the earth for 95 minutes.

It was also Leo Lehmann who provided Shaw's next acting job in a play he had written for the BBC, called *Success*. The play was transmitted live in March 1958, with Shaw, who could not play the piano, in the part of a classical pianist who finds his true bent in playing jazz music. Immediately after this Shaw was offered a film, after being sent to meet Cy Endfield for the first time, in *Sea Fury*. In the previous year Enfield, a writer director who had decamped to England after the purges of the House Committee on Un-American Activities in Hollywood, had met Sean Connery at Richard Hatton's suggestion and employed him in *Hell Drivers*. He was impressed with the quality of Hatton's young actors. *Sea Fury* starred Victor McLagen, in his last film, and Stanley Baker, whom Shaw already knew from *Hill in Korea*.

Making a film on a flooded sound stage is not the most pleasant experience for an actor. There were some dry scenes but most of the story of how the mate of a salvage tug saves a wrecked ship despite its drunken captain, involves a great deal of cold water being pumped down on to the actors day in and day out. To heat the water on a sound stage is not only prohibitively expensive (the 'tank' holds 60,000–100,000 gallons of water) but creates condensation and steam which are difficult for the cameraman to deal with. So filming is miserable.

For a well known stoic like Shaw it was, however, an opportunity to show what he was made of. While the other actors huddled against the cold, Shaw frolicked in the icy water and at least twice, pushed fully-clothed members of the crew into the tank as a 'joke'. In Stanley Baker, Shaw had found someone who was always prepared to accept a challenge. At a party during the shoot guests suddenly appeared to be congregating in an upstairs bedroom. On investigation Lesley Linder discovered they had gathered to watch Stanley Baker and Robert Shaw hanging by their fingers from the balcony of the bedroom on a bet to see who would be the first to give up.

Sea Fury was notable in Shaw's career for another reason; it was the first time he worked for producer S. Benjamin Fisz. Born in Warsaw in 1922, Benny Fisz had come to England to fight against Hitler. He flew with the Free Polish Squadron in the Battle of Britain and after the war decided he wanted to become a film producer. *Sea Fury* was his fifth feature: *Hell Drivers* had been his fourth. Benny's primary characteristic as a producer was loyalty.

With Sean Connery, after giving him a supporting role in *Hell*

Drivers, Fisz went on to feature him in *On the Fiddle.* Later he released Connery from a three-picture deal commitment to go and do the first Bond picture with Harry Saltzman and Cubby Broccoli. He had declined the percentage of the profits of the Bond picture they had offered him in return.

With Robert Shaw similarly, Benny liked him and recognised a screen talent. Shaw was to make three more films with Fisz and was offered two more.

Overall it looked as though 1958, with one television play and one supporting part in a film, would prove as disappointing in terms of acting as 1957. Shaw believed he had gained a reputation for being a 'difficult' actor and this was what was holding back his career. The place he most admired was the Royal Court and George Devine's English Stage Company. So he decided to write Devine a letter, in effect a begging letter. If Devine had heard he was 'difficult' then, he promised, ingenuously, he would not be, but he desperately wanted to work at the Court where he knew his talents would be recognised. Devine responded immediately. He invited Shaw to the theatre and asked him to give a reading of Blackmouth in the second John Arden play to be done by the English Stage Company, *Live Like Pigs.* Devine gave him the part. It was a strong cast led by Wilfrid Lawson with Alfred Lynch, Margaretta D'Arcy, Alan Dobie, Nigel Davenport and Stratford Johns. Blackmouth is described by Arden as, 'half-gypsy and looks it. He is 28, lean and sexy. He is both insolent and obsequious and can put on a kind of false joviality that does not take many people in . . . when crossed he gives clear indications of underlying mental unbalance.'

To date the demands on Shaw's acting ability had been negligible and that would include the parts he had been asked to play at RADA. His acting talent had never been tested. The bravado and charisma he had displayed spear-carrying were his own invention; it was not something that was required, indeed it was often surplus to requirements. None of his appearances in front of the cameras had required more than energetic mateyness and displays of British grit and determination, or thigh-slapping rope-swinging cocky guile. *Live Like Pigs* was the first occasion on which he had been asked to create a full character and be an equal member of an ensemble company.

What Shaw had experienced at the Old Vic and Stratford was the end of the old theatrical establishment and its way of doing things, star actors playing star roles. George Devine, at the Court, had set up something entirely different. Of course, when money was needed at the box office to bolster a subsidy never large enough for his plans, he had to hope star names would fill the theatre in the time-honoured way but Devine was interested in a different principle of theatre, a continental principle. Devine and his young associates – Bill Gaskill, Tony Richardson, John Dexter and Lindsay Anderson most notably – were very much aware of the theatre in Europe particularly in France (as Osborne noted in his autobiography, a command of the French language was *de rigueur*. For a time Lindsay Anderson's productions all began with *les trois coups*). Many have commented on how the Court under Devine was a writer's theatre, giving writers the freedom to introduce material that later became known generically as 'kitchen sink drama', but it also had a seminal responsibility in the development of a style of acting which not only allowed actors to throw off the shackles of received pronunciation and play leading working-class roles, but was rooted in a tradition of European theatre. The whole idea of an 'ensemble' company was not something that had been accomplished, though it had been much discussed, at Stratford or the Old Vic.

Play after play at the Court created an ensemble company though not, as with many of the European troupes, by employing a permanent company, which it did not have the resources to afford. The Court's company was unofficial and unpaid (in the sense that the casting was done from play to play and an actor was not paid a retainer if he was not cast) but a company nevertheless. The same actors kept turning up, sometimes in large roles, sometimes in small. But that was the point: there were no stars, only working actors, no 'leading' man and 'supporting' cast. There was a company of equals. This was true of the work so often seen as the turning point in contemporary British theatre, *Look Back in Anger*. A great deal has been said about its impact on play-writing but little about the fact that it was an ensemble company acting together as a unit and not highlighting a star performance. It is true that Mary Ure was rated as a 'star' in her treatment by the press; but that was not reflected in the company and the play was never intended to be a vehicle for her. Production after production used the same house style including all the Court's critical and/or commercial hits of the period, *Serjeant Musgrave's Dance*, *The Kitchen*, *Chips with Everything*, *The Knack*. Even *The Entertainer*, with Olivier as a star in the old-fashioned sense, was not a subordination to the idea of an ensemble company, and his performance benefited from it greatly. (When *The Entertainer* was tried in the '80s as a purely star vehicle it failed miserably.)

So *Live Like Pigs* was a totally new experience for Shaw. For the first time he was required to do something that did not come easily. It meant work and concentration but clearly the effort in personal terms, if not in public, was worth it. The play opened on 30 September 1958 and immediately became something of a *cause célèbre* in the popular press. The image of the 'angry young men' of the Royal Court was further advanced and the press persuaded the Mayor of Barnsley, who had never seen or read the play, but on whose council estate it was supposedly set, to 'emphatically repudiate it in the name of the people of Barnsley'. Behind the headlines the reviews were less sure what Arden was about, seemingly unclear as to whether he was attacking the Welfare State or defending anarchy and amorality. Shaw's performance was spotted and described as both 'unconvincing' and 'appropriately dissolute'. Despite the press controversy audiences stayed away.

Shaw particularly enjoyed the experience of working with Wilfrid Lawson. Lawson was a unique talent in the British theatre and a grossly underrated one. He was an old-fashioned scene-stealer but made no effort to hide it. He used his gravelly Yorkshire voice, sometimes so blurred with drink it took considerable concentration to understand it, to extraordinary effect. His wicked twinkling bright eyes could mesmerise an audience. He could also drink prodigious quantities of beer chased down by whisky and never let a performance interfere with his drinking. He would go to the pub next door to the Court *during* a performance to 'wet his whistle'. One day between the Saturday matinée and evening performances Shaw saw Lawson drinking particularly large amounts of beer before the show. Lawson had apparently taken a dislike to one of the female members of the company. During her major scene Lawson had an exit to the bathroom. As the scene unfolds the audience became gradually aware of a seeping pool of water coming from under what is supposed to be the bathroom door. Lawson had peed on stage. The actress's scene was ruined as the audience concentrated on how big the puddle of pee would get. It was a story Shaw loved to tell.

He also learnt from Lawson the ability to invest a smile with an air of deadly threat. In later years it was to become a characteristic of Shaw's performances particularly in Harold Pinter's plays.

At the Royal Court Shaw found his natural intellectual home. He loved the place. For the first time he was surrounded by people interested in ideas as well as theatricality. The theatre was crawling with talented actors, directors, assistant directors and writers. David Hockney and Patrick Proctor were used to paint scenery. It was unmitigatingly 'camp' in the sense that a high proportion of the people who worked there were homosexual, but Shaw found no difficulty with that. It was a gay world firmly rooted in reality, people went to prison for ideas – mostly in connection with CND though also for being homosexual – and when the Lord Chamberlain's office threatened closure (*A Patriot for Me*), there were barricades to man. It was exciting.

Shaw took to it like a duck to water. Though he only did three plays at the Court he was a member of the unofficial Royal Court company, a Royal Court actor, and was happy to regard himself as such. In the picture of the English Stage Company's 'writers, actors and directors', taken by Anthony Armstrong-Jones, Shaw stands at the back, his left shoulder characteristically dropped, with the other glitterati who made up the company – Anthony Page, Bill Gaskill, Miriam Brickman, Mary Ure, John Arden, John Dexter, John Osborne, Tony Richardson and George Devine. (Only Lindsay Anderson is noticeably missing.)

But Shaw's next engagement was not at the Court, though it was with a director whose influence on the theatre was to be as great. Peter Hall had directed Emlyn Williams and Peggy Ashcroft, with the Danish actor Mogens Wieth, in a play by the American writer Robert Ardrey describing the 12 years of communist politics in Hungary which ended in the revolution of 1956. The play, *A Shadow of Heroes*, had opened at the Piccadilly Theatre in October, but when Wieth had to return to Denmark after four weeks, Hall, having seen Shaw's performance as Blackmouth, cast him to take over the role, which he did in November. It was once again a taxing characterisation, particularly as Shaw did not have a full rehearsal period, involving the obtaining of a bogus confession by sustained physical and mental torture. His take-over was not reviewed; however, and did not last for long; the show closed in December 1958.

This was probably fortunate for Shaw as it meant he was available for another play at the Court. Lindsay Anderson cast him as Mitchum in *The Long and the Short and the Tall*, after Albert Finney, who had originally expressed an interest in the part, decided, instead, to make the film of *The Entertainer*. It was to be Shaw's largest stage role so far, in a cast that included Peter O'Toole – making a similarly big jump in his career – Edward Judd, Ronald Fraser, Alfred Lynch (again) and Bryan Pringle. Shaw's understudy was Michael Caine and O'Toole's was Terence Stamp.

There were high hopes for the play, though at rehearsals there was a great deal of tension between O'Toole and Shaw. It was not just a clash of personalities. While there was no question that Shaw's part was bigger than O'Toole's, it was quite obvious to Shaw, as rehearsals progressed, that it was going to be O'Toole who would get all the reviews. Shaw, playing the stalwart sergeant guiding an inexperienced patrol through the jungle, had little chance for histrionics, while O'Toole's character, the insubordinate, bawdy and lecherous barrack-room lawyer had endless opportunities to impress. And they were not opportunities he missed.

Shaw made every attempt to disrupt proceedings. He would talk constantly during O'Toole's scenes and make comments about O'Toole's performance and where he was going wrong. Anything he could do to undermine and upset O'Toole he would do. On several occasions Lindsay Anderson had to berate him like a headmaster with an errant schoolboy. O'Toole was not fazed.

The reviews were all good for Shaw. Milton Shulman found he made 'a hard anxious portrait of the sergeant', and the *Daily Telegraph* mentions him as 'particularly good'. But it was clear that it was O'Toole that the reviews favoured, most of them commenting on the emergence of a startling new talent. Shaw had been right.

The play, which had first been seen on the fringe at the Edinburgh Festival in 1958 (then called *Disciplines of War*) had gone to Nottingham Playhouse after the Festival (re-titled *Boys, It's All Hell*) before the new production at the Court opened on 9 January 1959 and was successful enough to be transferred to the New Theatre on 8 April 1959 where it ran until the end of June. It was Robert Shaw's longest run in the theatre to date.

Shaw's position had changed dramatically since the middle of 1957 when he was suffering from post-Dan-Tempest syndrome. He had now managed to establish himself in the theatre as an actor to be taken seriously and had got his feet under the table at the Royal Court. The slights and asides of his being a 'television' actor (then a term of opprobrium, now a prerequisite for theatrical employment) had been successfully dealt with and Shaw had proved himself as an actor of some considerable depth. Each of his three stage roles had been very different and his ability to transform each part into a real and rounded character had been established.

There is an element of luck, of chance, in any actor's career no matter what his talent, perhaps in all careers, but in an actor's it is more marked because the competition is so fierce. Shaw was quite aware of how haphazard and random the progression of an actor's career could be, how turning down one part to accept another, closing one door to open another, could lead not to new corridors but blank walls:

Well I'd just played Hamlet, do you see, and the old girl was very pleased and she said to me 'Henry, come back next season and play Peer Gynt.' But then I was approached to play in the new Galsworthy – at the Haymarket, it was – extremely fashionable do you see – bound to be a great success – social conflict. So I went to Lilian and I asked her to release me and she said she would – and it

was left to Arthur to play Peer. And I never played it. And I think
that may have been the time . . . (*The Hiding Place*).

Parts themselves have a life of their own. An actor can be chosen
from three hundred hopefuls to play a gigantic leading part in a film or
play and think it is an incredible stroke of fortune. But then the film or
the play makes no impact and he is immediately back to square one.
Shaw was lucky to be in the right place at the right time, to be cast as
Mitchem in *The Long and the Short and the Tall* but the luck was
compounded by the fact that the play seemed to hit a nerve in England
at the time, embroiled as it had been in a seemingly endless series of
post-colonial 'police actions' in Aden, Cyprus and Malaysia. John
Arden had dealt with the same subject in *Serjeant Musgrave's Dance* but
Willis Hall's was a more populist treatment of the difficulties of this
type of warfare and the effects of it on the individuals, either conscripts
or professional soldiers, placed in life-threatening situations far from
home. Though O'Toole effectively stole the show, *The Long and the
Short and the Tall* was an important step forward for Shaw.

In August Shaw was offered another theatre role at the New
Shakespeare Company in Liverpool run by the American actor/
director Sam Wanamaker. The play, *One More River* by Beverly Cross
was to be directed by Guy Hamilton (later to direct Shaw in two
feature films), and Shaw's character was very much the crux of the
play. The captain of a ship had died and the mate, Sewell, has to take
over. His brutal and cruel ways lead to near mutiny especially when a
young cabin boy is blinded by having boiling cocoa thrown into his
face by Sewell. But Sewell, called to account, proves that his actions
were necessary to save the ship and everyone in it, and that the incident
with the cocoa was an accident.

Shaw's performance as Sewell was highly praised when the play
transferred from Liverpool to the West End. It opened at the Duke of
York's on 6 October 1959 with Paul Rogers leading the mutiny. *The
Times* wrote that 'the brutal mate who becomes the victim of
circumstantial evidence' was played with 'energy and imagination'. It
was the sort of role Shaw could play with ease; a primitive violence
combined with a surprising logic and reason, hidden at first. The
production was presented by Laurence Olivier Productions. It was
not a success.

It seemed appropriate financially that the Shaws should move house
and they started looking for somewhere bigger and hopefully more
comfortable than the draughty flat in Haverstock Hill. They did not
move far. They had heard that Nigel Stock was moving out of his
rented house in Abbey Road to buy a place of his own. The house was

perfect for their needs, big enough for the growing children and to entertain friends. The rent was controlled and therefore low.

The first item of furniture purchased was a full-sized Jacques table-tennis table to which the front room was sacrificed. From that moment on a series of visitors to the house were put through their table tennis paces. Both Ronnie Fraser and Sean Connery were told, after dismal performances, 'just not worth playing you, boy. Just not worth it.' Philip Broadley was reduced to tears on one occasion after losing a marathon 100-set game.

By this time Jennifer was pregnant again. Shaw's desire – it might even be seen as a need – to have children had not been dulled by the responsibility and the effort of bringing up two small toddlers. They were both girls and Shaw, like Colonel Rimini in *Off the Mainland*, wanted a son. Whether consciously or unconsciously he wanted to re-create the relationship he had had and treasured, however briefly, with his father.

One day I shall my sin unravel
Because my child will aid me.

Shaw's third daughter, Rachel, was born in April 1959.

Chapter Five

One of Robert Shaw's favourite words was 'energy'. He used it constantly. In describing this period of his life Shaw would speak of the way the 'energy' generated from his acting fed into the 'energy' needed for his writing. It was an energy created from the adrenalin of success. For a brief period in his life the duality between his writing and his acting appeared to be resolved. The novel he had started in Suffolk in 1957 ('at the lowest point in my life' he once said) was polished and ready for publication, and Shaw had no doubt about quality.

By one of those coincidences that affect lives, Jill Balcon, one of the fairies in the Old Vic production of *A Midsummer Night's Dream*, had subsequently married the poet C. Day Lewis; who was also a senior partner at the publisher Chatto and Windus. During 1958 Shaw had been invited to their house and became a frequent visitor, talking to Day Lewis about his writing. As the book neared completion he would bring drafts around to be read and would accept any comments with surprising diffidence.

It was natural therefore that when the work was finished Shaw would submit it formally to Chatto's who, through Day Lewis, accepted it immediately. Shaw's first novel *The Hiding Place* was published in 1959, and was dedicated to his mother. It astonished the people who knew Shaw. It did not seem possible that this brash extrovert, boorish or boisterous man (depending on your point of view) could produce a first novel of such sensitivity, exquisite narrative delicacy and powerful character. It was an imaginative achievement, a triumph of characterisation.

Shaw had always been interested in the war and Nazi Germany. He had done his research well. The evocation of post-war Germany, the way the remnants of the Nazi party determined to give up the struggle in the face of the growing prosperity, the gaiety and energy of a country at the beginning of an economic miracle, are beautifully drawn.

But it is in his characterisation that Shaw shows most skill. Hans Frick, a dedicated supporter of Hitler and the Nazis, but a man who finds it difficult to deal with life, has saved two English bomber pilots from a baying mob of Germans, ready to lynch those responsible for the devastation all around them, by hiding them in his cellar. There he keeps them, at first for their own protection and then as his prisoners. Only when he suffers a heart attack does Frick realise he must release them. He has not told them that the war has been over for some years and Germany in 1952 is at the beginning of its post-war economic boom.

The reaction of the two men, Connolly and Wilson, as they try to make sense of what they see and come to fear the worst – that Germany has won the war since there are no air raids and everyone appears happy and prosperous – is wholly convincing. Finally, after a trek down the Rhine, they find an English newspaper dropped by a tourist and realise the truth. (The fictional ordeal of the two men and the imaginative way it is dealt with has curious echoes in the statements of the hostages released in Beirut in 1991.)

Shaw, in all his writing, was to use autobiographical material calling on large chunks of his own experience and ascribing them to his characters. Wilson and Connolly come from the Orkneys and Primrose Hill respectively, and Wilson visits an uncle in his dressing room at the Old Vic. But this material is never self-conscious or obtrusive, it is properly absorbed into the narrative. Shaw's own version of *carpe diem*, expressed so clearly in his poem to Barkworth is also reprised:

> this is where life is and not anywhere else. Now is the time and there's no other time but now. And this is your life and it's the only one you can be sure of . . .

The character of Frick is brilliantly drawn, a study in neurotic concentration (every detail worked out meticulously, leaving no means of escape for the men), an example of how an inadequate personality could be attracted to Nazi philosophy. For the prisoners the cellar comes to mean different things: for Wilson it has allowed him peace to write ('all your life you were looking for somewhere like this') while for Connolly it is a prison and he becomes obsessed with dreams of his wife and a presentiment of his own death.

The way the affection and attachment of the two men has built up over the ten years in captivity is convincingly portrayed but it is the quality of compassion that is the most telling aspect of the book. Shaw makes it entirely understandable that the two men do not want revenge on their gaoler but instead have a real and abiding compassion for Frick. The end of the book demonstrates Shaw's ability to convey a quality of infinite sadness and, at the same time, a real, not a romantic, joy.

There is one curious incident in the book that seems somehow out of place. After the airmen have discovered the truth, but before they are prepared to go into town and face endless questions and reintegration into a world that has passed them by, a step they face with understandable reluctance, they watch an Old Jew addressing a crowd of people about Jesus Christ:

> He was a spiteful man . . . and irritable too . . . Jesus was too much of a Jew. He always wanted to stick to the Old Testament and the Law and the Prophets . . . a bit of a prig . . . He didn't like the family much . . . very fond of wine. But you poor German idiots, what a great man eh? Not one of your Hitlers. A great man. And a Jew!

The themes raised by this character, the relationship between Judaism and Christianity, the irony that Christ was a Jew, seem only of marginal interest in *The Hiding Place* but they were themes to which Shaw would return.

Not all the reviewers of the book were enthusiastic and much of the criticism related to the ending. V.S. Naipaul found it 'tame and disappointing', *The Times* that 'it ends in mid-air'. But generally speaking the critics did the book justice. 'Odd, off-beat queerly haunting . . . an exciting new talent' was the *Daily Telegraph*'s comment, though they might not have used the word 'queer' today. 'The work of a real writer . . . particularly good . . . one of the most original novels of the year', was the *Observer*'s verdict. Penelope Mortimer wrote that 'as a novelist there is no doubt that Mr Shaw takes his place in the highest class with no qualifying talk of promise', and the *Guardian* found the book, 'the most impressive first novel I have read for some time. Original in its central idea, it makes compelling reading.'

The book was sold to Harcourt Bruce in America who were subsequently to publish all Shaw's novels. Rights were sold to France, Spain, Holland and Germany.

The story was to be sold to television twice and become a feature film starring Alec Guinness as Frick and Mike Connors and Robert Redford as the two (now American) flyers. Under the title *Situation Hopeless But Not Serious* it was produced and directed by Gottfreid Reinhardt, a German-born producer/director whose best-known films had been *The Red Badge of Courage*. It was Robert Redford's second feature film. Shaw had nothing to do with the script. In those days it was the custom and practice to sell the film rights in a book outright, especially if it was the work of a young unknown writer. Once the rights were sold the author expected little and got less as far as the artistic integrity of his material was concerned. Perhaps it was Reinhardt's German origin that made it difficult for him to see the book's potential, or merely Paramount executives' insistence, but the story was changed into a comedy and when the airmen eventually escape from Guinness' Hitler-like Frick they run into an American film crew filming a war movie in Germany. Paramount made the film in 1963, but were so unsure of its value it was not released until 1969.

But on television Shaw was more successful. In 1953 when Lew Grade put together the financial backing for what was to become ATV he had secured an investment from Hugh 'Binkie' Beaumont, the most successful West End producer of the time (and perhaps of any time). When they were awarded the franchise Binkie became, as well as continuing with his West End productions, the Head of ATV Drama. He formed a company, H.M. Tennent Television, to produce plays for ATV: at first classics or plays that had run in the West End (*Shadow of Guilt* by Patrick Quentin, *The Accomplices* by Paul Lee and *A Touch of the Sun* by N.C. Hunter for example) but then branched out into work original to television. Shaw was commissioned to adapt his novel into a television play for Binkie-vision, as H.M. Tennent TV was known.

Shaw had met Sean Connery at Richard Hatton's office and the two had become friends. As Sean had also appeared some months before in an ATV Playhouse, though not a Binkie-vision production, he seemed a logical choice for the part of Connolly, while Shaw himself played Wilson and Max Adrian played Frick. The play was directed live by Peter Wood and transmitted on Tuesday 11 October 1960 under the title of *The Pets*.

It was the beginning of a long and competitive professional relationship between Shaw and Connery. They had already had much of the same experience in the British film industry but Shaw's theatrical experience was much greater. Nor did Connery have any pretensions to write. At this point it was Connery who was hanging on the coat-tails of Shaw. Things were soon to change.

The Pets was not the end of the commercial exploitation of *The Hiding Place*. As already noted, Lew Grade had a successful relationship with CBS in America. He showed them the tape – a tape was made on Ampex at the time of transmission – of the play and they bought the rights. CBS Playhouse presented the play with Trevor Howard, James Mason and Richard Basehart.

The reception of the play in England was enough to convince

Binkie Beaumont that Shaw had a real talent as a playwright. He thought the adaptation had worked well and asked Shaw if he had any other material that would be suitable for television. Shaw responded by polishing up a play he had worked on for some time, *The Joke*.

The central theme of *The Joke* is a son's relationship with his father. The joke itself is an elaborate mock suicide staged by Harry, the central character, as an attempt to hurt his father ('he is trying to get back at me because of his mother . . . the only person who ever mattered to him and loved him') and, killing two birds with one stone, his girlfriend, who has been sleeping with another man. The plan is for father and girlfriend to find Harry's body swinging from a noose though it will subsequently be revealed as a dummy. As part of the intricate detail surrounding this plan a tape recorder is concealed so that Harry can hear everyone talking about him. Unfortunately he hears more than he might have wished when his father reveals he was, in fact, adopted. When father and girlfriend then arrive at the appointed place it is not a dummy hanging in the noose but Harry himself ('if a man should shed all his illusions . . . he would not want to live').

Apart from the improbability of the plot in purely critical terms, the play does not succeed because, other than the father's desire to re-marry and the vague talk of what he did to Harry's mother, Shaw never really establishes the psychological motivation for Harry's action, nor what is the raison d'être of the joke. The central character is obsessed with his father ('he can go on about you for hours') and the fact that the relationship between this obsession and the suicide is never properly explained in the play, though clearly inextricable, is probably because Shaw did not understand it himself. It is difficult not to jump to the conclusion that *The Joke* was more an attempt to work out the complex emotional nexus surrounding his own feelings towards his father, and to some extent his mother, rather than a fully formed and well-crafted play. The fact that the plot turns on the use of a tape recorder was also an example of a personal obsession; Shaw was fascinated by them.

Binkie Beaumont did not like the play and indeed it was IBA policy at the time, to deal with suicide in a very circumscribed way. *The Joke*, had it been produced, would have had to be severely cut.

With all this activity, with the sale of rights to television, film and foreign countries, Shaw thought it time to organise his financial affairs. In 1957, Richard Hatton had introduced him to Ivan Paul, a young accountant who looked after Hatton's accounts, to deal with the income from *The Buccaneers*, the first time Shaw had had to worry about tax. Now, with income from various sources, and good prospects of more, in October 1959 he was advised to set up a company which would (in a way already firmly established for successful performers, and tolerated if not exactly approved by the Inland Revenue) enter into a contract with him. This contract would state that Robert Shaw was exclusively employed by the company throughout the world for his acting services, in return for which he would be paid a salary and, from time to time, various bonuses. A 'shelf' company (a company already formed but with no share-holders, directors or finances – a quicker way of starting a company than forming one from scratch), Discoverer and Liberator Film Productions was purchased and renamed River Enterprises Ltd, which immediately became Robert Shaw's employer. Thus a company – e.g. the BBC – wishing to employ Shaw would enter into a contract with River Enterprises who would, as the jargon goes, agree to 'loan out' his services for an appropriate payment. This arrangement allowed Shaw to regularise his tax burden and increase his deductible tax expenses though it probably saved little, in the long run, in tax.

For Robert Shaw at the beginning of 1960 the world appeared to be his oyster. He had established himself as an actor of quality, he had a certain degree of public fame, his writing, once heavily criticised, was now applauded internationally, he was mixing with people he admired intellectually, he was earning almost as much money as he could spend and he was getting regular offers of employment. During 1960 he had substantial parts in three plays for ITV companies, *Misfire*, *A Place of His Own*, and a *Night Run to the West*, and one, *Hindle Wakes*, for the BBC. At Abbey Road, too few people could beat him at table tennis and at the Hampstead Squash Club he had rapidly become the number one player and was talked of as a possible amateur champion. He had a good marriage, a beautiful wife and three healthy children. From the trough of 1957 he was now riding the crest of the wave.

What happened next is open to interpretation. If man is the architect of his own fate, then Shaw either consciously, with malice afore-thought and out of a sense of cussedness or boredom or both, or unconsciously for reasons he did not understand and made no attempt to master, decided this cosy arrangement did not suit his deeper needs and went in search of adventure and destabilisation. If, on the other hand, man is the helpless pawn of the gods, then it was Fate that placed him in proximity to Mary Ure.

In March 1960 Shaw played the part of a journalist from the 'yellow' press, as it was then called, in Patrick Kirwan's *Lodging for the Bride*, directed by John Fernald at the Westminister Theatre. The play, with strong echoes of Hecht and McArthur's *The Front Page*, dealt with cheque-book journalism: a convicted murderer is used by Shaw's character to increase the circulation of his paper. With Roger Livesey and Jane Hylton in the leads, the play opened on 18 April 1960 and was a moderate success. Shaw attracted another set of good notices for 'skilfully delineating the stirrings of conscience' with 'an excellent and subtle sketch' (*Daily Telegraph*).

During the run of the play Shaw was asked to appear on the ITV programme, *Bookman*, which was chaired each week by the critic J. (Jack) W. Lambert, and made at Twickenham Studios. As a fledgling novelist himself he was asked to review Edna O'Brien's *The Country Girls*, while the author herself, rather embarrassingly it might be thought, sat watching, on camera. As it happened Shaw was very flattering about the book. After the programme he offered her a lift back to town in his, by then, Jaguar. He had, she recalled, a 'magnetism' and was a flirt in an understated way. In the car she put her hand on the dashboard. 'You're very nervous,' Shaw commented. 'So are you,' she retorted. But she found him an attractive man, and when he asked for her telephone number she gave it. In the interval of *Lodging for a Bride* he called her, but by this time she was regretting having given him her number and he was not able to convince her to come out with him. Ms O'Brien was, she said, 'a frightened woman (still am) and married at the time'.

This was not the first sign that Robert's relationship with Jennifer was beginning to show strains. A few months earlier at the end of 1959, Shaw had been with Tony Richardson at a party given by Joan Plowright. The party, Shaw declared, was boring and he was going to drink too much. As the two friends got progressively drunk their conversation became more and more salacious, turning to which of the numerous actresses – and in Richardson's case actors – they would most like to fuck. Richardson mentioned Mary Ure, who had married John Osborne in 1957, and Shaw immediately exploded into a series of graphic mimes as to what he would do to her, in what position and for how long. She was, in his view, the sexiest piece of arse he had ever seen. In fact, he said, why didn't they go right round and see her this very minute. As Richardson had directed all of Osborne's plays and was his partner in Woodfall Films, there seemed to Shaw absolutely no reason why Osborne would not welcome a visit from his friend, despite the fact it was already two o'clock in the morning.

Arriving in a taxi the two men stood outside the Osbornes' house in Woodfall Street. Unhappily for the neighbours the next morning was refuse collection day, so the street was lined with metal dustbins waiting to be emptied. These provided an ideal instrument for Shaw to beat out a merry tune to accompany himself as he sang Mary's praises and begged her to come out and play. After some minutes the front door opened and there was John Osborne standing in his dressing-gown. He invited them in, suggesting that ringing the doorbell might have been a more succinct way of gaining admittance. Osborne was a good deal taller than Shaw, but this did not intimidate him from explaining that he had developed a passion for Osborne's wife and actually wanted to fuck her. Osborne gave them both another drink. The appearance of Mary in a long white – reputedly diaphanous – robe did not calm matters. Shaw started moaning with delight and rolling on the floor. Osborne, giving Tony Richardson the icy look for which he was renowned, retired to bed. Shaw lost no time in telling Mary what he had already told Richardson, and her husband, and giving her his telephone number.

Mary called him the next morning.

There is no question that as well as being an attractive woman Mary was a star in Shaw's firmament. She took leading parts in films and in stage plays. She was frequently featured in all the popular papers with and without her husband. Their wedding had hit the headlines, since when they were second only to Laurence Olivier and Vivien Leigh as the couple the press most liked to feature – and pursue. Since the two couples' lives overlapped, there were frequent story opportunities. Any headline that could include the words 'ANGRY YOUNG MAN' seemed to carry a particular appeal for sub-editors. In addition Mary Ure was, like Vivien Leigh, eminently photogenic.

In 1951 Shaw had set out his stall for Jennifer, the most beautiful member of the Old Vic Company. Now not only was Shaw setting a stall for Mary Ure but he was making Osborne an Aunt Sally. At the Court, Osborne was king. Shaw, with his ever-present desire to compete, wanted to dethrone him. He was never going to beat Osborne at the playwriting stakes (Osborne, two years his junior, had two plays on Broadway by the time he was 30); but giving Mary babies, which Osborne had not been able to do, was a game Shaw knew he could win. Nor was Shaw unaware of the enormous amount of publicity that would be generated if he stole Mary away from Fleet Street's favourite eponym. If his motives were a sort of schoolboyish devilment, a wish to give the Head Boy of the Royal Court a bloody nose, he was certainly adult enough to realise that the concomitant press furore would push him into a public prominence that at the moment he had only enjoyed fleetingly. The glitter from Mary's stardom would undoubtedly rub off on him.

Mary Ure was born in Glasgow in 1933, the daughter of an engineer. She had been educated at the Quaker Mount School in York. At the Lyric Hammersmith she had starred in Jean Anouilh's

Time Remembered with Paul Scofield in 1954 ('what *Ring Round the Moon* did for Claire Bloom, *Time Remembered* did for Mary Ure', the *Daily Mail* said in its review of the play) and the following year she had played Ophelia to Paul Scofield's *Hamlet*, directed by Peter Brook. During the run Alexander Korda had walked into her dressing room and offered her a two-picture deal with his 'studios'.★

In 1956 Mary had had a considerable success in *Look Back in Anger* and then in the first English production of Arthur Miller's *View From the Bridge* for Binkie Beaumont to whom she was also under contract. The Broadway production of *Look Back in Anger* was equally successful, by which time she had married its author. After doing the film of *Look Back* in 1958 with Richard Burton she had gone on to star in Jack Cardiff's filmed version of D.H. Lawrence's *Sons and Lovers* for which she was nominated for an Academy Award, as Best Supporting Actress (Shirley Jones won for her performance in *Elmer Gantry*). At Stratford in 1959 it had been decided to repeat Paul Robeson's earlier success in *Othello* and Mary was asked to play Desdemona, whom Peggy Ashcroft had played in the previous production in 1930. She also played Titania to Charles Laughton's Bottom and Virgilia to Laurence Olivier's famous *Coriolanus*, both directed by Peter Hall.

In New York Osborne had already begun a series of affairs and in England continued with the Australian designer Jocelyn Richards. Mary was quite aware of the situation. Her father had provided the money for her to buy the house in Woodfall Street which was, as the lawyers say, the marital home but, when Mary returned to Broadway to play in another Christopher Fry adaptation of a Giraudoux play *Duel of Angels* with Vivien Leigh, Osborne moved into Richards' flat.

It was during the run of *Duel of Angels* that Vivien Leigh announced to the press that Olivier was 'dumping' her for Joan Plowright. Osborne had not made any such intention clear to Mary Ure but the parallels between the situation of the two women were obvious. Mary thought of Vivien as a friend. A great deal had been said about Vivien Leigh's histrionics and affairs but to Mary she was always kind and sensible. She had, Mary said later, been treated outrageously by Olivier.

Mary was being treated equally outrageously by Osborne, who had

★ Mary was quite taken back by Korda's offer but not enough to lose her wits. 'Do I get script approval?' she asked surprising Korda in turn. The charismatic Hungarian was not used to people asking him any sort of questions, especially not twenty-one-year-old blondes. 'Of course my dear, anything you want.' And he was as good as his word. Mary starred in Korda's remake of the Four Feathers story, *Storm Over the Nile*, in 1955 (with Antony Steele) but another script was never found to meet her approval before the studios collapsed in 1957.

clearly taken the marriage very lightly. If we are to believe Osborne her outward calm never cracked, whatever was going on under the surface. Mary was plunged into the deep end of celebrity very much as Osborne himself was. It is a difficult thing to cope with but for the young especially so. No pattern of life has been established, no preferences explored. Mary had lived a comparatively sheltered life in a happy family, the only cloud in her youth being the death of her mother and the arrival of a step-mother. Nothing had prepared her for the internecine intrigue and sexual politics of the Osborne circle.

Mary's way of dealing with stress was to adopt an attitude of severe unconcern, as if nothing Osborne did touched her. Everything else was suppressed. That was not to say that she was incapable of fighting her own corner. In New York, during the run of *Look Back in Anger* while Osborne was away on a Caribbean idyll with his newly acquired mistress, she told her friends she was pregnant. Osborne was called by Harry Saltzman, then a partner in Woodfall Films, with the news, but on his return Mary made no reference to it and was clearly not with child.

Robert Shaw's early morning entry into her life was extremely well-timed. Shaw would always claim, incidentally, that they had been introduced, prior to his impromptu visitation, by a mutual friend, the critic Penelope Gilliatt, who ironically was to become Osborne's third wife, but Mary had no recollection of meeting him before the night in Woodfall Street. Their first venue for dinner together was chosen by Mary – Au Père de Nico where Mary's wedding to Osborne had been celebrated.

In the brief Tangled Triangle of Ure/Osborne/Shaw, 'babies' were to become an issue and a weapon. Mary, according to her friend, the painter Zsuzsi Roboz, had always genuinely wanted a baby. Osborne's preference is not stated. Shaw's philoprogenitiveness, from the evidence of his life with Jennifer, verged on the obsessional. When on New Year's Day 1961 Woodfall Street caught fire and the Osbornes were only saved from a drug-induced sleep by Mary's dachshund, Mary was already pregnant with Shaw's child. During the run of *The Changeling* she announced to the press that she was going to have a baby but declined to name the father. Mary did not tell her husband who the father was either, so Osborne was left to draw his own conclusions. Such was the reward for unfaithfulness.

A Lodging for a Bride closed in June 1960. As well as planning his affair with Mary, Shaw was busy. Chatto and Windus had commissioned his second novel, after he had described his idea to his newly appointed editor, Nora Smallwood. Ms Smallwood, then in her late forties, who was later to become the literary guide and mentor for

Dirk Bogarde, with her tall slender figure and strong features was the sort of woman Shaw could respond to at once. Her authority, like the Headmistress of a girls' public school, left him almost intimidated – a considerable feat – but he was able to talk to her, and take suggestions from her, without it ruffling his masculine pride. Over the next three novels it was Nora Smallwood's opinion he most valued, and her reading of the manuscript he most respected and feared. Shaw, now earning freely, refused an advance for the second novel but instead asked for a bigger royalty. He got 12½%, instead of the more normal 10%, and an option for a third book.

In July Shaw, who had graduated to being asked to contribute articles to the national papers, mostly on the subject of first novels, was asked by *Queen Magazine* to cover the Rome Olympics. He jumped at the chance. He attended every subsequent Olympic Games spending weeks beforehand obtaining tickets for the various finals.

As well as working on his new novel, Shaw delivered the television adaptation of *The Hiding Place* which was transmitted in October. He then re-worked *The Joke*. Meantime, he could pursue Mary on the familiar territory of the Royal Court where she was appearing in *Trials by Logue* directed by Lindsay Anderson which opened on 23 November 1960.

Tony Richardson, like everyone at the Royal Court, knew about the affair between Ure and Shaw. His friendship and partnership with Osborne did not prevent him from suggesting Shaw play de Flores in *The Changeling* with Mary Ure as Beatrice-Joanna.

In the programme note Richardson quoted from T.S. Eliot's essay on Thomas Middleton:

> It is the tragedy of the not naturally bad but irresponsible and undeveloped nature, caught in the consequences of its own action. In every age and in every civilisation there are instances of the same thing; the unmoral nature, suddenly trapped . . . and forced to take the consequences of an act which it had planned light-heartedly.

This was an apt description of what was about to take place in the Tangled Triangle. Richardson knew all three sides; his choice of play suggested that life was about to imitate art.

It is an indication of the new couple's position in the theatrical hierarchy at the time of *The Changeling*, that Shaw had to accept billing – the generic term covering all the ways in which an actor's name is presented to the public in relation to a production, on posters, programmes, paid advertising and 'on the neon' – in the second position, with Mary first.

MARY   ROBERT
URE   SHAW

JEREMY BRETT

He had no grounds for arguing that his name should come first. But he did not like it and when a friend made reference to it the remark was met with a cold silence. Billing was crucially important to Shaw. It always would be. The next time Mary and Robert appeared together it was Shaw's name that would come first, with Mary relegated to subservience, one of the many prices she would pay for their relationship.

By the end of 1960 Mary had brought a house in Cliveden Place. Jennifer decided that this was one winter in England she was going to escape and took the children to Jamaica leaving Shaw to go his own way. For the first time Shaw could be with Mary without arranging accommodation or having to rush back to Jennifer. At Cliveden Place they began to entertain as a couple long before the fiction of Mary's marriage to Osborne was ended by the fire on New Year's Day 1961. Shaw's marital arrangements were less easy to resolve.

Just as Shaw had feasted and fêted Jennifer, so with Mary. He was all over her. He swore undying love for her and was, apparently, exceedingly jealous. Knowing what *they* had got up to at Zsuzsi Roboz's Eccleston Place studios – which they had used for amorous liaisons – he was particularly suspicious when Mary announced she was going there to be painted by Zsuzsi. 'Where Mary Ure goes, I go,' he would say.

Mary, certainly, was more reserved and, possibly, undecided. After her bruising experience with Osborne her caution was understandable. Her pregnancy was a cause of great delight to her. She never doubted for one moment that Shaw would leave Jennifer and come to her, but Mary was an intelligent woman. In an age before the phrase 'woman's liberation' had been coined Mary was already very liberated. She earned as much as a man, she had her own house and she was independent. In a different climate of opinion Mary might not have chosen to marry Robert despite her pregnancy.

Any reticence on Mary's part became a challenge he had to overcome. He had already made her pregnant and, he wrote – in a letter Osborne found – he would do it again immediately after their first child was born. (In the Tangled Triangle, leaving the letter for Osborne to find was clearly not accidental.) Mary's desire for children was real and even after her fourth, when her friends thought she was fulfilling Shaw's agenda rather than her own, she made it absolutely clear to them that she was doing it because she wanted to – deeply and happily. Shaw had found the right 'weapon'.

The problem for him was that he had used it indiscriminately and, after her return from Jamaica in January, Jennifer Shaw announced that she too was carrying Robert Shaw's child – 'irresponsible and undeveloped nature, caught in the consequences of its own action' was an apt description. Shaw found himself sharing his time between his wife and his mistress, both of them bearing his child, and whose stage of pregnancy differed by no more than five weeks.

Chapter Six

The Changeling opened on 21 February 1961 and was a success. The press notoriety of Mary and Robert helped the box office receipts considerably, but it was a brilliantly conceived production by Tony Richardson, and Shaw's de Flores was a performance that confirmed his acting abilities in what was his most demanding stage role to date. The essence of Shaw's successful performances as an actor was always in his ability to convey an extraordinary energy, often sexual energy, combined with charm and a quality of crude, almost psychotic, violence. De Flores was the perfect role for such a talent, beguiling Beatrice-Joanna with a sexual innuendo she does not understand, 'if you know/How sweet it were to me to be employed/In any act of yours . . .' despite his physical repulsiveness (his twisted posture was exaggerated to fit the part) before revealing a gift for unrestrained violence. In some productions the sexuality between de Flores and Beatrice-Joanna is subsumed; in this production Richardson was helped by the offstage intrigues to make the sexual menu clear, the closeness of sexual repulsion to sexual attraction evident.

Shaw's best moment, however, was the affront to his sense of equality:

Look but into your conscience, read me there,
'Tis a true book, you'll find me there your equal.

The idea that a servant was not worthy of a lady was delivered with biting irony. It was a perfect reflection of Shaw's own attitude. Any sort of snobbishness was alien to him. His belief in social equality was one tenet of faith he never breached.

Richardson, curiously, was critical of Shaw. Though he admired his performance he felt ultimately that he lacked 'genius'. Shaw's energy had come to annoy him, and his competitiveness he found childish. It was a symptom of gigantic insecurity, in his opinion, and demonstrated only that Shaw had vaulting 'ambition without achievement'. The two men never worked together again. *The Changeling*, which closed after a record-breaking run at the Court in

April 1961, was to be Shaw's last appearance on the English stage.

Before resolving his personal problems, which were growing daily, Shaw had to deliver his second novel. *The Sun Doctor* was published in the autumn of 1961: ironically it was dedicated to Jennifer. 'Mr Shaw succeeds in making a commentary on the whole human condition . . . a virile and compassionate novel which lifts the spirit', was the *Guardian*'s view. Kenneth Allsop in the *Daily Mail* found it 'consolidates his place as a writer, whole and proven, and one of the powerful individual talents . . .', while Francis Wyndham thought it 'full of ideas, feelings, vigour and imagination. Mr Shaw's outstanding talent is for the bizarre story of action, rich in implication.'

The novel was based on a play Shaw had written before starting on his first novel in 1957. The play, *Strange Providence*, has little to recommend it but does contain the character of Dr Halliday; the idea on which *The Sun Doctor* is based, was taken from an account by Robert Graves of what were called 'Whittaker's negroes', which Shaw had read in the magazine *Encounter*. In the play Shaw is once again concerned to rehearse a father-son relationship:

> I've seen my father so drunk . . . he lay on his back in the main street by the market-place, kicking his legs in the air and shouting and singing, and quite sure he was walking up the side of a hill.

Halliday as a boy carries his father home thinking him dead drunk and stopping halfway to steal a swig from his brandy flask. In fact the father is dead.

> When they told me he'd been dead . . . I felt guilty about that brandy for years . . . I wished he'd lived longer. I might have pulled down the barrier between us.

By the time he came to write the novel, four or five years later, Shaw's ability to transform emotional concerns into beautifully crafted writing was complete. Any personal issues in *The Sun Doctor* are artfully subsumed. And once again the novel astonished those who knew Shaw as an apparently insensitive and boorish man, with its delicacy, compassion and truth. It was, for some, like imagining a boxer in boxing gloves crocheting in lace.

There are obvious similarities in technique to *The Hiding Place*, mainly in the use of memory. As the two prisoners, are, perforce, obsessed with their memories, so is Halliday, for no other reason than that they haunt him. Shaw now has no need for an external motivation. Most of Halliday's memories centre on his father:

'whatever you do for God's sake don't get like me.' As in *The Hiding Place*, Shaw uses autobiographical material freely (to those who knew him it is almost like an in-joke):

> Three schools he had been to: Ladock Church, Stromness Academy and Truro. He'd liked Truro . . . Back from Orkney, back from Cornwall his mother led him to Ladock Church to pray for his father's soul.

And, of course, the character of Halliday is taken up with the idea that his father committed suicide. He remembers his drunken father 'crying, hugging him, burying his face in the pillows'. Halliday, from boyhood had believed that his father's death at sea was suicide and naturally believes it was his fault, that he was to blame, that his father was intent on leaving *him*. That this powerful writing was based on Shaw's own complex emotions in relation to his own father is clear, but it does not detract from the power of the novel.

What Shaw has done is to take this emotional nexus and combine it with a parallel and imaginative story to achieve something of a resolution. Dr Halliday, working in Africa ('he had sworn to do all he could to relieve human suffering') in the heart of the jungle discovers a tribe who have a disease that makes it impossible for them to sweat. The members of the tribe who suffer from the disease have established hegemony over the majority who don't, creating a religious totem to instil the idea that heat, and the sweat it will produce, is death. In breaking this totem Halliday discovers he has merely replaced one tyranny with another – the undiseased members of the tribe now depend on him. His despondence at this mistake is inextricably involved with his memories of his father but when he returns to the Orkneys and is told that his father did not commit suicide but was killed when his ship went down at sea, he decides he has no alternative but to continue to work with the tribe and cure the disease.

What Shaw has done is to create a mirror image of Halliday's feelings – and by implication his own feelings – for his father. Here is a tribe who have not evolved a pattern for survival, just as the father figure – supposedly – did not want to survive.

> Drinkers are never romantic. My father was a drinker and in the end he wasn't romantic at all. He destroyed himself like you lot [the tribe]. He had an instinct for self-destruction.

The book is a struggle with the romantic. Much of it is hard and bitter; Halliday's neurotic reaction to sleeping with Kamante, a young member of the tribe, his loveless encounter with a girl in London, his desire to throw Kamante's dead body into the rocks after her heart attack but, ultimately, romance, that his father's death is accidental, that the tribe will adapt, and that he will find love, makes the ending profoundly optimistic. It is not a false optimism. It is rooted in psychological truth and immediately counterpointed in external reality as a 'mushroom cloud' from a nuclear test is seen over the jungle.

In transposing his play into a novel, there is no doubt that Shaw was influenced by Conrad's *The Heart of Darkness* and, indeed, he even quotes from the book. But at the heart of Shaw's darkness is not evil but guilt and confusion. In comparison to his first novel, the depth and scope of the writing are startingly enlarged. This is a book that through profound and detailed characterisation manages to raise metaphysical questions, questions of life and death, religion and morality.

The novel won Shaw the Hawthornden Prize for novels by writers under the age of 41. The £100 prize money was of less significance to Shaw than to be counted among such previous winners as Sean O'Casey, Robert Graves, Evelyn Waugh and Alan Sillitoe. His ability as a writer was unquestioned; his dream, in this respect, had come true. It came true at a point when his life was in total turmoil. He had no time to take a breath, to consider his good fortune. He may well have wondered like Halliday 'when the pain might grow less – if ever again in his life he would spend a whole day cheerfully, naturally'.

Once again Harcourt Brace picked up the American rights, this time paying $1,250 and the book was sold for translation to France, Sweden, Denmark and Holland.

In Robert Shaw's own character there was always a desperate need to be noticed, to stand apart from the crowd. In sport this manifested itself in his desire to win at all costs and by any means, fair or foul, as long as he ended up the winner. He had no moral objection to cheating outrageously if it would win him the game, though it should be said his cheating was always unconcealed. In a social situation he would achieve the same result by introducing a subject calculated to shock. If he sensed a reluctance, a weakness, a distaste he liked to reveal it, expose it to the public gaze and root around in it. Ralph Michael, who appeared in *Off the Mainland*, recalls a dinner with his then-wife Joyce Heron and Googie Withers when Shaw asked both women to 'describe the female orgasm'. In the play too, he recalled, Shaw would always insist on kissing him full on the lips. Out with friends for dinner at Don Luigi's in the King's Road, Shaw asked a wife, whom he had never met before, 'Have you ever been buggered?'. When she replied that she had not, he seized on this as an opportunity to describe the whole procedure in technical detail – 'You see, you have to be very hard, it's no good unless you're really hard . . .' A deathly hush had fallen over the whole restaurant while everyone tried not to listen to the conversation.

It is not surprising that among friends and acquaintances he would describe his situation with Jennifer and Mary quite openly and often, seemingly, with delight. When asked the question as to what he was going to do he would reply, 'I'll take the one that gives me a boy.' The fact that this is precisely what he did, in the end, does not detract from the feeling that Shaw's remark was made more for its shock value in a social situation, then for its factual content. Whatever the truth the dichotomy of the man is apparent. A man who could write:

A crimson glow above London had seemed to be a reflection of his own adolescent distress. Alone in the dark he had cried out in sympathy at human suffering, and had sworn to do all he could to relieve it . . .

and yet he was as crass as to tell his friends that his future lay in the random arrangements of chromosomes.

Among his friends there was unanimity as to what he should do – stay with Jennifer. Philip Broadley was particularly vehement in his opposition to Mary, not because he did not like her, but because he felt she was not right for Shaw. On one occasion Philip had shared a taxi with Mary, after visiting the couple at Cliveden Place, and had told her that they should not get married. By all means have an affair, he had told her, but marriage would be a 'disaster'. His opposition was based on the fact that he felt, in Jennifer, Shaw had exactly what he needed. She was a good mother, lover and friend; she had long since given up any ideas of continuing her career. She was no competition. Mary, on the other hand, was a working actress, a strong and determined woman (behind the 'wilting flower' look as Broadley put it) who was an intellectual equal to Shaw.

As with John Osborne's affairs, the idea of keeping matters secret seemed to be very much out of fashion and Jennifer was by now perfectly aware of what was going on. She decided that having to look after three small children might cramp her husband's style somewhat, so she packed her bags and headed out, on her own, to Jamaica, where the situation could be discussed with her family.

It was Harold Pinter, long a friend of Shaw's, sharing the problems of poverty and young babies at virtually the same time, who provided the catalyst. He had achieved a significant breakthrough as a playwright with the production of *The Caretaker* at The Arts in 1960, Donald Pleasence in the title role. The play had transferred to the Comedy Theatre for a 16-month run, and was now being moved to Broadway. The part of Aston, originally played by Peter Woodthorpe, was to be re-cast and Shaw naturally came to mind. In fact he had been considered for the original production but had already accepted *A Lodging for a Bride*. But when the Broadway production was mooted Shaw was only too keen to accept. Jennifer had been away for three weeks and the antics of a trio of young children were beginning to pall even on Shaw who enjoyed his infants greatly in short bursts. It was the ideal opportunity to escape his domestic situation and the perfect excuse to persuade Jennifer to come back to look after the kids. She agreed.

In the last week of August Mary moved in with Zsuzsi Roboz at her Eccleston Place studios while Shaw flew to New York. On 30 August 1961, as Zsuzsi was painting, Mary came down from the bedroom and gaily announced that her waters had broken. A few hours later her gynaecologist Dr Spicer delivered Colin Osborne into the world – Robert Shaw's first, and long-awaited, son. The tabloid headlines marked the event with a degree of confusion: 'FOR MARY URE – A SON', 'JOHN OSBORNE'S A SHY DAD.'

Five weeks later on 4 October 1961 Jennifer Shaw gave birth to Katherine Shaw, the newspapers marking the event with slightly smaller headlines – 'HER BABY IS BORN WHILE HUSBAND WORKS IN NEW YORK'.

On 14 October, her six-week-old son and a nurse in train, Mary flew to Philadephia. Asked by reporters why she had come to America she replied, 'for a rest'. She was not pursued to New York, where she joined Robert who had opened in *The Caretaker* on the very night his daughter was born. The need for discretion at this point was not merely for Jennifer's sake, nor an aversion from publicity. The divorce laws in 1961 still carried the notion of a 'guilty party' who could be punished by the courts when the settlement came to be discussed. Presumably the main reason for Mary's careful subterfuge was to ensure that the caster of the first stone was seen to be Osborne and that matters were not confused by subsequent pictures of her with another man, clutching his baby.

It was also a defence. Mary was far from a fool. If she had announced to all and sundry that she was having Shaw's child and he returned from New York to hotfoot it back into Jennifer's arms, despite his avowals of love for her, Mary would have been left facing a very public humiliation. She had no intention of doing that. Her public posture of sublime unconcern served her well. She played a waiting game, and won.

Shaw's performance in *The Caretaker* was remarkable. The part of Aston was probably the most difficult acting role he had attempted. Unlike the part of de Flores where his flamboyance and charismatic ability to catch and hold the eye could be given full play, the character of Aston required a minimalism of performance with very little dialogue. The play called for a whole new acting style far from the mainstream English theatrical tradition of bravado, articulation and showmanship. Shaw was cast against type but was superb nonetheless, as the film version confirms. It was his ability to invest Aston with a brooding quality and a feeling of concealed power that made him so effective in the role. The menace (a word that seemed to characterise Pinter's early plays) and power the character exudes is matched only by the character's seeming inability to come to terms with the world. Instead he had created a world of his own, with its own strictures and its own dynamic, understood only by him. It was unquestionably a part that required a huge effort from Shaw and he was quoted as saying that it was the most tiring role he had ever played.

Despite this effort of will Shaw was not the kind of actor who required a regimen of absolute concentration during a performance, just as he was not a writer who had to have peace and quiet – let alone emotional tranquillity. Seconds after leaving the stage in the role of the uncommunicative Aston he would revert to the flamboyant character he had made his own.

After a month of the Broadway run, Alan Bates had to return to England to start filming on *A Kind of Loving*. Shaw, always the first to remember his friends, had immediately suggested Alex Davion for the part and Donald MacWhinnie, the director, had agreed. With Bates in the audience to watch his replacement on the Saturday matinée (before giving his last performance on the Saturday night), and having been rehearsed by a very drunken MacWhinnie for only a week, Davion was understandably nervous. During one of the play's many silent blackouts Shaw came up behind him and goosed him comprehensively. Davion only just managed not to cry out. 'Thought that would relax you boy,' Shaw hissed characteristically through clenched teeth.

It was Shaw's first appearance on Broadway. The critical reception for the play confirmed the London notices and all three performances were praised. Shaw enjoyed the celebrity, eating at Sardi's and staying at the Algonquin for the first time. It was not an easy life however. Jennifer was at home with his family of four and Mary was in New

York with his family of one. Petitions and cross-petitions were filed. Osborne petitioned for divorce citing Shaw, Mary petitioned Osborne citing three women. Penelope Gilliatt's husband petitioned his wife citing Osborne. The Tangled Triangle still had some months to run.

If Shaw had ever considered going back to Jennifer after *The Caretaker*, it was quite clear that his time in New York with Mary solidified his intention of doing no such thing. Had he been living at home with Jennifer and the children, the eldest still only seven, with nothing to do (there was an actor's strike in England at the time) he might not have been able to walk out so easily. But his career had taken him to New York and, in a sense, made the decision for him. He had also reached a point where he could just afford, with the help of Mary's larger financial resources, the alimony he was going to have to pay.

The end of the run of *The Caretaker* came at the beginning of 1962 and Shaw returned to England with Mary travelling separately to avoid the press. Willis Hall, author of *The Long and The Short and the Tall*, had written a screenplay based on *L'Equipage Au Complet*, a play by Robert Mallet, which Roy Ward Baker was to direct and now retitled *The Valiant*. It was to be made on location in Torrento, southern Italy, with John Mills starring as the captain of a battleship forcing captured frogmen to reveal where they had placed their time-fused limpet mines. Shaw accepted the part of the trusty NCO with alacrity, no doubt delighted to distance himself from his personal problems once again.

The domestic turmoil had not dulled his sporting instincts. The ship used in Torrento harbour was rat-infested and Shaw was only too happy to show other members of the cast how harmless rats were, running around the hold trying to see how many he could catch. On days off Shaw would organise a day of sporting events, sprints, five-a-side football matches, table tennis and arm-wrestling.

Shaw had not made a film since *Sea Fury* in 1958. In that year it had looked as though he might become one of a handful of actors who made up a kind of British film repertory company living entirely on film appearances. It is the existence of this 'company' that explains why the same faces turn up over and over again in the British films of the period (between 1950 and 1965 when the industry suffered a major set-back with the phasing out of 'B' movies). Film directors were not known for inventive casting. Richard Attenborough, Victor Maddern, Harry Andrews, Gerald Sim, George Baker and Lionel Jeffries were all regular members. But Shaw's career had taken off in the theatre after *Sea Fury* and now with some notable critical successes it looked as though the film industry was going to take a subsidiary role in his career.

Back in England after the eight weeks on *The Valiant* the priority was to find a place to live. Shaw's finances were capable of supporting his daily life and that of Jennifer and the children, still living in the Abbey Road house, but he had never succeeded in saving any money and still did not own a house. Fortunately Mary had the profits from the sale of Woodfall Street plus her investment in Cliveden Place. The need for a new house was made more urgent in July 1962 when Shaw fulfilled his written promise to Mary and gave her a second child. As neither Mary nor Robert worked again until the autumn they had plenty of time to look at properties and in August they bought, with Mary's money, Porch House in Amersham, Buckinghamshire.

The house was an ideal place for a family, surrounded by garden and in a quiet rural setting. It was not particularly beautiful, rather square in proportions with an attic extension that made it seem top-heavy. But there were eight bedrooms and, eventually four bathrooms, which made it suitable for what was soon to be (when Jennifer's children came to visit) a family of six children. Later they would add a swimming pool and, inevitably, a tennis court. There was also plenty of room for the prized table-tennis table.

The house became a haven for Shaw. It was a home. Mary, surprisingly to some, was also a home-maker. Shaw developed an interest in the large garden and begun to plan plantings. Later they would buy an adjoining orchard where a succession of fruit trees would suffer a series of pestilences and never develop into the hoped-for cottage industry. Most of all, Porch House gave Shaw unlimited opportunities to challenge guests at whatever game he was currently playing, as well as all the old favourites. Boule, for instances, had recently been added to the list.

One evening, Shaw had invited Philip Broadley and Alex Davion, together with Leo Vala, a wealthy businessman who ran an industrial photography company and had been a card-carrying member of the Communist Party despite his Rolls Royce, to play Subeteo table football. It was, as it turned out, not a game that suited Shaw because flicking the ball with the tiny players required a degree of delicacy that Shaw did not possess. Shaw was in goal, his player attached through the goal to a wire at the back of the board. The stake was five pounds. Broadley scored twice almost immediately and was then awarded a penalty. This time Shaw moved the wire so violently the whole board tipped over on to the floor. From then on every time his goal was threatened. Shaw used this ploy to avoid goals being scored against him. Finally Broadley lost his temper at these antics and told his friends he had no intention of playing any further. In that case, Shaw retorted, the game is forfeit and, 'you better hand over the fiver, boy.' Broadley stormed out of the house and back to London swearing he would never have anything to do with Shaw again. The next morning his phone rang. It was Shaw. 'Well, boy, glad we got a little spirit back into the game, boy,' he said laughing. Broadley found he started to laugh too.

On another occasion Shaw bought an expensive set of badminton equipment, complete with nets, rackets and shuttlecocks. But badminton was not like tennis, in which power could overcome most subtleties. Like Subeteo it requires a certain delicacy, a snapping action of the wrist, which Shaw did not possess and could not learn. Invited to play the moment the new equipment arrived from Harrods Philip Broadley found he could score freely off Shaw and, after some practice, was able actually to hit Shaw with the shuttlecock. An infuriated Shaw lost the match. The badminton set was never seen again.

Shaw's achievements in the theatre had certainly wiped away, at least in the minds of the profession, the image of Dan Tempest. His reputation as a classical actor was further enhanced in 1962 by two performances in plays for the BBC. In April he played Leontes in *The Winter's Tale* for director Don Taylor in which *The Times* said he 'possessed a driving intensity that seemed naturally to express itself in a brooding quality of delivery' and in June earned similar praise in the BBC production of Strindberg's *The Father* with Daphne Slater.

Shaw's next employment was an interesting 'B' movie, *Tomorrow at Ten*, directed by Lance Comfort, in September 1962. It was a cut above the usual run of 'B' movie pictures mainly because of a well-plotted script and excellent performances from Alec Clunes and Shaw. Shaw played a kidnapper who is killed before he can reveal the hiding place of his young victim. He invested the character with qualities very similar to Aston in *The Caretaker*; his sparse dialogue exuding menace gave the film an element of reality that might otherwise have been missing.

Porch House provided Shaw with the perfect writing environment. In the attic extension a room was designated as his study, bookshelves installed together with his drop-leaf desk and a black leatherette swivel chair placed in front of the window to reveal a panorama of Buckinghamshire countryside. But the dawning of contentment in his domestic life at Porch House seemed to militate against his writing. *The Sun Doctor* was delivered to Chatto and Windus in spring 1961. It would be 1965 before his next novel reached them. The long climb to the attic room was undertaken with less frequency than writing perched in the bedroom in a house where he could not be so easily isolated from the family.

Due almost entirely to her successive pregnancies Mary had not worked since *The Changeling* in April 1961. Now in November 1962 she starred in *The Mindbenders* directed by Basil Dearden, as the six-month pregnant wife of a scientist involved in 'brainwashing' experiments. She was then, three months into her own pregnancy.

Harold Pinter and his producer Michael Birkett were making frantic efforts to raise the money to film *The Caretaker*. It was never going to be a picture that would appeal to traditional sources of film finance, so Birkett set about creating a private syndicate of investors to finance a budget pared of everything non-essential. The three actors and Pinter all agreed to do the picture for a 'notional' fee which would be subsequently paid out of profits (i.e. they would receive no money at the time of making the film). Letters to potential investors were sent out and Noël Coward, Peter Sellers, Peter Hall, Harry Saltzman and Richard Burton all contributed various sums. The film, directed by Clive Donner, was shot in a derelict house in Hackney. It took some years for the money to be repaid but eventually it was, and the actors too got their fees. (As the American language has no exact equivalent for the word 'caretaker' the film was released in America under the title of *The Guest*.)

In January 1962 Sean Connery had been driven to Pinewood Studios to start the first day's filming on a picture produced by Harry Saltzman and Cubby Broccoli, and directed by Terrence Young, but due to a heavy fall of snow the car was late and the start of filming delayed. The film was *Dr No*, the first in what was to become a record-breaking series of James Bond films. Its success, when it opened in the autumn of that year, was to take everyone by surprise including its two producers. Fortunately they owned an option for the rights in all Ian Fleming's Bond books (with the exception of *Casino Royale* and the short story on which *Thunderball* was based) and a second film was immediately planned to exploit the success of the first.

As Richard Hatton was Sean Connery's agent he had done the deal for the first film, and seeing the script for the second, suggested another of his clients, Robert Shaw, for the part of the killer, Grant. The situation between Connery and Shaw was neatly reversed. It was Shaw who was now hanging on coat-tails.

Shaw's role of Grant, the blond killer in *From Russia With Love*, is certainly well remembered. His sneering dismissal of the effete Bond ('you may know which wines to drink with your fish but it's you who are on your knees') and his silent threatening presence through the first two-thirds of the action brought out Shaw's best characteristics as an actor – the ability to suggest a capacity for unlimited violence (Grant is described as a psychopath) in a character on the lower rungs of life, in conjunction with some sort of moral, physical or spiritual superiority, however fleeting.

The key to the instability of the role in popular terms was how it was written in the screenplay, however. The character was central to the development of the plot of the film and though, in effect, Grant gets little screen time, the fact that everything leads up to the confrontation on the Orient Express in Yugoslavia, until which time Grant is given no dialogue, gives the part its impact. A comparatively small but crucial part may often count for more than a good performance in a large part which is less integral to the film. In addition of course, the film was a phenomenal success on the back of the expectations raised by *Dr No*. Saltzman and Broccoli had managed to tap a vein of sentiment and communal psychological need, that no one knew was there. The elegant, slick, womanising, smoking, fast-car driving, gadget-ridden, gambling and ever-witty Bond was an image that appealed to a generation of men *and* women. It led to a series of films which will probably never be equalled in their money-making capacity or their ability to provide escapist entertainment. *From Russia With Love* was one of the best of the series, with a reliance on character, a straightforward plot and none of the massive set-pieces of the subsequent films. Shaw was paid £1400 for his work with no participation in the profits.

Mary Ure delivered Shaw his fifth daughter on 29 April 1963 by which time he was in Istanbul filming the interiors at the Saint Sophia Cathedral. As soon as she was able to travel she took Colin and the new baby (Elizabeth - Lizzie) out to Turkey to join him.

The actual filming of *From Russia with Love* was beset by a series of disasters. At Sinkeci Station in Istanbul the train driver couldn't hit his mark and ran over and cut the generator cables. In shooting the sequence where Bond is chased by power boats – filmed in a Scottish loch – the helicopter carrying the director Terence Young crashed after two minutes in the air. He walked away with only light bruising and continued the shoot. In addition Pedro Armendariz, who played Kerim Bey, was dying of cancer. He had begged to be allowed to continue the part when he was given the news so that his wife would be left some money and the film was re-scheduled to shoot his scenes at Pinewood Studios first. Afterwards, a 'going-away' party was held for him at Terence Young's house which Ian Fleming, who was also gravely ill, attended.

Shaw always liked to tell his friends that in the climactic fight in a railway carriage between himself and Connery he had 'bested' Connery. What precisely this meant, especially as he repeated it to actors who were quite aware that most of the fight was done by stuntmen (Jackie Cooper for Shaw and Bob Simmons for Connery), is not entirely clear but there is no question that Shaw did not enjoy being second to someone he had 'bested' for several years professionally. It rankled with him. That is not to say that the two men were not, and would not remain, friends. Shaw admired in Connery qualities he did not himself possess. Connery was straightforward, no-nonsense, direct. To Shaw, Connery's life looked amazingly simple and uncomplicated.

Connery, on the other hand, was aware of Shaw's problems and occasionally would lose patience with him. Golf, Connery's passion since he had been sent away to learn the game for the golf match with Gert Fröbe in *Goldfinger*, and a game that Shaw had played since he was a boy, became a natural extension of friendship and they played together whenever circumstances permitted. Gradually, however, Connery ceased to enjoy playing with a friend who was constantly arguing and challenging every shot, especially when he was losing.

On the 13 April 1963, just before filming began on *From Russia with Love*, and two weeks before Lizzie was born, Mary Ure and Robert Shaw were married in Amersham Registry Office. And it was immediately after the filming that Shaw met the woman who was to play a remarkable role in his life. Virginia de Witt Jansen (to be known henceforward and by everyone as Miss Jay). She was working as a temporary secretary for Richard Hatton's agency while she tried to sort out the mess that had become her life. Her father, Clinton, had been a plantation manager in Malaysia before retiring and returning to England to live. The world Miss Jay had experienced as a child was very different from the one that awaited her on being shipped off to an English boarding school. In Malaysia there were servants to pick up her clothes as she undressed at night, servants to turn back the bed, servants to dress her in the mornings, servants to wash, iron and cook. As she grew older the contrast in her life increased, holidays from school spent in tropical comfort, compared with the necessary stoicism of poorly-heated boarding schools. She was one of many such children sent halfway across the world by parents anxious to make sure that their children did not 'go native' and got a proper education. They stood in ranks on railway stations, small leather suitcases clutched in their woollen mittens, big wooden trunks stowed away, brown paper labels tied around their necks. It was the last throw of the Empire, before plantations were nationalised by emergent governments, and international jet flight put packet steamers out of business.

This may not have been the best preparation for dealing with the London of the 1960s and Miss Jay found herself pregnant by a Frenchman who had no intention of marrying her, and whom she had no wish to marry. When her parents discovered her situation she was told 'never to darken their door again'. She could expect no help from them.

As the time approached to have the baby she would have to leave the temporary job she had at Richard Hatton Ltd. A cousin in Denmark had offered to help and there, in the land of storks nestling in chimneys, her son Charles was born.

It was Hatton who mentioned to Robert Shaw, whom he knew was thinking of hiring a secretary, that Miss Jay was in a difficult predicament. Obviously a traditional secretarial job was out of the question. It would cost more to have a nanny for the baby and a flat to live in than she could possibly earn as a secretary. How could she find somewhere to stay with a baby and pay for all the many necessities? Robert Shaw came to her rescue. Shaw asked Hatton to send her up to see him and hired her on the spot. It was a perfect solution. One more baby made no difference in the Shaw household. Mary was only too keen to help Miss Jay with the finer points of motherhood. Miss Jay could type up Shaw's manuscripts, answer his letters, and generally be useful in arranging his life for which she would receive 'bed and board for herself' with her baby son and earn a small salary.

Not many people would have taken a stranger into their home in quite the same way. It was a gesture of kindness on Shaw's part – and on Mary's.

Jennifer, a thoroughly sensible woman, saw no point in inflicting any bitterness she might feel on her children. Nor did she blame Mary for what had happened, or, if she did, she kept it to herself and did not let an animosity develop. In this way it was soon common, while Jennifer went back to Jamaica for holidays or needed the children looked after for whatever reason, that the family at Porch House would swell to seven children, the eldest still only 10.

Shaw's slowness in writing his next novel was partly explained by diversions into other areas. It was not unnatural in an industry not renowned for its subtlety that the reaction to an actor who wrote novels should be to imagine that this could devolve into a talent for writing screenplays. Richard Hatton began receiving enquiries for Shaw's services as a screenwriter, and in response started suggesting him for the role. Shaw had no objection and indeed, was not at all averse to the idea of earning £2,000 for a first-draft screenplay. But writing for the screen was not something he took particularly seriously; for him it was not of the same order of things as writing a novel. It was essentially frivolous and he spent none of the time and painstaking effort he used on the novels.

With the success of the Bond films Harry Saltzman was now flush with cash. He called the Richard Hatton office to ask if Lukas Heller, an established screenwriter, would be available to write the screenplay of a book by Len Deighton to which he had just acquired the screen rights. Heller was heavily involved in the follow-up to *What Ever Happened to Baby Jane?*, which he had written, but Hatton suggested that Shaw might be an appropriate choice to write the screenplay for *The Ipcress File*. Saltzman and Shaw met for lunch. *The Ipcress File* offered an opportunity to create an entirely different sort of spy, a counterpoint to the suave, elegant and fantastical Bond, a working-class spy, worried about his pay scales and so firmly rooted in reality he even did his own cooking, Saltzman explained. Shaw, having read the book, was enthusiastic and was hired to write a first draft screenplay. It was his first commission for a film.

Robert Shaw was now 36 years old and had six children. He was in demand as an actor and as a writer. The success of *From Russia with Love* had given him a profile in the international movie industry, namely America, for the first time. Just after the success of *The Buccaneers* Shaw had returned to Cornwall with Jennifer in his 1933 Rolls Royce, and subsequently taken her to the Orkneys. Now he took Mary to see the Orkneys in the wake of the release of *From Russia with Love*. He liked to re-visit the scenes of his childhood at a point when he was enjoying public success. The popularity of his latest film, and the clutch of interviews he had done certainly assured him of that, even in Stromness. But while this can be seen as a sort of bragging, there was a serious point to these visits. His return to scenes of profound unhappiness were a way of using his success to lay the ghost of his past. He used his childhood as a touchstone of how he felt about himself, and the glittering prizes of success proved to be only a temporary balm. Later, when the meaning of success was less clear, when the fame he had sought and savoured, had turned sour, he would not go back to Cornwall or the Orkneys.

Chapter Seven

The momentum of Shaw's career was now considerable and 1964 would be his busiest year so far in both acting and writing. At the end of 1963 Irving Kershner, an American film director, had arrived in England to cast a film based on Brian Moore's book *The Luck of Ginger Coffey*, set amongst the Irish community in Montreal. He had seen Mary Ure in *Sons and Lovers* and felt the qualities she had portrayed made her ideal casting for the part of Ginger's wife in his film. After some initial conversation with Mary's agent, Kershner was invited to Porch House for lunch, where he was introduced to Robert Shaw. He had only a dim awareness of Shaw as an actor, which probably went for all Americans up until the release of *From Russia with Love* in the USA in January 1964, but became increasingly aware, as the lunch progressed, that Shaw could well be suited for the part of Ginger. The innocent childlike delight that consumed his whole face when he beat Kershner at table tennis convinced him. It was the essential quality for Ginger Coffey, a character of childlike naïvety and enthusiasm. It would be Shaw's first leading part in a film and his first film together with Mary.

Taking Miss Jay with them, Mary and Robert and the children set off for Montreal in the middle of winter. It was freezing. The filming took place in an old warehouse due for demolition which Kershner had temporarily turned into a sound stage. But no matter how many heaters were employed the warehouse never seemed to get warm, the icy wind seeping in through every broken window.

Ginger Coffey is an Irish immigrant to Canada who finds it difficult to keep a job because he has an exaggerated sense of his own importance. His wife, Vera, not finding Canada to be the country of her dreams, wants to go back to Ireland, but Ginger, always the optimist, thinks Canada will finally recognise his talents. So Vera leaves him though their daughter refuses to go with her mother. Ginger works during the day delivering nappies and at night on a newspaper. He is convinced the paper is going to promote him, so he leaves the day job only to be fired by the paper for insolence. He goes on a drinking binge and is arrested for indecent exposure when he is caught pissing against a wall. It needs all his charm and innocence but he manages to talk the judge into letting him off. Outside the court Vera and his daughter are waiting for him.

This slight story needed the power of Shaw's characterisation of Ginger. Given the opportunity to create a leading character Shaw gives Ginger an infectious charm, and manages to put a gloss on the less satisfactory elements of the story. It was a carefully judged and mature performances and showed, again, that Shaw was capable of bravado and flamboyance as an actor while at the same time reaching emotional depths and portraying matters of great sensitivity. The background of the Montreal winter, with Arctic temperatures and heavy snow matched the story perfectly.

Like most actors Shaw was very realistic about his performances and indeed this was to become a problem in later life. He knew perfectly well when he was bad, using tricks and mannerisms to suggest a character ('a bucketful of clichés') rather than something more substantial. He also knew when he was good and for him Coffey was one of his best screen roles. In an interview with the *New York Times* he described his pleasure in playing a leading role and his hope that the film 'will mean a breakthrough for us'. It did not. The film had a very limited release in America and an even smaller one in England. The critics were enthusiastic about his performance and about the film but the subject matter was never going to make it more than an 'art house' film. It is the sort of film, as a character study of one man, that would have sat better in the French film industry.

Writing commitments were mounting. Working on his new novel which Nora Smallwood had agreed to postpone from delivery in January 1964 and on *The Ipcress File*, Shaw had also had the idea to adapt an unfinished Oscar Wilde play, *The Florentine Tragedy*, for television. The play, which was completed by the poet T. Sturgis Moore, concerns the story of an ageing merchant and his young wife who falls in love with a penniless younger man – a triangle not dissimilar to *Off the Mainland* – and provided excellent roles for Robert and Mary. It had been sent to Sydney Newman at the BBC who agreed to do it immediately and brought in Herbert Wise to direct. James Fox was contracted to play the young lover.

But after the first week's rehearsal it became increasingly clear that Robert Shaw and James Fox were never going to be able to co-operate as actors and James Fox decided he had to leave the production. It was a clash of temperament, the braggart Shaw against the sensitive Fox or the wimpish Fox against the impassioned Shaw, depending on your point of view. Shaw, always loyal to his friends, once again suggested Alex Davion to fill the breach. The play was transmitted on 11 March 1964.

The next project was also for the BBC. 1964 was the quarter-centenary of the birth of William Shakespeare and Sydney Newman planned a *Hamlet* to be shot on location at Elsinore Castle. A co-production (with WNET in America and Danish Radio) was arranged, Peter Luke brought in to do the adaptation and Philip Saville sent off to do a 'recce'.

Saville assembled what is called an 'international' cast: Alec Clunes as Polonius, Christopher Plummer as Hamlet, Jean Tobin as Gertrude and Jo Maxwell Miller as Ophelia. Among the rest of the cast several names would subsequently become national and international figures – Steven Berkoff as the Player King, Michael Caine as Horatio, Lindsay Kemp as the Player Queen and Donald Sutherland as Fortinbras. Despite being only two years older than Christopher Plummer, Shaw was cast as Claudius.

It was a major television event and a major production problem. This was long before the days of light-weight cameras; the huge and heavy turret cameras had to be manhandled through the corridors of the gothic castle. For convenience the shooting was divided between two units nicknamed Nina and Frederick. Inside the castle walls a television city of 150 people grew; wardrobe, properties, construction and catering.

Saville had told Newman the whole production would take four days. Newman said it had to be done in three. In fact Saville knew perfectly well it would take eight and secretly scheduled accordingly. On the fifth day he got a call from Newman who was panicking. It must be finished the next day he shouted 'even if you shoot it like a football match'. On the sixth day the head of television, Kenneth Adam, came out to the location. Saville expected the worst but Adam looked round with interest and made no comment whatsoever. The shoot finished after eight days on Saville's original hidden schedule.

The players' scene was shot in the 100-metre ballroom of the castle and, with all the technical complications, meant a long day's work. Shaw had insisted that his chalice be filled with whatever the modern equivalent of 'rhenish' ('as he drains his draughts of rhenish down') was. By rather torturous reasoning it was decided the modern equivalent was schnapps and the chalice was filled accordingly. It was a large chalice encrusted with 'jewels'. By the time he got to his lines, after the various takes and re-takes, Shaw was calling for the chalice to be re-filled. His make-up, planned to be reddish, now appeared beetroot. But he got through his lines perfectly, without hesitation, until on 'O my offence is rank, it smells to heaven' his elbow slipped off the arm of his chair. As the line was well-known Saville had to 'pick it up' (re-shoot the line later) but this time, try as he might, Shaw could not get it out. The schnapps had finally won. It took a great deal of work before the 'pick-up' was successful.

The production also had to negotiate a new agreement with Actors Equity since at the time television was only allowed to use actors for continuous recording for three times the length of the programme. The *Hamlet* production was based on what later became known as 'rehearse-record' and needed entirely different criteria.

The new agreement did not see the actors out of pocket, however, especially not the principals. Some weeks later, after the shoot, Saville had lunch with Shaw at Alvaro's in the King's Road. After lunch Shaw showed him his new car, a sparkling Mark Ten Jaguar. 'That's my overtime from Hamlet,' he told him.

Shaw was earning good money. But he was also following the advice he had given to Peter Barkworth in 1948: 'live above your income'.

He was generous with friends, lent and gave money freely and, as the new Jaguar showed, could be wildly extravagant, especially when it came to cars. He was fascinated by expensive cars, not through any mechanical bent (he knew absolutely nothing about the workings of a car engine – he had no practical skills), but because they were an easily understood status symbol. A car, for Robert Shaw, was a statement. He liked his statements to be unequivocal. His car needed to proclaim his success and loudly. He was particularly found of white cars. He owned three Rolls Royces, two Jaguars, and a Cadillac prior to 1968.

After *Hamlet* was finished Shaw had a screenplay and a novel to deliver and was approached by E.J. Arnold to edit an anthology of modern poetry, hoping, no doubt, that his name would help sales. Shaw had continued his interest in poetry – in fact he never wrote anything that did not include verse, however brief, somewhere, whether his own or someone else's, including verse by his daughters Deborah and Penny in *The Flag* – but under the pressure of time merely handed the publishers a list of material, unedited and with no preface. A co-editor, Jon Silkin, had to be brought in to sort the book out and write an introduction. Silkin received a flat fee and no royalties: the royalties went to Shaw. *Flashpoint* was published in 1964.

In the summer Shaw delivered his second writing commitment, the screenplay of *The Ipcress File*, to Harry Saltzman. As with most screenplay contracts a writer is commissioned to write a first draft for which he is paid a sum of money (in this case £2,000) after which there is a 'cut-off' should the producer decide he does not want to have the writer proceed to a second draft incorporating the producer's notes. Saltzman was not impressed with Shaw's efforts and told him he did not want to go to a second draft. There was a double disappointment for Shaw, who had cheerfully announced to Penguin Books, who were publishing the paperback edition of *The Sun Doctor* in July 1964, that he would be playing the part of Harry Palmer in the forthcoming film. Harry Saltzman told him he had now cast Michael Caine in the part.

The delivery of his third novel, *The Flag*, to Nora Smallwood and Chatto and Windus was greeted with a great deal more enthusiasm. Nora Smallwood called Shaw to tell him that she was delighted; it was, she said, his best book so far and a book of real quality. It would be published in 1965.

In August Shaw was approached by Peter Brook to go to Broadway in his production of Frederick Dürrenmatt's *The Physicists*. After a three-month run at the Aldwych in the previous year the production was being revived to take to New York with Irene Worth – who had played Helena in *A Midsummer Night's Dream* with Shaw at the Old Vic in 1951 – expected to be billed first. Shaw refused. Using his success in *The Caretaker* on Broadway as ammunition he demanded to be placed first. He had no intention of doing the gentlemanly thing and letting the lady go first, as was suggested. The impasse was resolved when Irene Worth withdrew and her role was taken by the American actress Jessica Tandy. Shaw got his first position billing, for the first time on Broadway.

Shaw disliked flying, though it never became a phobia with him. By preference and if time allowed, however, he would always elect to go by sea. Indeed crossing the Atlantic on a liner, he would often say, was one of his greatest pleasures, seeing New York emerge from the early morning mist, the stark outlines of the skyscrapers behind the welcoming figure of the Statue of Liberty. On this occasion he decided to take a German boat over since the play was set in Germany and written by a German-Swiss and it would help him, therefore, get into the play – or so he reasoned, always liking to justify extravagance.

The trip provided more interesting than he had imagined. In the bar one night he heard a man saying that England was spiritually the weakest nation in Europe and West Germany (as it was then) the healthiest. Shaw interrupted and said if that were the case why was it inconceivable to think of Nazi atrocities happening in England. An argument developed, the sort of thing Shaw loved, and the two men became friends. The man was Dr John Huess, the pastor of the richest church in New York, Wall Street Church.

The Physicists opened at the Martin Beck Theatre on 13 October 1964. It was not a success. The *New York Times* critic Howard Taubman did not like the play but found Shaw 'splendid, spirited, intelligent . . . intellectually and emotionally alive'. Shaw, not being surrounded by friends as he had been in *The Caretaker*, spent time wandering the streets of New York soaking up the atmosphere and the speech. He went to a tailor in the garment district and had a jacket made and was going back for a fitting the day the Pope announced that the Jews had been forgiven for killing Christ. He asked his Jewish tailor what he thought of the Pope's announcement. 'Who needs it?' was the reply. It was this reaction and his experience on the streets of New York, together with a comment Leo Lehmann had made some years earlier when Eichmann was being tried in Israel in 1961 – 'What would it be like if the Jews had got the wrong man?' 'They'd soon find out about it so there's no book,' Shaw replied – that gave Shaw the central theme for his next novel *The Man in the Glass Booth*. It would be his first book set outside England and its authentic New York feel and idiom would come from this period.

It was from this period, too, that Shaw began his association with one of the 'characters' of the Broadway theatre scene, the agent Milton Goldman. Goldman, a gossipy, dapper homosexual, who had developed a long-term 'marriage' with a New York attorney, Arnold Weissberger, represented most of the stars on Broadway. A confirmed Anglophile – he took a suite at the Savoy Hotel every year to entertain his British friends and associates – had come to specialise in British actors and actresses working on in New York. He had met Shaw at the time of *The Caretaker* and thought his performance in *The Physicists* confirmed his talent. When Shaw told him he was keen to work on Broadway again, Goldman rang Richard Hatton, as always acting with due regard to the proprieties, who agreed that he should look after Shaw's interests in the States. Hatton knew and trusted Goldman from the work he had done for other clients of his agency, including Donald Pleasence.

Shaw, in common with his other clients, was fond of Goldman. It was difficult not to be. Immaculately dressed, softly spoken, Goldman knew everyone and everything that happened on Broadway, from gossip to business. He worked subtly introducing actors to directors and producers at cocktail parties in his own East River apartment, held two or three times a week. Arnold Weissberger, a keen amateur photographer was often present and a book, *Famous Faces*, published in 1974, makes a fascinating document of the passing of the years on so many well-known writers and performers. Robert Shaw and Mary Ure are featured many times.

Goldman got Shaw a job immediately he had taken him on as a client. Joe Mankiewiez was directing *Another Christmas Carol*, a screenplay by Rod Serling adapting the Dickens classic, for NBC.

Shaw was offered the Ghost of Christmas Past in company with Sterling Hayden, Eva Marie Saint, and Peter Sellers, with his then-wife, Britt Ekland. Sterling had adapted the story to be propaganda for world peace with Scrooge transformed from miser to warmonger. To convert him to peace rather than war he is taken on a journey to see what happened when peace failed in the past (Shaw's role) and then through the blasted wasteland of the future should peace fail again. The proceeds of this enterprise were to be donated to the United Nations.

Shaw was back in England in time for a more seasonal Christmas at Porch House: 1964 had been his busiest and most lucrative year. He had crossed the line drawn at the point where an actor no longer has to look for work: work, instead, comes looking for him. He was now in the position of being actively sought by directors and producers. In terms of his acting career, however, using an analogy he was fond of using himself, he was still in the second division of the league, though definitely at the top of that division. He had a comfortable and secure life, relatively, but he did not look like being promoted to the first division as so many of his contemporaries had already been. At 37 this was not enough.

For a lot of people what he had achieved would be a cause of satisfaction but not for Shaw. It was here that his truly obsessional competitiveness which he wore like a heart on his sleeve, leaked into more profound areas of his psychology. It appeared that this aspect of his personality was something more than a social habit; it was a deeply ingrained *need*, a need that was not satisfied by winning a sprint up a mountainside, a bout of arm wrestling, or a holding-your-breath-under-water contest, or any of the hundred other games he would devise and play on a daily basis. But applied to other areas the game-playing syndrome and the need to win made very little sense. The analogy between the 3.90-minute mile or the 10-second 100 metres and an award-winning novel or an Oscar-winning film. There would always be some book that was better, some performance ranked higher, some actor paid more. Shaw was an intelligent and sensitive man and rationally he may have understood that there was no such thing as 'best' in his profession (accurately professions). But he did not understand it emotionally. He was in competition with everyone.

At the beginning of 1965 these concerns were very much to the fore in Shaw's mind and perhaps with some external justification.

All around him he saw his contemporaries leaping ahead of him in terms of film 'stardom'. Sean Connery was firmly established as James Bond, a part that had made him an international star commanding an enormous salary; Michael Caine, Shaws' understudy in *The Long and the Short and the Tall*, had made *Zulu* and *The Ipcress File*; Peter O'Toole, whose flashy performance in *The Long and the Short and the Tall* had led straight to *Lawrence of Arabia* and *Becket*, was well established, and even O'Toole's understudy in the Willis Hall play, Terence Stamp, had broken through with *Billy Budd* and *The Collector*. Albert Finney, another Old Vic and Stratford graduate, had not looked back since the success of *Saturday Night and Sunday Morning* and *Tom Jones*, Laurence Harvey was already in Hollywood billed above the title with Elizabeth Taylor; and this was to say nothing of Richard Burton. Shaw, it appeared, had been left behind.

Shaw wanted success in films and he wanted the money that went with it. But he also wanted to write. Indeed he would repeat to friends and journalists alike, over and over again, that he was at his happiest and at one with the world only when he was sitting in his black leatherette swivel chair at his drop-leaf desk in front of a red spiral exercise book. But it was becoming increasingly clear to him that he could not do both. In addition, the rewards from the one talent were so different from the rewards of the other. The rewards from acting were fame and money both of which he loved. The rewards from writing were critical acclaim, which he loved, and very little financial reward, which he did not love at all.

Shaw liked to compare himself with Denis Compton, the great English cricketer. Early in life Compton had played football for Arsenal as well as cricket for England. Fortunately, Shaw would say, his talent for football had been eclipsed by his cricketing skills. 'But what if,' Shaw would insist, 'What if he'd been able to do both? What would have happened then?' The implication was that had his talents for both been equal he would have failed at both. Though for a time it appeared that the adrenalin of success in one field fuelled his 'energy' for the other, this effect did not last. As 'tiredness' became a word used more frequently in his vocabulary to describe his state of being, he came to believe he could not do both. It was this conviction that made the duality a problem, not the duality itself.

'What I try to achieve in acting – flamboyance – would be self-indulgence if I tried it as a writer,' he was to say. In all respects the two talents seemed to be contradictory. Novel writing is a lonely business; acting entirely social. In his writing Shaw was meticulous in his attention to detail; in his acting he would often make the script up as he went along. About his writing he was diffident and modest; despite his startlingly good reviews he would not regard himself as a writer he said, until he could look up at a shelf full of books that he had written – like Dickens or Tolstoy. About his acting he was boastful and vain; there was no actor, he claimed in the same interview, that gave him cause for humility. He would never have dreamt of prostituting his writing talent by trying to write a 'commercial' book, yet he was to constantly abuse his acting talent by appearing in films for which the only quality threshold was the size of his fee.

It was at this point that the larger-than-life figure of Phil Yordan marched into Robert Shaw's life. Yordan was an American writer/ producer straight out of the Hollywood of the '30s. Physically a cross between John Huston and Humphrey Bogart, his voice, no doubt affected by the large cigar permanently clamped between his teeth, sounded as if his vocal chords were made from barbed wire, so gruff and husky it was sometimes difficult to understand what he was saying.

In Hollywood in the '50s Yordan had written some notable movies – *Detective Story*, *The Naked Jungle*, *Man from Laramie*, *Broken Lance* (for which he won an Academy Award), and *Studs Lonigan* – and also became known as a script 'fixer', someone who would come in to put a script right without necessarily doing much more than changing a line here or there or adding a new scene. He was very good at it. Naturally the smaller contribution went uncredited, though not unpaid. He would say that he had 'fixed' the script of *The Maltese Falcon*.

By the '60s Yordan had decided that there was money to be made in Europe. Producing films in Europe, especially, he argued, Spain, was cheaper than producing them in American where, at that time, movie unions were insisting on minimum crewing standards, set working days and overtime payments that made the more laissez-faire attitude of some European countries – but not England – seem unbelievably attractive. Yordan's film-making philosophy was simple. He was in the business to make money. He was not concerned for the quality of the picture. After writing *El Cid*, *King of Kings*, *55 Days in Peking* and *The Fall of the Roman Empire* he had come to the conclusion that 'people would rather go and see a bad big picture than a good small one.' Making a 'big bad picture' in Europe was cheaper than it would ever be in Hollywood.

That any producer should not care about the quality of his product was, and is, a fact of life in the film industry, arising from the way films are financed outside the major studio system. Most independently funded films are financed from a variety of sources, companies specialising in making movies together with individuals who just want to dabble in the film business, rich men who want to be photographed on set with the 'stars'. A producer sets up an often complicated network of finance, like a delicately poised house of cards, on the basis of the script. Obviously the script is available to be read by any or all of the participants but generally they have little experience of reading scripts and none in assessing innate problems. Often their financial decision is made on the track record of the other elements of the 'package' i.e. the director and the actors. As long as the leading actors are famous enough – 'bankable' – then the money for the picture will be committed.

What is also presented with the script is a budget of the film – how much the script is going to cost to make. Within the budget the producer will have built in a considerable sum for himself in what are called 'money-finding fees'. This means that he charges, for instance, people who put up one third of the finance a fee to find the other two-thirds. Naturally when he finds the two-thirds he then charges the participants for finding the remaining one third. Which means the producer cannot lose.

So from the first day of principal photography – the day the shooting begins and payments in relation to copyrights in the screenplay are contractually made – the producer has made a considerable sum of money and it is really not important how the final film turns out. The psychology that would argue that if the film was of high quality it might make a great deal of money simply does not apply. 'Might' is not good enough. Besides, if the original budget presented to the financiers can be pared down there is more profit for the producer.

This is by no means the only game that was and is played with film financing. Yordan reputedly inflated the size of one film's budget to enable him to build an entire sound stage in Almeria, out of the amount designated for the construction of sets. Subsequent films made by him were budgeted as though the studio didn't exist, thus inflating their budgets with extra construction costs.

That is not to say that the people involved in the actual movie-making are not dedicated and clever professionals. But the problem they are presented with at the beginning of the film is not how to make the script into a marvellous film, but how to make the script into any sort of acceptable film at all. It is to their credit that they often manage to do just that. Nor, it must be added, are all independent producers as unscrupulous.

Yordan was in the process of setting up *The Battle of the Bulge*. He had got wind of the fact, in the way that such 'operators' have, that Robert Shaw was a name to be conjured with. His performance in the Bond film had been duly noted among the heads of the Hollywood studios, and cards had been marked. Shaw's inclusion in a project, Yordan felt, would do no harm at all to its prospects of getting a distribution deal with one of the major studios – an agreement to advertise and sell the film to exhibitors in the USA or Europe or worldwide. This, in turn, would encourage his financial backers. Yordan called Richard Hatton and a meeting was arranged the moment Shaw returned to London from New York. Filming was due to start at the beginning of January 1965 so there was no time to waste. Yordan had already lined up Henry Fonda, Charles Bronson and Robert Ryan as his main leads, with Telly Savalas, George Montgomery, Dana Andrews and Ty Hardin filling the featured roles, and Ken Annakin (fresh from the enormous box office success of *Those Magnificent Men in their Flying Machines*) as director to impress his money-men. As soon as he met Shaw he offered him the part of Colonel Hessler, a tank commander of brilliance gradually becoming embittered with Nazi methods of command. The script was un-impressive, however, using historical events as an excuse for a rather obvious plot resolved by a cinematic cliché – tanks lined up against each other like gun fighters in a Western shoot-out – having absolutely no historical basis.

But any reservations Shaw may have had about the quality of the screenplay were overcome by two factors. Firstly, he was enormously taken with Phil Yordan, his bluff personality and endless store of aphorisms ('Always tip big, kid. Then you get treated like royalty and everyone wants to know royalty.') Secondly, Yordan's offer for the film was $350,000, practically the equivalent of the entire amount he had earned from his acting and writing career so far. The film was to be made on location in Almeria and Madrid and filming would have to start in January so the snow on the mountains would imitate the conditions in the Ardennes. There was no time for second thoughts. Shaw accepted.

Faced with such a comparatively large fee, Shaw and his advisers went ape. As the film was to be made entirely abroad, there was, as the tax law stood in 1965, an opportunity to take advantage of a major loophole and extract the fee from the UK tax net thereby considerably reducing the amount of tax payable on a fee that would normally have attracted a high tax rate. *The Luck of Ginger Coffey* would have qualified as it was made in Canada but Shaw's fee of $50,000 did not make setting up a scheme worthwhile. *The Battle of the Bulge* and $350,000 was a different matter and Shaw's solicitors were immedi-ately enlisted to work out an appropriate scheme of what is euphemistically called tax avoidance. What happened next, in the scramble to get this scheme in place, was to effect Robert Shaw's life irrevocably.

By 1965 tax avoidance had become a major preoccupation with most film stars. As early as 1957 Richard Burton had made a very explicit public statement as to why it was necessary for him to become a tax exile and move to live in Switzerland. He had said that the tax system in England was grossly unfair to actors because in one year an actor might earn a million pounds, and be taxed at the rate of 90%, but in the next it might be half that and, possibly, in the following year, he would earn nothing at all. Burton himself had earned £80,000 and kept £8,000. He felt it should be possible to reclaim some of the tax paid in good years to offset the bad. Though this statement was probably self-justifying, after the mauling he had received in the press for his decision to go abroad, it was undoubtedly true that the tax system for high-earning performers, in whatever field, contained a number of inequities and did not take account of the vicissitudes of their careers. The main motivating factor in tax avoidance was, however, the 90% rate of tax at the top of the UK income band.

By the beginning of the '60s an expectation had been fostered that tax schemes could be created by highly paid lawyers and accountants which should save performers large amounts of tax money. The main loophole in the tax law, now ended, was what was called 'remittance basis' taxation. A person domiciled in the UK was subject to income tax on his income worldwide. However, if it could be established that an agreement existed for his employment wholly outside the UK then he would only be taxed on the money sent back – 'remitted' – to this country. So what happened was that an actor contracted his services to a company abroad who agreed to pay him a salary each year plus bonuses. That company would then loan his services to a film company for the purposes of making a film. The film company would pay the loan-out company who would then pay the actor his salary and bonuses calculated on what they had been paid for the film, less their administration charge. It was obviously important to prove that this intermediary company was not owned by or controlled by the actor or the Inland Revenue would merely regard the whole scheme as a fiction and tax the actor on the money paid from the film company and nothing would be achieved. A number of these 'arm's length' companies grew up, mostly based in Liechtenstein, to fill the need.

At that time sterling was subject to strict regulation. Even the amount available to change into foreign currency for holidays was strictly limited and each such transaction entered in the tripper's passport. One of the other provisions of the Exchange Control Act was that money due to a UK resident from a foreign company had to be remitted as it became due; it could not be held abroad. If this had meant that the money earned from the arm's length company had to be remitted straight back to the UK then clearly the schemes would have had little effect. But this is where the aforementioned loophole operated. Money earned had to be remitted back to the Sterling Area, which was defined as England, Scotland and Wales, the Republic of Ireland, the Isle of Man, Gibraltar and the Channel Islands. But the Channel Islands were not, for the purposes of taxation, within the revenue's bailiwick, so the procedure was simply to open an account in Jersey, pay the foreign earnings into it, which satisfied the requirements of the Exchange Control Act, and then 'remit' money to the UK when and if the need arose – hopefully in years when domestic income was low and in such amounts as not to attract the higher levels of tax. If the need did not arise, of course, the money could be kept in the Channel Islands, spent abroad and therefore never taxed in the UK.

Under the impetus of the 90% top tax rate even more ambitious schemes were invented to meet the expectation of star performers that they were somehow not liable to the tax law governing ordinary mortals. One of the companies providing arm's length foreign employment decided it would initiate a UK tax scheme to exploit what it saw as a loophole in the domestic tax laws. The top rate of tax on income was 90% but on capital gains it was only 30%. If income could magically be transformed into capital a huge saving would clearly result. The company, Constellation, had a performer form his own company with a contract for his exclusive services worldwide. Constellation would then buy this company but instead of paying cash would pay with loan-stock redeemed with cash when the profits of the company it had acquired reached previously agreed levels. The value of the company was hypothetical and could be grossly inflated since the loan stock would only be turned into cash once actual profits – e.g. the fee from a major film – had been achieved. If the actor's company was purchased by Constellation for £1 million of loan stock and the actor received £100,000 for his next project then £100,000 (less administrative expenses) would be redeemed. This redemption was a capital gain and not income, and would be taxed at 30%.

The problem with the scheme was that Constellation, being a public company, had to make an announcement every time it bought a new company and the agreed purchase price was often excessive enough to make headlines. The press was full of stories of how much performers were worth. And the press is read by the Revenue, who acted quickly to close the loophole by stating that performers would be taxed on the loan-stock as if it were income. As the amount of loan-stock issued for any particular company was often grossly inflated, what started as a tax avoidance scheme cost some performers a great deal of money.

It is against this background that Shaw's advisers were working in

1965. Zsuzsi Roboz had introduced Mary Ure to a Hungarian lawyer, Laszlo Gombosh, part of the Hungarian mafia including herself and the Kordas, back in 1955. Gombosh was, to many, an intimidating figure. Always impeccably suited with a carnation in his buttonhole, his English perfect though heavily accented, he was a senior partner at Theodore Goddard, a firm founded by the solicitor who had represented Harold Macmillan and who, reputedly, had been the man upon whose word Macmillan had acted in making his statement to the House of Commons that there was no truth in the allegations against John Profumo (also a client of Goddard's). With his brusque manner Gombosh gave the impression of authority. He handled Mary's divorce from John Osborne and, in doing so, greatly impressed Robert Shaw who consigned all his legal work to him from henceforth.

Chapter Eight

Taking Mary and the children with him, Shaw set off for Almeria, unaware of the problems that *The Battle of the Bulge* would later create for him. He was in high spirits and was quite sure that this film and this part would allow him to play catch-up with his contemporaries. His good humour did not last long. *The Battle of the Bulge*, in retrospect appeared to be what it was not. It appeared to be a big American war picture of the type so popular in the mid-50s – *Here to Eternity, Sands of Iwo Jima,Operation Pacific*, even *South Pacific*. It had an American producer, American writers (Yordan, Milton Sperling and John Melson) and American stars. But the American stars, once bright, had lost their lustre, and were working for what they could get. Henry Fonda, Robert Ryan and Dana Andrews were no longer in the top echelons of Hollywood. In fact, *The Battle of the Bulge*, though not cheap to make, was to war films what Sergio Leone had been to westerns; it was a sangria war film based firmly on Phil Yordan's principle that people would rather see 'bad big films than good small ones'.

The film was no more than moderately successful at the box office, which meant that, considering its cost, it would never go into profit, and it was critically slated. It did not do for Robert Shaw what *Dr No* had done for Sean Connery or *Lawrence of Arabia* for Peter O'Toole. It raised his public profile, it was good for him to appear in a leading role with his name above the title in a big picture, especially in America, but that was about as far as it went. No significant offer emerged as a result of *The Battle of the Bulge*. It was not a 'breakthrough' movie. It did leave Robert Shaw $350,000 the richer, however.

In May 1965 Shaw returned to Porch House from Spain after his 16 weeks' work. During his stay in New York in *The Physicists*, Paramount Pictures had approached him to write the screenplay of *The Judge and his Hangman*, another Dürrenmatt project to which they held the rights. Shaw had hoped to work on it while filming but had achieved little, so he plunged into the project in his study at Porch House to meet the delivery date of July 1965. He was also working on a film for Karel Reisz under the general title of 'Divorce'. After a few weeks, however, this was abandoned. Reisz wanted to make the story of *his* divorce, Shaw would say later, while Shaw's divorce, he thought, was more interesting.

Shaw's screenplay for *The Judge and his Hangman* was not what Paramount was looking for and they rejected it at the first draft. The main problem with converting the novel to the screen was to make the sort of overt German expressionism that characterised Dürrenmatt's work into a form acceptable on screen. American ideas of what is acceptable differed widely from European. The problem with hiring Shaw, in particular, to accomplish the feat was his interest in this sort of writing. In his novels he had managed to avoid the overt symbolism it required but his plays were full of lines reminiscent of the abstract concepts found in Dürrenmatt: 'On your gravestone it will read: "Here lies one for whom Evil Was Freedom"', 'I am driven by an overpowering desire to taste life to its last drop. I feel my life is unique.' There is even verse:

> The Devil goes around
> Beating the people
> Down to the ground.

which could well be a quote from *Off the Mainland*. Indeed the title itself is of the same order of abstraction. The central problem appears to be one of mortality but it is as though the mortality were being discussed at one remove, like discussing the morality of taking the Queen with a Bishop in a game of chess. It is not a real moral issue but a constructed one.

Shaw's involvement with the work of Dürrenmatt in 1964–65 was important in the development of his writing. From conceiving the idea of *The Man in the Glass Booth* in New York while appearing in *The Physicists* to working on *The Judge and his Hangman* and in the process reading most of Dürrenmatt's novels and plays, Shaw saw how Dürrenmatt used the techniques he had attempted in *Off the Mainland* and *The Joke*. There would be several scenes in *The Man in the Glass Booth* that reflected this influence and certainly the complexity of the moral message very much echoes the way Dürrenmatt constructed labyrinthine moral dilemmas through overt symbolism.

Shaw felt no real disappointment at the rejection of his script; he was realistic enough about the film business to know that the material was not then going to be made into a film, and that the prospects of a film script being approved, let alone filmed, were slim. In his agent's office in Stratton Street he had once looked at two shelves of scripts covering a large wall. Each had the name of the project neatly written in block capitals on the exposed binding. There were probably two or three hundred scripts. Each represented an investment – including the acquisition of the original material (book, play, short story), a first-draft screenplay by one writer, another version by a second, and perhaps even a third, legal fees to draw up all the necessary contracts – of not less than £20,000 and often more than £100,000. Of the scripts on the shelf only one in 70 had actually been made or would be made. Scripts to film producers were like feathers to a bird: it was necessary to have several in order to fly and the more you had, the greater the chances of getting off the ground. Shaw had sat in the office counting every script, estimating the average cost and calculating the investment the two shelves represented. No doubt his script for *The Judge and his Hangman* would soon be joining the others on the shelf.

The publication of *The Flag* in 1965 brought Shaw a new level of critical acclaim. As Nora Smallwood had said, it was his best book so far. He was now to be referred to as a writer in the top flight of young British novelists. Tom Maschler, a Royal Court 'groupie' and now head of publishers Jonathan Cape, regarded him as an important talent. Just as *The Sun Doctor* had been a very different and much more mature book than *The Hiding Place*, so *The Flag* was to take Shaw into a whole new area of both form and content. In common with the other two books, he used autobiographical material with references to Westhoughton and Walberswick (where he wrote *The Hiding Place*), but for once he escaped any discussion of his father and, though the book is once again concerned with the nature of men in relation to religion, it is not pervaded by the same sense of guilt and regret that run through Halliday's character in *The Sun Doctor*. The image of suicide, though present in the book, is presented in an entirely different way.

Originally tilted *The Wrong Parish*, and dedicated to Mary Ure, *The Flag* is set in England in 1925. It was a period at which the political life of the country was riven with contradictory influences, the raw memories of the First World War, the Fabian Movement, women's suffrage, the experiment with communism in Russia, all posing the question of whether England would swing to the left or whether the rigid class system, the English devices for deflecting revolution into institution and the onset of the depression would maintain the status quo. The Reverend Calvin's determination is that it should not, that religion and the church should be at the centre of the debate, that the red flag should fly over England:

If a system is based on justice and generosity, revolution is madness, if a system is based on injustice and greed, revolution is necessary as wise and proper.

Against this political background it is Shaw's characterisation that is the primary force behind the book. All the characters are drawn with subtlety and complexity. Calvin himself (based on the real-life figure of Conrad Noël, vicar of Thaxted), so sure of his faith, but trying to deal with his wife's apparent madness (Shaw's best portrayal of a woman); Lady Cleeve, the local patron of the church; the General weeping for losses in the war and his clever, existentialist son Andrew, playing life and death games in front of an express train; and Rockingham who brings the red flag to the village from Lancashire, are all characters whose attitude to life is thoroughgoing. Shaw portrays Calvin's children well too, all in their various ways trying to make sense of their parents' relationship and their mother's unhappiness.

Shaw illustrates how the English class system survives by dealing with revolution not by repression but by a sort of benign irritation, by an established process which makes disestablishment seem unthinkable. Letters to *The Times*, petitions to bishops and archbishops, questions in Parliament, organised protests, allow the steam to escape. Nothing actually changes. Eton, as Andrew says, has made him snobbish, but Lenin is quite fashionable there.

Shaw places religion in the centre of the political ferment ('to be equal isn't to be the same . . . the test of religion is how much it pertains to the world . . .') but he makes a distinction between faith and God. *The Flag* is about faith, about religion in its proper sense. It is not a book about belief in God. It is about how people have come to have faith, why they need faith, what that faith means, what it can mean if held collectively, as a power for change, and how it can be lost.

Though the book deals with political issues it is not a polemic. If it is biased towards the left that is a bias based in the characters. Shaw is never tempted to propagandise, indeed, in modern terms, his way of addressing socialist issues had an uncanny relevance to the world that has seen the end of the Russian experiment in socialism and asks questions that still have to be answered:

Three questions: why should production be left in private hands? Why should there be a free market when it makes for inequalities? Is the only reason a man will *strive*, to put money in his purse?

The overall impression left by the novel is the poignancy of its many characters: infinite sadness, sweet sadness, and a feeling of the delicacy of life. It is a major novel.

The critical response was no less enthusiastic. Harold Hobson wrote: 'It is a very long time since I read a novel which has so excited and so moved and so disturbed me.' The *Times Literary Supplement* found it, 'Admirably uncommitted and impartial. Mr Shaw stands in the middle of it all, reporting long, subtle conversations between faith and reason, being admirably sympathetic to and understanding of young people, seeing how comical as well as how noble the do-gooders of this world can be, and writing at all times with originality and imaginative truthfulness.' In America, too, the book was praised. The *Saturday Review* saw it as 'the clash of reason and faith, of ideas and emotions' written with 'the believable blend of humour and pathos, of anger and pity'.

The book was intended to be the first part of a trilogy under the overall title *The Cure of Souls*. Some of the critics looked forward to the future volumes. Iain Hamilton, for one: 'This masterly first volume makes it clear that the trilogy will be a work of major importance.'

After *The Battle of the Bulge*, Shaw, the actor, was out of work. Offers of employment came and went, most involving roles as psychopathic killers or, once *The Battle of the Bulge* opened in autumn, Nazi officers or both. As it had become common, with his continuing prestige as a novelist, for offers for Shaw's acting services to be accompanied by offers for him to work on the script, Shaw had to make a rather unusual choice as an actor. Was the part something he wanted to play and could he change it into something he would want to play by agreeing to write the screenplay? The answer seemed to be in the negative on both counts. He also turned down offers to adapt material to the screen from scratch. Offers to write the life of Donald Campbell for instance, and, from Clive Donner, to script his film of *Alfred the Great* were both rejected.

Porch House was filled with guests. Shaw, generous to a fault, anxious to share his good fortune with others, wined and dined them extravagantly before, after and sometimes during the meal, testing their sporting skills. After one weekend at Porch House a visiting producer was asked whether he'd enjoyed himself. 'You must be joking,' he replied, 'It's too much like the bloody Olympic Games.' With the swimming pool now in place and a tennis court, the variety of games available to torture his guests had greatly increased. In fine weather tennis, boule, three- or five-a-side football, running – a hundred-yard dash marked out on the lawn – and swimming were the competitive sports as well as the holding-your-breath-under-water test. If rain stopped play outside, there was always table tennis, carpet bowls, arm-wrestling and, for the less well-endowed, poker.

Shaw played squash for Buckinghamshire, driving into Hampstead Squash Club if the Bucks courts were too busy for regular practice. He was keen to play more golf so rang Noël Coleman who, he knew, was a member of the conveniently placed Denham Golf Club. Noël was in fact a sort of honorary member by virtue of the fact that his back door opened on to the course and so was not in a position to sponsor Shaw's membership. However, he managed to find one of the full members to propose Shaw and his application was duly accepted. It was a tradition of the club that the new member should play his first game with his proposer so Noël, knowing Shaw was a good player, suggested he go easy on the man who had kindly proposed him. The suggestion was not greeted with much sympathy. 'I'm going to hammer him, boy.' And he did. Noël had also asked Shaw not to order more than a beer in the bar after the match since the man was not well off. This suggestion met with a similar response and when asked what he wanted to drink Shaw replied, 'Champagne'. Shaw hated champagne.

With Philip Broadley in a pub in Amersham before Sunday lunch Shaw ran into the film director Basil Dearden (who had directed Mary in *The Mindbenders*) and his beautiful wife actress Melissa Stribling. Conversation turned to table tennis and Dearden, not realising the consequences, told Shaw proudly in front of his wife that he had never been beaten. A match was arranged on the spot for the following Sunday: Dearden and his partner against Broadley and Shaw on the Davis Cup system, a double match, two singles and reverse singles. Dearden was never able to repeat his boast. Broadley and Shaw won all the matches. Melisa Stribling was not impressed.

A similar fate awaited the players at the Chalfont St Peter's Table Tennis Club Invitation Tournament. Shaw read of the event in the local paper and rang Broadley keen to enter. 'Got to see how good we really are, boy, test our metal against the real world.' They turned up to find themselves playing against the club's two best players, a woman who played lawn tennis for Bucks and the Captain of the Chalfont St Peter's Table Tennis Club who happened to have an artificial leg. Broadley played the woman and won easily while Shaw played the one-legged man.

'How did you get on?' Broadley asked afterwards.

'Once I spotted he had a wooden leg,' Shaw replied grinning from ear-to-ear, 'it was easy. Just played from corner to corner. He fell over twice!'

Both Broadley and Noël Coleman remember vividly a game of three-a-side football at Porch House with Conrad Philips – known on British television as William Tell in a long-running series made on the same principles as *The Buccaneers*. If a goal was scored against an opponent a shilling was paid. Shaw charged in against Philips and scored, knocking him to the ground in the process. Philips stayed down screaming in agony that he had broken his leg. But Shaw stood over him unmoved. 'Give me my shilling, boy. You're not getting up till you give me my shilling.'

Shaw did not enjoy sports at which he did not have any expertise. Broadley's victory at badminton had done away with that game at Porch House. Mary Ure's interest had always been sailing, taught to her by father and brothers. Noël Coleman, a keen sailor, arranged to take them both out on his boat from Lymington Marina. Mary loved the experience but Shaw could not get the hang of tacking and jibbing, was hit by the boom, and retired hurt to the cabin. They never went sailing again.

Shaw was anxious to pass his sporting prowess on to his son. Colin was a good sprinter but did not, his father felt, have the killer instinct. As the boy breasted ahead of the others in an impromptu race on the lawn, he looked back to see where the competition was. Shaw was furious with him despite the fact that he had won the race. 'Never look back. I never want to see you look back. I never look back.' Philip Broadley, who was watching, had never seen Shaw, normally an equable and indulgent father, so cross with the boy.

On 9 August 1965 Robert Shaw was 38. It was the age at which his father had committed suicide. In September Mary Ure had her second daughter (Hannah), Shaw's seventh child of which six were girls. Mary had for all intents and purposes turned into the mirror image of Jennifer, the earth mother, child at her breast, content with her lot. But Mary was not Jennifer and there were inherent strains in their relationship. Mary's career had been subsumed – willingly according to friends – into the joy of motherhood. From being the toast of Broadway, the West End and even Hollywood – she was nominated for a Tony and for an Academy Award (Oscar) – by 1965 she had only made two films in five years. It was Shaw's career that took precedence and to which everything was sacrificed. She arranged her life around him and appeared quite happy so to do. As often happens, however, what starts naturally and casually in a relationship, can harden into a custom and practice that goes without question, accepted as the status quo until there is a sea change and the custom turns into a cause for profound resentment.

Robert simply ignored Mary's career. He did not want it to exist so it did not. For once in his life he did not relish competition from his own wife. He wanted compliance. At the Royal Court he had gone out of his way to woo and win her. Having gained the prize, however, he did not want it to be able to get up off his trophy shelf and move away of its own accord. From the early days Shaw was never able to accept a woman as equal. He could accept a woman as an object to worship and admire, to beat easily at tennis, to conquer, to brag about, but never to treat as merely equal. All Shaw's long-term friendships were with men, all his professional advisers throughout his life were men though he did allow himself the services of a woman dentist.

In January 1966 Shaw was offered the part of Henry VIII in Columbia Pictures' *A Man for All Seasons*, their filmed version of Robert Bolt's play, previously turned down, though not to Shaw's knowledge, by Richard Burton. As Burton noted in his diary. 'Robert Shaw, who might be consigned to playing ageing actors at ping-pong, played it.' As it appeared at the time Burton was in danger of being right about Shaw's career. There had been many offers since *Battle of the Bulge* finished in May 1965 but none of them could be regarded as a positive step forward in career terms. Playing the leading role in the Yordan film had, if anything, had a negative impact.

But the part of Henry VIII, though obviously not the lead, offered Shaw the opportunity to shine again. The part of Henry is a comparatively small one in the script but, as with the killer in *From Russia with Love*, it is a crucial one. The gusto and exuberance that Shaw was to exhibit in his first appearance, jumping ashore from the Royal barge into the mud, made a huge impact on audiences and critics alike. His long scene with More as he tries to get him to change his mind ('come with me in this matter') over his opposition to divorce, as the character goes from almost childlike good humour to bouts of barely controlled and tyrannical rage, suggesting the power of an absolute dictator, is one of his best screen performances, making, in turn, the dilemma of Paul Scofield as Sir Thomas More, seem only too real. His later carousing – in song – with Vanessa Redgrave as Anne Boleyn is appropriately suggestive.

In terms of screen time (no more than 12 minutes) it was his smallest part since *Sea Fury* but in terms of his public profile it was to be a memorable film.

A Man for All Seasons took up three weeks of Shaw's life from the end of May 1966 almost exactly a year after his last acting job on *The Battle of the Bulge.* Problems over billing the very distinguished cast – Leo McKern, John Hurt, Nigel Davenport, Susannah York, Orson Welles, Wendy Hillier (but not Vanessa Redgrave who was only credited in the cast list) – were solved by the simple device of putting the billing in alphabetical order. Even Scofield was billed in this way, though his name was 'boxed'. Shaw was paid £15,000, a far cry from his last fee of £350,000, but in addition to this he was given 2½% of the producer's profits from the picture. Normally percentages of the producer's profits, or even the picture's profits – the two are slightly different, the latter more than the former – is a meaningless incantation, a nod to the actors contribution to the film, a gesture of good faith when 'up front' money is restricted. The accounting procedure for films is labyrinthine. From the money that comes into the cinema box office, the cinemas (exhibitors) take their cut, usually 30%, and then hand the remaining 70% to the distributors. This is then set against the enormous cost of prints (the actual copies of the film) and advertising which is calculated to be 2.4 times the cost of actually making the film. Only when this huge sum of money has been recouped by the distributors do they pass anything on to the producers to set against the negative cost of the film (i.e. the cost of producing the negative). Only after this cost is fully recouped does the film go into profit. As the money to make the film is treated like a bank loan and interest accrues from the first day of principal photography recoupment may seem like a very distant goal ever receding into the future as interest is charged on interest.

Not surprisingly, therefore, actors given percentages of the profits rarely see a further penny unless the film is a huge success commercially. From *The Battle of the Bulge* on, Shaw was often to receive a percentage of the profits as part of the deal but *A Man for All Seasons* was the only film from which he actually received pay-outs in this respect. Over the years the film probably earned Shaw an additional $50,000 and, with its release on video and television showings the profits continue to accumulate.

As often the exhibitor, the distributor and the producer of the film are one and the same company actors often feel the system is open to abuse and profits can be hidden. All actors with percentages have an 'accountancy clause' in their contracts entitling them to look at the accounts for the film but the cost of sending in accountants to go over all the financial statements is prohibitive and is only contemplated when it is suspected large sums are hidden. Sean Connery successfully discovered undisclosed profits on *The Anderson Tapes* in 1972.

Shaw's exuberance in *A Man for All Seasons* was apparently matched by his exuberance in general. In posing for the press he decided to run through the long grass with Susannah York trailing in his wake. As he ran the expensively made rings, replicas of historical artifacts, dropped from his fingers. If they were not found it would be a disaster for the film as, with the continuity problem it would create, no further shots would be possible until replacements were made. The whole unit fell on its knees in the long grass looking for the rings. Shaw's cry of 'a case of champagne to anyone who finds them' soon got the whole press corps looking too.

A Man for All Seasons earned Shaw a nomination for an Academy Award (Oscar) as the Best Supporting Actor of 1966.

Phil Yordan had kept in close touch with Shaw since the end of *The Battle of the Bulge* and, with the reviews of the American opening, he sent Shaw a script for his next Spanish project, *Custer of the West*. With the Vietnam War in full swing and protests against American involvement escalating from university campuses to the streets of Washington, Yordan had the idea that a film about Custer would be a hook on which to hang various simplistic morals about the evils of war. The script, making little attempt to delve into Custer's historical character, and rehearsing spurious Freudian motivations for his behaviour, had little to recommend it. It did, however, have a part for Mary Ure as Custer's wife, and Yordan, once again, was prepared to pay Shaw $350,000, with $50,000 for Mary, and an option on his services for a further picture at the same price.

The style of living to which Shaw had become accustomed needed large infusions of money. Deborah Shaw was about to go to Wycombe Abbey, an expensive girls' public school, and all the other children would be privately – and equally expensively – educated. There was the alimony due to Jennifer, cars to be bought and sold, friends entertained, lawyers, accountants, agents and private doctors to be paid. Shaw employed a secretary and a nanny and a gardener. Shaw had little choice but to accept Yordan's offer. There was nothing else likely to pay him so much. He would talk of the freedom the money would give him, freedom to write. But it never did. As if creating a version of Parkinson's Law, the more money he had the more he spent, his spending simply expanding to match the money available. Shaw was on a treadmill of expense from which he would never escape.

The idea of making Custer's Last Stand in the hills of Almeria in Spain with an English actor and actresses playing Mr and Mrs Custer might not have seemed a terribly good bet but once again Yordan's ability to finance a film with an unlikely assemblage of personnel was never in question. In addition, Shaw's name helped him get a distribution deal with Twentieth Century Fox then run by Darryl Zanuck who had expressed a firm belief in his potential as a 'star'. Yordan had hired the veteran Hollywood director Robert Siodmak whose credits included *The Spiral Staircase*, *The Killers*, and *Cry of the City*, though the Civil War sequence was directed by Irving Lerner, as Siodmak had to return to America on another engagement. The rest of the cast included Yordan's usual collection of fading stars and might-have-beens, Robert Ryan, Ty Hardin and Jeff Hunter.

Yordan had also decided to make the picture in Cinerama, a

technique that involved the use of three synchronised cameras and three synchronised projectors to produce a screen image three times wider and twice as deep as the conventional ratio. He argued that the film would get a great deal more publicity and be pushed harder by the distributors because they were keen to publicise the process in general which was hoped would be an antidote to the flagging audiences that were now beginning to beset the film industry. Though this was true, the fact that so few cinemas in the world were equipped with the necessary projectors (only one in England) meant that, for the film to recoup its cost, it would have to run to full houses for months on end. Nor would it be available for showing on television as the ratios were incompatible.

Custer of the West attempted to exploit the new screen width with scenes of runaway trains, shooting rapids, and spectacular horse stunts, but it was not a success. Among Americans Shaw's accent seemed phoney. The pseudo-psychological motivation imposed on a story that everyone was familiar with was not convincing and, though anti-war sentiment may have been emphasised in the publicity handouts, it was not apparent in the film. Shaw both rewrote a great deal of the dialogue (later exaggeratedly claiming 'I rewrote every line of that picture without credit') and composed the song *Follow Custer*, the music for which was written by Bernardo Segall (who, by coincidence, had composed the score for *The Luck of Ginger Coffey*). But his efforts did not manage to lift what was basically second-rate material. The film was launched with an appropriately grand publicity campaign emphasising the visual effects, but it was nevertheless a critical and commercial flop. After the triumph of his small role in *A Man for all Seasons*, his performance in the title role of *Custer of the West* was heavily criticised.

His second association with Phil Yordan was a disaster in everything but the fee he earned. He would need it. During their stay in Spain the swimming pool heaters had been left on at Porch House and an unused outdoor pool had been kept at a constant 84°F for nearly three months. Not that this stopped Shaw buying himself a new James Mulliner coachworked Rolls Royce drop-head coupé in white with black leather upholstery.

Shaw returned to Porch House in September 1966 and delivered the manuscript of *The Man in the Glass Booth* to Chatto and Windus at the beginning of October. He had already conceived the idea for his next book, which was just as well because there was nothing to distract his attention on the acting front. In fact it was not until April 1967 that Shaw was to receive paid employment again, and the £200 per programme that he then received for five appearances on *Three After*

Six, an ITV discussion programme, was hardly going to pay for the servicing of his Rolls Royce.

The programme had been running for three years and was intended as a 30-minute general discussion programme with three 'celebrities' on subjects, sometimes arising out of the news and sometimes from issues in general. Shaw appeared articulate and cool, arguing the left's point of view persuasively and with charm. Nancy Banks Smith in *The Guardian* remarked that it was not his 'lucid humane opinions' that made him fascinating but his 'sex appeal'.

While Shaw cast around in the film industry for a part to further his ambitions, the publication of *The Man in the Glass Booth* in the spring of 1967 was not greeted with quite the same enthusiasm as his previous novels. The *New Statesman*'s verdict that the book was 'bewildering' was typical. The *New York Times* found it 'original' but ultimately that it 'fails to convince'.

In the novel, Arthur Goldman, wealthy New York property tycoon, is a man obsessed with Nazi Germany and the concentration camps. He has a secret room filled with Nazi memorabilia. Goldman proceeds to set himself up as Karl Dorf, a concentration camp guard responsible for killing thousands of Jews. The Israelis arrest him and take him to Israel for trial where Goldman rails against them, accusing them of cowardice as they were led to their deaths in the camps and is ready to be executed for his crime when it is realised he is not Dorff at all but was one of the inmates of a camp.

The book represented a profound change of style in Shaw's work. *The Hiding Place*, *The Sun Doctor* and *The Flag* were a straight line of development, refining and honing techniques based in the tradition and conventions of the English novel. It is a style where the quality of writing comes from the delicacy and sensitivity with which it portrays its characters. *The Man in the Glass Booth*, set in a very Jewish New York, is written in an entirely different tradition; Shaw has taken to heart the American Jewish novels of Bernard Malamud, Saul Bellow and Philip Roth. It is a change from a narrative-based style to a style based on dialogue and monologue. Previously in his books people who knew Shaw had been literally shocked to find he was capable of writing with such sensitivity and measured effect. In *The Man in the Glass Booth*, for the first time in his writing, it is possible to hear Shaw's actual voice, his cadences, his way of changing conversations to shock, his interest in the vocal effect of words. The gentle, quiet voice of the previous novels had become strident; Shaw's bluff personality had merged with his writing style.

None of this is to say that the book does not have as much power and resonance as *The Flag* or *The Sun Doctor*. The writing has a brilliance of its own. What Shaw had done was to match form and content. The character of Goldman, with the Jewish appetite for words, presented almost in a long monologue occasionally broken by a visual image of haunting power, an image echoing the past, echoing the stark realities of the concentration camps which have come in time to haunt Goldman:

> Leaving the ice he walked with a monotonous rhythmic step. He reached the trees again. There he stopped, took off his fur coat, his jacket, and his socks and threw them into the snow. He took off his black tie, bound it round one of his bare feet, retrieved his silk handkerchief from the breast pocket of his jacket, bound that round the other foot, looked about him, and set off again, staring at the ground . . . He walked as if he had sores on his feet.

Shaw throws many complex issues into the book. As in *The Sun Doctor*, guilt is on the agenda but this is not the guilt of the family. In general the book is asking who actually bears the guilt for what happened to the Jews in Germany. Was it the Germans? But the Jews they murdered were Germans too, and they let themselves be murdered by obeying so compliantly as they were led to their deaths. And then there were the atrocities committed by the liberators – 'I saw the Herrenvolk hanging from the girders . . . every lamppost in Danzig a gallows.' Goldman, among his imaginings, sees himself as a sort of Christ; 'he wants to be crucified', 'take me to Calvary'. If there is any reason for his deception it is because he, like Christ, wants to shoulder the sins of man. And thus to the starting point: 'The Pope has forgiven the Jews!' and an echo of the themes Shaw first mooted in *The Hiding Place* where the Old Jew tells the crowd, 'Not one of your Hitlers, a great man. And a Jew.'

The book throws up enormous issues, metaphysical, political and moral. Whether, in the end, Shaw manages to resolve them in the character of Goldman is a matter of opinion. What is certain is that he manages to make Goldman's suicidal desire to hang for crimes he did not commit seem utterly convincing and that Goldman's character and Goldman's voice is writing of great power.

Shaw was fond of telling people that it was his sister Joanna who gave him the idea to turn the novel into a play but it is difficult to believe that the idea had not already occurred to him, especially as Harold Pinter, his closest Jewish friend, was enormously enthusiastic about the book. Whoever was responsible Shaw realised it would take little effort to turn the extensive dialogue of the novel into a two-act play.

By April 1967 his agent in America, Milton Goldman, was taking the play to David Merrick in New York, Shaw assuming that because of the subject matter the play should start on Broadway. Merrick, the top producer on Broadway at the time with a string of hits, turned it down without comment. Pinter, having read the novel and worked extensively with Shaw on the play – Shaw actually told one interviewer that Pinter had 'adapted' his novel – volunteered to direct the play in the West End. It would be the first time he had directed work other than his own. Further, Pinter thought Donald Pleasence would be ideal for the lead, though Shaw had privately imagined he would play the part himself. As the three of them had previously been involved in setting up the film of *The Caretaker* it seemed natural that they should put on the play themselves. With the help of Terance Baker, an agent who had joined Richard Hatton's office to deal with literary matters, they formed Glasshouse Production. The veteran West End producer Peter Bridge, was approached to be Glasshouse's co-producer and with his help there was no trouble in securing a theatre, especially with the 'marquee' value of the three main participants.

On 15 July 1967 the play opened at Nottingham Playhouse and a week later went to the Theatre Royal, Brighton. Last-minute adjustments were made before the play opened at St Martin's Theatre on 27 July. Its reception was mixed. Irving Wardle found it 'over-ambitious . . . emotionally indulgent' and added that 'the production by Harold Pinter is painfully slow and does nothing to conceal the inertia of the supporting parts or the childish improbability of the trial scene.' Philip Hope-Wallace thought it had intriguing ideas but was 'not . . . my idea of a good theatrical evening. I miss otherwise the touch of melodrama which the theatre if not the printed page demands.' Peter Lewis obviously saw a different play as he complained it was too melodramatic 'certainly hypnotic but . . . an exercise in confusing the mind.' All agreed Donald Pleasence's performance was outstanding.

A gloom set over the directors of Glasshouse Productions until Robert Shaw opened his copy of the *Sunday Times* on the following weekend, Harold Hobson had had more time to consider the complex issues raised by the play and had long been an admirer of Shaw as an actor and writer:

Donald Pleasence is astounding. He begins upon a low note and gradually increases the volume of his voice until one hears all over again the frenzy of Nuremberg, and the diabolical ecstasy of marching and stamping jackboots. When he finishes, there is a

moment of horrified silence that is one of the most dramatic
experiences I have ever known in a theatre. This silence is broken by
the revelation that this man who has just spoken with such adoration
of the Führer is not a former SS colonel at all. He is not Dorf, but
Goldman, a Jew who has himself suffered in the German camps.

To know this beforehand, as everyone knows it who has read Mr
Shaw's fine novel, does not injure the effect that the play makes. For
one thing, it is not so much the revelation itself that is sensational as the
manner of its making and its timing, with that quiet that is, in certain
circumstances, more stunning than any noise; at this point Sonia
Dresdel, through whom the revelation comes, is very remarkable.

But the essence of the matter lies elsewhere. The important
question is not whether Goldman is Dorf, but why, with so much
to lose, and with such racial memories, he should say that he is
Dorf. Why should he speak of Hitler in words that burn with
worship? Why should he rejoice in the murder of so many men,
women, and children of his own nation and religion?

. . . the crucial philosophic problem of the play [is]; the problem
of absolution. If the Jews are absolved from the killing of Jesus,
should not the Germans be absolved from the killing of the Jews?
Goldman knows what his answer is, and it is No.

. . . *The Man in the Glass Booth* is a tough play. It is not marred by
any of that central softness and self-pity which spoil so many plays
that think themselves tough. It is hard on the Germans, for whom,
through Goldman, it says there is no redemption; and it is hard on
the Jews, maintaining that they would behave like the Germans if
they got the chance. It is hard, too, on the conventional notions of
Christ, whose mantle this strange man is ready to assume. He will,
he says go one better than J.C. taking on his own shoulders the
sins of other men, not so that they may be washed clean, but in
order that the men who committed them may be rendered eternally
hateful . . .

Mr Shaw does not ask us to agree with Goldman. He does not
even imply that he agrees with him himself. He shows us
tremendous passions; and if they shake us, if they frighten, if they
destroy the glibness of a facile optimism, that is as it should be.

Shaw was ecstatic. Hobson seemed to have genuinely understood
what he was trying to achieve in the play and the issues he was trying
to address. The play ran for four-and-a-half months closing on 6
December 1967 with the distinct possibility of a Broadway transfer
the following year, but the heavy running costs of a cast of fifteen
meant that it barely recouped its production costs.

Chapter Nine

While all this activity was going on there had been several developments in Robert Shaw's film career. In May 1967 20th Century Fox,
no doubt through Darryl Zanuck's continued enthusiasm, had offered
him the lead in John Kohn and Stanley Mann's screenplay of the John
Fowles book *Nine Tiger Men*. The film was to be shot in July for 10
weeks and Shaw was to be paid $250,000 – dollars being the only
currency used in the film world for major deals. It was a big film for
Shaw, his first lead in a film produced – as opposed to distributed – by
a major American studio. The project had originally been intended for
Sean Connery and Diane Cilento. When Connery dropped out after
an argument over money, Zanuck needed little persuading by Richard
Hatton that Shaw should step into the breach. Not only was the
money good but it was an interesting and demanding part in a well-
written script. Nor could there be any argument about Shaw's first-
position billing.

Meantime Elliot Kastner had approached Richard Hatton for Shaw
to play Martin in the film of Iris Murdoch's novel *A Severed Head*
which had been successfully adapted as a play and had been running in
the West End for some time. The film, with a screenplay by Frederic
Raphael, would not start principal photography until after *Nine Tiger
Men* in September 1967. A fee of $200,000, plus $100,000 deferred out
of net profits, was agreed, with Shaw to be billed in the first position
above the title, in the same size as the title and with his having approval
of director and actresses. This deal was struck after several lengthy
telephone calls and letters. At lunch at The Bull in Gerrards Cross,
Shaw and Kastner discussed casting. Anouk Aimée was Shaw's first
choice followed by Leslie Caron. Approved directors were John
Boorman, Peter Medak and Bryan Forbes. Hollywood had at last
come to Buckinghamshire.

It is axiomatic that, in dealing with actors' contracts, 'my word is
my bond'. Rather like the diamond business, hundreds of thousands
of dollars are committed by word of mouth. An actor may be sent
half-way across the world on the purely verbal agreement between his
agent and a producer. As in all sorts of business where the word is

crucial there is a special jargon so that no misunderstanding arises. A producer 'makes an offer' which is an irrevocable commitment should the actor accept it. An 'availability', however, is only an enquiry as to whether the actor is available for the job and does not commit the producer in any way. If the actor through his agent accepts the 'offer' he is similarly committed to the film just as the producer is committed to pay him. At this point the deal is 'pay or play' meaning the actor will play the part or, if for no fault of his own he doesn't, he will be paid anyway. And that is that. Contracts follow later. Often contracts are not signed until after the film is completed.

As far as Richard Hatton was concerned Elliot Kastner had made an offer which had been accepted and therefore the deal was 'pay or play' just as was the deal for *Nine Tiger Men* with 20th Century Fox. It was not to be quite that simple.

Harold Pinter had been talking to Robert Shaw, as they worked on *Glass Booth*, of plans to make a film of *The Birthday Party* in which he wanted Shaw to star. A young American director William Friedkin (later to direct *The French Connection* and *The Exorcist*) was interested in directing it but for the finance it was felt they needed at least one 'name'. Shaw expressed an interest but pointed out that he would not be available until the end of the *Severed Head* in February.

It was the beginning of June 1967 when Stuart Lyons, the British head of 20th Century Fox called Hatton to tell him that the Americans had cancelled *Nine Tiger Men.* Obviously they would honour Shaw's 'pay or play' commitment but hoped that it would be possible to find a part for Shaw in one of their other properties. There was, for instance, he went on, a part for him in *Prudence and the Pill* and he was sending over the script immediately. Shaw was slightly dismayed, but, as he would still get the money, and was preoccupied with *The Man in the Glass Booth*, he was not overly depressed.

He read the script of *Prudence and the Pill* and turned it down immediately. In his entire career on stage, television and film Shaw never played in a comedy, with the insignificant exception of early days in Shakespeare, and his tiny part in *The Lavender Hill Mob.*

Elliot Kastner, hearing the news, thought he would send *A Severed Head* to 20th Century Fox. If they liked it and were prepared to finance it, their problem in relation to Shaw was solved and they would virtually 'save' themselves $250,000. (The position was that they had to pay Shaw the money by default. If, however, they could substitute another film in the place of *Nine Tiger Men* they would only have to pay additional money if the film went into dates not covered by the *Tiger* contract – and they could not force Shaw to accept any film. The reason for this is that in law damages for default can only be awarded against proof of actual loss. Shaw could have proved he had actually lost $250,000 between July and September 1967 by not doing *Nine Tiger Men*, but if he worked on any film for any part of that time the fee he earned would be deducted from his claim for loss by default. Obviously if the substitute film was for 20th Century Fox, so much the better.) But 20th Century were not interested in *A Severed Head*. Kastner told Hatton that he was doing a deal with CBS.

A few days later Lyons called to say that Fox were doing a film in America based on the book of *The Boston Strangler* and Shaw, they felt, would be excellent as the detective. At the moment however the film was scheduled to start in December and would interfere with Shaw's commitment on *A Severed Head*. Lyons sent the book over anyway.

From the book it was impossible for Shaw to tell whether the detective would be a good part in the film or a small subsidiary role. He would need to see the script. And anyway it was academic because the dates clashed. Lyons conveyed this information to the director Richard Fleischer in New York and was told it now looked as though the picture would be rescheduled to go in January, so Shaw's commitment was not a problem.

On 9 August 1967, Shaw's 40th birthday, Richard Fleischer called him direct to ask if he would be interested in playing the part of the strangler and not the detective. Fleischer had gone away and seen a copy of *The Caretaker* and was enormously impressed. Shaw agreed immediately provided he got first position billing and the script was right. Fleischer promised he would call Fox and ask them to make a formal 'offer' once the script was ready.

Meanwhile plans to film *The Birthday Party* were firming up. ABC (in America) and Paramount were prepared to finance the film on a budget of $500,000 with a four-week rehearsal period, (it is not usual to have any rehearsal period for a film though some have a week when it is felt there is an emphasis on the acting. Four weeks indicated that the idea was to film a production of the play rather than fully convert it into a movie) and a four-week shoot starting in mid-February, there would be a direct clash should *The Boston Strangler* materialise.

At this point, after taking Mary to the centenary fête of the Ladock Church School, which he had agreed to open in early July, Shaw decided he needed to have some peace and quiet to get on with his novel, now that *The Man in the Glass Booth* had opened. The book was provisionally entitled *The Telegram*. He left for a tour of Norway on 12 August, planning to return in time for *A Severed Head* which was also going to rehearse prior to shooting, though this time only for a week. For the first time Shaw had sold his new novel to his American publisher first. Harcourt Brace had paid him an advance of $7,500 for the rights (to the book they knew as '*Two Gentlemen from Madrid*') and an additional sum if sales of *The Man in the Glass Booth* exceeded royalties of $7, 500, which Shaw felt they would. They never did.

Before leaving, Shaw completed a recording of an LP reading of the *Prefaces of George Bernard Shaw*, produced by Robin Richardson and Peggie Smith. It earned him £150 and 6% of the wholesale price after the sale of the first 100 discs.

Shaw's wanting to escape to write was unusual. Some of his best work had been undertaken under high emotional pressure in cramped, noisy and uncomfortable surroundings. Wanting peace and quiet was a departure from his normal practice. The truth was the book was not going at all well. Shaw was stuck. He hoped the mountains of Norway would help him get on.

But if he wanted to escape the telephone he was to be disappointed, there was too much that required his attention. If he were to do *The Birthday Party* in the spring it would be necessary to ask Phil Yordan to release him from his option on Shaw which he had acquired at the time of *Custer of the West*. Yordan had now acquired the rights to Peter Shaffer's enormously successful stage play *The Royal Hunt of the Sun* for which Shaw was ideally suited to the part played by Colin Blakeley on the stage. Fortunately Yordan still didn't have a director so a delay was possible, provided Shaw agreed to start immediately after *The Birthday Party*.

After two days in Norway, Shaw called Richard Hatton to ask what the situation was with his play *The Joke*. It was a strange request, as it had been some years since Binkie Beaumont had rejected the play and Shaw had not mentioned it since. The agency had tried it with the BBC but had received no reply. Shaw was delighted. He wanted a copy sent out to him to Norway straight away. He had thought of the way to finish his book.

On his arrival in Oslo there was a message to say that it looked as if 20th Century Fox was going to make him an offer for *The Boston Strangler* at $300,000 for 12 weeks. It would mean that *The Birthday Party* would have to be postponed slightly but if that could be arranged – which it could – Shaw would do three films in a row plus *The Royal Hunt of the Sun*, possibly making four in a row, depending on Yordan getting his director sorted out. It was a big commitment especially in terms of his favourite word 'energy'. Did he have the 'energy' to do three films, all leading parts, all very different characters, none of them easy, all good scripts?

From the Norge Hotel in Bergen Shaw phoned Hatton with his decision. He could see the way to the end of his novel. He could almost finish before leaving Norway (now that *The Joke* had arrived) and with that out of the way he did have the 'energy' to do three films in a row, and earn over $½ million. His decision was not unexpected.

Within three days his future career looked very different. Stuart Lyons called to say that Fleischer had had second thoughts and was not going to make an offer on *The Boston Strangler*. He did not say, of course, that the part had gone, very much against type, to Tony Curtis. On top of this, rumours were circulating in America that Elliot Kastner had not got the financing for *A Severed Head*; Ben Benjamin, head of Ashley Famous in Los Angeles who looked after Shaw in Hollywood – though they had never met – called to tell Hatton the news. It was true.

On 19 September Kastner called Richard Hatton to say he was having great trouble with financing the picture and would Shaw consider doing it for nothing (i.e. for a percentage of the profits and no money 'up front'). Shaw's reaction was immediate. He would – and had – done such a thing with a masterpiece but there was no way he was going to do it with *A Severed Head* which he regarded as a purely commercial picture. Conveying this message to Kastner, Hatton also added that as far as he was concerned he regarded the deal as having been done, that it was a 'pay or play' deal and if Kastner was not going to produce the film and let Shaw play then he would have to pay.

So from the prospect of Shaw having three films and earning over $500,000 there was now only one, the least financially rewarding – *The Birthday Party* for which he was to receive just $25,000 plus 8½% of the gross after break-even – which had been postponed until April 1968. At a meeting with Kastner, Shaw, who might have thought to have been a frightening prospect in such a situation, sharp of tongue and hard of eye, reversed his previous position and said he would do the picture for nothing. But it was too late. Kastner could not get financing even on that premise. He knew he was in a hole and that there was very little he could do to dig himself out of it. He offered to find parts for Shaw in his other projects. Hatton noted it was 'pathetic'.

A few days later Kastner's attitude changed and, through his lawyers, he stated that Shaw's deal had always been subject to confirmation of a distribution deal for the picture. The only way Shaw was going to get his money was to sue and the file was passed to British Actors' Equity for them to take the matter up. A settlement was finally reached out of court. The film was eventually made in 1970 with Ian Holm playing Martin Lynch-Gibbon.

Though financial pressure was eased by the payment from 20th Century Fox for *Nine Tiger Men*, it looked as though 1967 was going to be a year in which Shaw did no acting whatsoever. On the Frost

Programme which he did on 6 October he talked animatedly of his writing and how he was quite happy not to have acted since finishing *Custer* in September 1966. 'It is no good you see, accepting any film, I've made that mistake before. It's got to be the right film. Otherwise I just write my books.'

But by the end of October he was offered an acting job. ABC Television in New York – who were financing in part *The Birthday Party* – were producing John Osborne's *Luther* (sponsored by Xerox). As Finney, who had played the part on stage, was now massively too expensive for a television-only production they were looking for a Luther. The English director, Stuart Burge, knew Shaw from his stage work at the Royal Court and a deal was struck at $40,000 for two showings in the US only. Burge directed with Robert Morley as Pope Leo and Alex Davion rowed into the cast with Shaw. The four-week schedule was completed on 1 January 1968. John Osborne did not attend the rehearsals or the recording.

The production was nominated for an Emmy but strangely in a project that is so much about the performance of the central character, Shaw was not nominated in the Best Actor category. Perhaps there was a degree of naïvety and innocence required by Luther that Shaw could not conjure: the scatological themes so well developed in the language of the play were certainly very much to his taste, however. The production was never seen in England.

Despite the cancellations of the previous year, 1968 was going to be very full for Shaw. He had to deliver his novel to Harcourt Brace, he was booked to do *The Birthday Party* starting on 25 April 1968 and Phil Yordan had now decided that Irving Lerner would direct *The Royal Hunt of the Sun* which would start in the summer in Spain. The deal for the latter, $350,000 and first position billing above the title again, was quite a contrast to the $25,000 he was getting for *The Birthday Party*. Whatever else could be said of Shaw he was certainly flexible when he came to his fees, especially when it was a question of helping a friend.

The Birthday Party had first been presented as a play at the Arts Theatre in 1958 to an indifferent reception. It was Pinter's own production at the RSC in the Aldwych Theatre in 1964 that had revived interest in the play. For the film Friedkin was to direct, only one member of the Aldwych cast survived, Patrick Magee as McCann. Robert Shaw took over from Bryan Pringle as Stanley with Sidney Tafler as Goldbert, Dandy Nichols as Meg and Helen Fraser (taking over from Janet Suzman) as Lulu.

Shaw's performance confirmed him as an actor perfectly suited to Pinter's writing. The layers of meaning necessary to give the script its validity, to make it appear to have an overall rationale, are supplied by the actor and it therefore requires a particular sort of acting persona to fill out what is not given in the dialogue. Shaw's ability to switch so quickly from charm to menace, the word most over used in relation to Pinter, from apparently touching concern to apathy, from tenderness to violence, was exactly the depth needed to flesh out the character. Patrick Magee, Sidney Tafler and Dandy Nichols were all actors of the same type, carrying with them the baggage of a personage already well established.

During the filming Benny Fisz reappeared in Shaw's life after a break of 10 years and sent him a script of *The Battle of Britain*, a multi-million dollar epic he was producing with Harry Saltzman to be directed by Guy Hamilton, another figure from Shaw's distant past. Fisz, as an ex-fighter pilot, had always been keen to make a picture of the Battle. He had enlisted the support of the RAF and promised a percentage of the profits of the film would go to a RAF Charity (the picture cost so much that it never went into profit). The script by James Kennaway (whose distinction as a young novelist was almost as great as Shaw's, based on the reception of his book *The Cost of Living Like This*), and Wilfred Greatorex, was written to accommodate a large number of stars playing relatively small 'cameo' roles with only one or two actors going through the whole picture. The theory was, and the concept was becoming increasingly popular, with many films around this period made in the same way, that the large number of stars would increase the 'marquee' value and generate publicity, while the smallness of their involvement would mean that their cost was kept comparatively low.

Shaw's role took 12 days in May and earned him £12,000 plus a deferment out of profits. Among the other names to grace the film were Christopher Plummer, Susannah York, Michael Caine, Trevor Howard, Patrick Wymark – Shaw's best man – Ralph Richardson, Laurence Olivier, Harry Andrews and Michael Redgrave. Shaw gave a jaunty performance, allowing the steely glint in his eyes and the suggestion of mischief under the white Aran roll-neck sweater and compulsory fur-trimmed flying jacket, to imply that underneath the Boy's Own qualities of the battle there was something more profound, like fear.

Once again, though Shaw's part in the film was small, when it opened in November with one of the heaviest promotions for a purely British film, and a gala première, it increased public awareness of Shaw as a film star, more than *Custer of the West* had done, and had much the same effect as *A Man for all Seasons*. In the public perception, Shaw's massive leading roles had gone largely unnoticed. It was his three smaller roles in *From Russia With Love*, *A Man for All Seasons*, and *The Battle of Britain* that had bought him *public* notice.

As it happened Phil Yordan had been searching for a partner for his company, Security Pictures, to complete the financing on *The Royal Hunt of the Sun.* While in England in April he had been introduced by Shaw to Benny Fisz. Taking the opportunity he pitched his plans to Benny; the advantages of Spain, his distribution deal in America, the studio complex in Almeria. Benny was impressed and *The Royal Hunt of the Sun* became a Security Pictures/Benmar co-production.

In the appropriate heat of the sun in July in Spain Shaw realised that he had chosen the wrong role. Yordan had offered him either part and perhaps through want of 'energy' he had opted for Pizarro. But Atahuallpa was actually the key part in the script and the one requiring acting histrionics, and with Christopher Plummer in the part there was now nothing Shaw could do about it except regret. There was a great deal of tension on set. Shaw, always popular with crew and any visiting press corps, was an exact opposite of Plummer whom he regarded as effete and affected. Plummer refused to accept any of Shaw's athletic challenges: like Achilles, he sulked in his tent, or rather his air-conditioned Winnebago, and refused to come out to play.

The film of Peter Shaffer's imaginative play had none of the excitement of the theatrical production. Phil Yordan's screenplay, unconcerned with subtleties, turned the story into a sort of Hollywood bio-pic. Irving Lerner shot the script as a job of work not a work of art, with the usual priority being to see that the film is made on time and on or under budget. The deals had been done, the money made, long before the cameras rolled. As long as the picture was delivered any gesture to excellence was surplus to requirements.

Shaw's third involvement with Yordan proved that it had been downhill all the way. Not only was the film a critical failure, as the first two had been, but *The Royal Hunt of the Sun* was only given a very limited release. Suspecting from its title that this might be esoteric material for local cinema audiences only, a few prints were made and when the cinemas showing these failed to report good business no more prints were produced and the film was pulled. In America only a New York and Los Angeles release was planned, again to test the water, and when the water was found to be distinctly cold, the film was withdrawn.

Shaw's attitude to Yordan was curious. He was besotted with the man, more so than anyone he had met. His trust in him was absolute. In August Yordan suggested that he offer Shaw a three-picture deal with Security Pictures for $333,000 per film with 5% of the producer's profits and $1,500 per week expenses. In other words the mythical $1 million dollar contract. The deal would not include script approval, i.e. Shaw would, like studio stars in the Hollywood of the '30s, have to accept the script and the part he was given. Astonishingly, Shaw was quite prepared to agree to this provided the contract *guaranteed* that Yordan was the producer of all of the films.

Yet Shaw knew perfectly well that when friends like Joe Losey and Harold Pinter expressed their concern about the obvious lack of quality in the work that was taking so much of his precious 'energy', he knew they were right. *The Royal Hunt of the Sun* was, as he would later categorise it, a 'piece of shit' and his performance bore little resemblance to the haunting performances he was capable of turning in under the right director in other circumstances. Indeed though he would try to hide it publicly by a swaggering bravado at press conferences to launch such product (Shaw was never an actor to bite the hand that feeds during pre-publicity campaigns for a film. He always tried to appear enthusiastic and always succeeded) there was no doubt that his inability to feel that his time was spent in a worthwhile way depressed him deeply. 'Worthwhile' in this context clearly did not include – nor would it in the future – making large sums of money.

It was this, however, that was at the crux of the relationship with Yordan as well as at the heart of the problem with himself. His faith in Yordan was ultimately because Yordan was the first man to come along and put his money where his mouth was and give Shaw the chance to be a film star, however inferior the product. Without Yordan, Shaw may well have been even further behind his rivals – Caine, O'Toole, Stamp et al. That was the reason for his trust and loyalty and faith in Yordan: Yordan had trust and loyalty and faith in Robert Shaw.

The problem remained that there was a side of Shaw that despised money, especially easy money. He wanted to do good work – and because he was an intelligent well-read man with notably successful friends renowned for the quality of their work – he knew precisely what good work was, both in writing and acting. It was becoming increasingly difficult to deliver. For the time being Shaw ignored this problem. There was a feeling, with all the activity of 1968, that he had reached a 'tide in the affairs of man, which taken at the flood . . .' It was only when the flood tide began to ebb, when Shaw had more time on his hands, and when circumstances conspired to take away some of the foundations of his life, that the problem re-emerged and re-doubled.

The '60s had been a Golden Age for the British film industry. American producers, the carpetbaggers of their time, had flocked to London, on the back of the success of The Beatles on the world stage, to test whether Britishness was a marketable quality in other areas of the entertainment business. Money flowed with them and during the period there were probably more truly dreadful films made in England with American money than at any other time. It seemed that as long as the script had the requisite number of pages it would be made (*What's New Pussycat, I'll Never Forget What'sisname, Work is a Four Letter Word, Here We Go Round the Mulberry Bush, The Magic Christian, Casino Royale, The Wrong Box, The Jokers*: the list is endless). Some important movies had been made too and several important careers launched, but with less frequency.

Robert Shaw had been a figure largely on the sidelines of all this activity, consigned to make bad Phil Yordan movies in Spain and given no real opportunity in a leading role to star in a film that would make a real impact on the public and on his career. His successes had all been in minor roles. He was perceived more and more as a 'character' actor (an idea he would hate) on one hand, and on the literary and intellectual field, on the other, as someone who could be relied on, in an article or a chat show, to come up with lively controversial opinions. He had not made the 'breakthrough' to become a major star on the international stage. In the court of the '60s, Shaw was often cast as a sort of Jacques ('Did he not moralise this spectacle?').

Quite suddenly in 1969 the Americans had enough and disappeared taking their money with them, tired of waiting to see if British films and British talent could produce in the film industry what The Beatles had produced in music. The Golden Age was over. The British film industry would never recover.

With the New York production of *The Man in the Glass Booth* opening in September 1968 and Shaw's obsession with the Olympics, immediately after the filming for *Royal Hunt* was over, Robert and Mary and the youngest in the family flew to Mexico where, with the help of his American agents, tickets had been acquired at greatly inflated prices for the Mexico Olympics. It was the Games in which a notoriously unfair decision was made in favour of a local boxer. Shaw, he later recounted to friends, had protested so vigorously he was hauled out of the stadium by Mexican police and almost spent a night in jail. On the way to the stadium in Acapulco one afternoon they were witness to an event that left a more lasting memory: their car pulled up behind a road accident that had happened only minutes before. As Mary later wrote:

The pale yellow face of the driver dying
Killed instantly by the driving wheel
His wife holding a daughter dying too
The other car was worse
All eight people lay dead and crumpled

'What about the helicopter from Acapulco?'
'That,' he said, 'is only for the tourists.'

The event did not stop Shaw attending several cock fights which
were not part of the Olympic schedules.

The New York production of *The Man in the Glass Booth* opened at
the Royale Theatre on 26 September 1968, with Donald Pleasence
repeating his performance as Goldman and otherwise an American
cast (including F. Murray Abraham doubling as Rudin and
Tzelniker). Clive Barnes, then the most influential critic on Broadway
was enthusiastic: 'a simple melodrama, engrossing at its own level,
and a fantastically effective vehicle for bravura acting'. There were
echoes of the London critics who found the play confusing but
generally speaking the production was a success and Donald
Pleasance's performance was greeted with real enthusiasm. The play
was nominated for a Tony Award (*The Great White Hope* by Howard
Sackler won that year) and ran for 269 performances. Jack Warden
took over from Pleasance in the last four weeks. Shaw enjoyed his
celebrity and was very much the man about New York, doing
interviews and talk shows and eating at Sardi's and the Russian Tea
Rooms. Among the people he was to meet was Thornton Wilder who
had come to the show and told Shaw afterwards it was one of the most
moving theatrical experiences he could remember. Shaw took an
instant liking to the quiet New Englander. Wilder said he would love
to read Shaw's next book and he was subsequently sent an advance
copy of *Card From Morocco*.

Glasshouse Productions, the company that had presented *The Man
in the Glass Booth*, were also busy. As well as the New York
production Terence Baker had involved them in another play. As the
agent for John Hopkins – a writer who had established new ground
with the television series *Z Cars*, dealing with policemen with a degree
of realism previously unthought of – Baker had been trying to sell a
play he had written for three years. But in those days theatre managers
were very suspicious of 'television' writers whose experience in the
theatre had been limited. Finally the Royal Court had agreed to a
production of the play, *This Story of Yours*, provided a West End
management could be found to sponsor the production.

The triumvirate of Pinter, Shaw and Pleasence readily agreed once
they had read the script. The play ran to packed houses at the Court
before transferring to the West End. Glasshouse Productions recorded
a small profit.

Aside from this production activity it was very much a time when
star actors were encouraged to take control of their own destinies and

produce their own films. Shaw was not in the same position – a 'bankable' star – as O'Toole, Richard Harris and Albert Finney (who all had their own 'producers', Jules Buck, John McMichael and Michael Medwin respectively). In 1967 he did pay George Bluestone, an American writer $5,000 to write a screenplay of *The Sun Doctor* with a view to producing the film himself and starring as Dr Halliday. He felt he was too close to the material to write it himself. Bluestone's script was not a success and the project was abandoned but, following the success of *Far from the Madding Crowd* in 1967, and with an abiding interest in Thomas Hardy – much of whose poetry he had included in the poetry anthology *Flashpoint* – Shaw decided to buy the rights of *The Mayor of Casterbridge* as a vehicle for his acting talents. Looking for a screenwriter, Terence Baker suggested John Hopkins who went to work immediately under contract to River Enterprises. If all else failed, at least these items were tax deductible.

Mary Ure had not worked since her appearance in *Custer of the West* with her husband in 1966. In September 1968 she was offered the female lead in *Where Eagles Dare* with Clint Eastwood and Richard Burton, directed by Brian Hutton. Leaving Shaw and Miss Jay with the children she set out for Austria in December but sitting in her caravan on the second day of shooting she received a call from Laszlo Gombosh to say that Warner Brothers had reneged on the agreement for her billing and that they would not bill her above the title as previously agreed. Over dinner Burton asked her why she was so depressed and she told him. What could she do? Burton called his agent immediately. Neither Miss Ure nor Mr Burton would appear before the cameras until Ms Ure's name was reinstated above the title of the film with his own. By the morning Laszlo called with news of Warner Bros' complete capitulation. Filming was not delayed by so much as a minute.

Shaw came out on a visit for a weekend. It was the first time Peter Barkworth, who was also in the film, had seen him since 1950. Barkworth was telling a story of having been to an Austrian inn where the owner had a huge store of Nazi memorabilia, which he proudly displayed to all and sundry. Shaw was outraged. 'Didn't you tell him,' he demanded, 'didn't you tell him what the Nazis did, how evil it was?'

The film was produced by Elliot Kastner and was hugely successful. Part of the profits would pay for Shaw's settlement on *A Severed Head*.

It was to be tax that was very much on the agenda in 1969. Following his 1966/67 and 1967/68 tax returns, Shaw's accountant, Ivan Paul, received a letter querying the arrangements that had been made in respect of Robert Shaw's overseas employment contracts.

Tax inspectors are, after all, human beings who go to the pictures and read newspapers like other individuals and were therefore quite aware that Robert Shaw had made three pictures abroad for reportedly large sums of money that were not reflected in his annual tax returns.

Though the returns had been quite proper, the letter called for more details in reference to Shaw's employment agreement with a Liechtenstein company, Art Productions AG. It was only when Ivan Paul began to try to answer some of the Revenue's questions, that his long experience of tax affairs led him to believe that there was going to be trouble ahead, and considering the amounts of money earned through Art Productions since 1965 – well over $1 million – which would be affected, it was not going to be trouble easily dismissed.

Shaw's loyalty to another figure in his life over the past 15 years was also proved to be unquestioning. In 1969 Richard Hatton had decided that the pressure of running what had become one of the most successful agencies in London, together with the burgeoning career of Sean Connery, made it impossible to continue to handle Robert Shaw's affairs personally. Another agent had been brought into the business, Shaw was told, so he could be given as much attention as in the past. Surprisingly, considering the main reason for the change must have been quite obvious to him, and he might well have interpreted the decision to mean he was being sloughed off with second best, Shaw took the decision with equanimity. Donald Bradley, the new recruit, was dispatched to Porch House and after a bout of drinking and arm-wrestling took over Shaw's representation with scarcely a hitch.

Joe Losey, another of the Hollywood directors chased from Los Angeles by the Committee for Un-American Activities (but not one of the Hollywood Ten) was introduced to Shaw by Harold Pinter who had worked with him on *The Servant* in 1963 and would later effect an award-winning collaboration of L.P. Hartley's *The Go-Between*. Losey, moulded in the Bogartian tradition of Hollywood heroes, pockmarked face, hardlined by hard drinking, gruff 60-cigarettes-a-day voice, had become a friend. Every child of Shaw's – quite a list after all – would receive a birthday card from Losey each year with a little ink sketch drawn on the card. In 1969 he called Shaw to say that he was now directing the film of Barry England's book *Figures in a Landscape* which Columbia Pictures were producing. Shaw already had the script and had expressed doubts about its value. The impressionistic title, indicating a symbolism for which Losey's work was well known, might explain why the film was eventually so successful in France. *Figures Mis en Scène*, a fair translation, was almost a definition of some French film-maker's technique. It was this quality that had worried Shaw, but once he heard Losey was to direct, he expressed his delight. Losey told him he knew exactly how to get the film right and would like Shaw's help in fixing the script.

It is not difficult to understand Shaw's initial concern. The script, set in an imaginary country, has two prisoners, having escaped from prison with their hands bound behind their backs – conveniently with rope not handcuffs – fleeing three helicopters. As they trek across country in an attempt to reach the border and freedom, they gradually gain respect for each other (what the Americans called a 'buddy' movie) and save each other's life as the helicopters close in. Finally McConnachie, the older of the two, is killed while Ansell, a man just out of his teens, escapes over the border.

Columbia's offer certainly made the job worthwhile financially. Shaw was to be paid $326,000 plus 7% of the gross receipts from the film over and above the first $7 million from the box office. If the film grossed $6 million Shaw would get nothing from this percentage. If it grossed $8 million he would get an extra $70,000. With the exception of *The Birthday Party* it was the first time Shaw had received a percentage of the 'gross', i.e. the amount taken at the box office before any deductions of any sort are made. It was also the first time Shaw was, finally, to play a leading role for a major American studio and be paid at Phil Yordan rates.

Shaw had delivered his next novel, now called *A Card from Morocco*, at the end of 1968, so he could set to work on the screenplay of *Figures in a Landscape* with no impediment. His main contribution was to add a degree of reality to the characters. Bearing in mind his own penchant, it is the element of competition between the two men, McConnachie's constant taunting of the younger Ansell ('Town boy aren't you . . . brought up on a bloody bottle . . . never saw a cow . . . all those bloody women you've had . . . all those dirty doorways . . . I must be old enough to be your father . . . Sorry I forgot the toothpaste.') that Shaw has added. But most typical of all is the song McConnachie sings:

> What are you waiting for, my handsome young son?
> What are you staying for, my lovely young one?
> For your arms to hold me, father
> For your lips to kiss me, father
> Make my bed softly for it's dark down below
> And I'll soon be gone.

Losey did not want to characterise the men too much, however. He wanted them classless, making the only difference between them their age and their attitude to sex (McConnachie married, Ansell constantly relating his conquests). By not placing them in a country, by not allowing us to know their crimes, their guilt or innocence, every time there is a reference to something specific – Harrods, Fortnum & Masons, Americans in the war – it jars. The men speak as if they are English but they are clearly not in England, though they make no reference to being in a foreign country. To judge from Losey's extended conversation with Shaw, however, this is precisely the effect he wanted to achieve. The only other characters in the film are the three helicopters, equally anonymous, painted black with no markings and black reflective windows so the pilots are never seen. The question of whether they are justified in their pursuit of the two men – who may be mass killers for all the audience is told – is never raised.

Shaw's contribution to the script was disputed by the original screenplay writer and eventually in December 1969 there was a Screen Writers' Guild arbitration to decide who should receive what credit on the film. This arbitration involves various representatives from the producers on one side, and the writers on the other, reading the various versions of the screenplay and comparing them with the final film. Shaw was awarded, as a result of this process, sole screen credit.

Shaw seemed to be destined to make films in Spain. The filming of *Figures* was done entirely on location in Granada. Before he set out in June 1969 on what was to be a physically gruelling picture, he faced what he came to regard as an equally gruelling prospect. He had been asked by the BBC if he would agree to be the subject of their *Omnibus* arts programme. The main theme the director, John Ingrams, wanted to pursue was how Shaw managed to be both a highly successful actor and a prize-winning novelist. Shaw had been flattered and readily agreed, but as the date of the first interview approached he became increasingly nervous. The plan was to film an interview at Porch House in May, another during the making of *Figures* in Spain, then to do the final interview back in Buckinghamshire in the autumn. It didn't quite work out that way.

At the first interview Shaw talked of his childhood, with obvious pain, and then of his writing. It was only through writing 'that I began to function as a person,' he said. There is no actor to whom he feels inferior but there are many, many writers. Writing 'fills me with an enormous sense of well-being.' Nor is he worried if he cannot write for the next few years, the writing will always be there. He could retire from acting, 'after 10 years at the top' and start to write in earnest. His performance, in front of the *Omnibus* cameras, was polished, articulate and controlled, sitting in a chair in his study by a full bookcase, his eyes bright, a certain worried concern in his face, a sense of wanting to get at the truth. His nerves seemed to have disappeared.

His belief in socialism had not been affected by his wealth, he goes on to say. How does he reconcile the two? 'You see I've made all my money myself, by working. I've never done it by investing, unearned income.' Clearly he had forgotten, in his enthusiasm, the list of investments River Enterprises in England, and Art Productions in Switzerland had made and his often persistent enquiries to find out how much these investments were worth and how much they had earned. He was forgetting also the time and trouble that had been spent on tax avoidance. It was a curious double think.

In Spain two months later and well into the filming of *Figures* the image was very different. Joe Losey had chosen Malcolm McDowell, the star of Lindsay Anderson's *If . . .* , to play Ansell. McDowell's experience of filming, and life, was necessarily limited in comparison to Shaw's and Shaw was not in a generous mood. He had discovered, for instance, that McDowell had a phobia about snakes, and since there were many where they were filming one particular sequence, where the helicopters pursue them through a field of maize, he chased McDowell with one in his hand while the cameras were rolling. Losey included the sequence in the film. Diana Sullivan, the PA on *Omnibus*, remembers Shaw taunting McDowell on his inabilities, 'I've beaten you at running, my son's beaten you at chess, isn't there anything you can do, boy?' McDowell was close to tears. Sensing that Sullivan was less than impressed with him, Shaw told her that he had thrown his one-year-old son into the swimming pool in order to teach him to swim – a scene from *Reflections in a Golden Eye* but not from life – to provoke a reaction. He did not get one.

Shaw's cruelty was based on his own unhappiness. *Card from Morocco* had just been published and, for the first time since *Off the Mainland* in 1956, he had received a unanimously bad press. Some of the reviews of *The Man in the Glass Booth* had been less than complimentary but he could always console himself with Harold Hobson. The response to *Card from Morocco* could be summed-up as a feeling of disappointment on the critics' part. The *New Statesman*'s 'tediously insubstantial . . . endless conversations mannered and repetitious' was typical. It was a blow because, as he said in front of the *Omnibus* cameras, he had convinced himself it was his 'best book'. Nobody has understood, he complains, that the book is about 'sexual insecurity'. Instead it has been described as a 'travelogue'. The standard of literary criticism is appalling, he continues, not allowing the interviewer to escape to talk of other things, only wanting to talk of the book. In England, reviewers are paid £25 to review a book it has taken a writer perhaps years to produce. He continues:

> I don't quite know what I was expecting. I don't think any writer ever does know what he is expecting. Critics upset me very much because I care so much about my novel. I hate these flip glib critics, the sort of disenchantment, the awful, awful debilitating effect of realising that hardly anyone reads your novels, hardly anybody. It is true that if I were to write the greatest novel that were ever to have been written, by any standards, I doubt very much whether more than 15,000 people in England, if the whole press was totally with me, praised it on every level, would buy it in hardback [*The Hiding Place* sold 10,000]. Well you've got to be awfully courageous to keep on wanting to do that when you can get more immediate comeback as an actor obviously in films . . . I'm too good a novelist to have instant appreciation. Everybody wants it all ways, we all do. I'd like to be appreciated by the intelligentsia, the fools, the comics, the alcoholics, everybody. I would then have to guard against, as I do as an actor, too much adulation . . . But by God it's depressing to be a novelist at the moment, it's not easy, I'm sure it's never been easy. Could I write a really great novel, could I not? Some days, a long time ago, I used to think I could . . . As much as talent is important to any form of writer so is energy . . . and anyway you know bloody well in a few years time you'll be dead and so what in my case, there'll be nine books on a bookcase that nobody's reading anymore. I know a lot of people look on me as successful and when I complain they think: how dare he complain, what's he getting so angry about? But from my point of view I don't feel successful at all. Of course failure always makes one reshape one's pattern. What is sad in life is the people who've got genuine talent whom failure knocks into the ground. No, failure isn't going to knock me into the ground till I'm too tired. Yes, the fact that *Card from Morocco* has been a failure might make me write a better book, it might not. I believe in the parable of the talents, I really do believe in that . . .

The fact that the *Omnibus* cameras were present to record this particular crisis in Shaw's life was a coincidence; what they captured on film was a spontaneous reaction, a raw nerve exposed. The way, on camera, he worries away at his disappointment, that he cannot put it aside, that he has to find a way to come to terms with his despair, is typical of his reactions in general. He was never able to cope with a hurt, to leave it unresolved and accept the pain. It had, instead, to be compartmentalised, tidied away, turned into something that could be dealt with, that didn't hurt. This rationalisation worked only on the surface, however; it had the effect of driving the actual problem deeper. It was exactly the way he had dealt with the death of his father as a boy, the event that established the pattern.

Shaw's reservations about the standard of literary criticism were only partially justified. *Card from Morocco* is certainly not Shaw's best work. In fact, Shaw was mortified by the critics' reaction because he sensed the criticism contained more than a grain of truth. Anger is often in direct proportion to the amount of responsibility borne in its commission and Shaw knew that, despite the bravado of calling it his 'best book', it was one he had written without the care and attention to detail he had lavished on his earlier novels, and had delivered the book ignoring his better judgement that it needed more work.

Card from Morocco uses the techniques Shaw developed in the novel of *The Man in the Glass Booth* but without the huge moral and metaphysical issues raised in the latter. That is not to say it is not successful in a much more limited area. All Shaw's other novels had dealt with large themes but the principle theme of *Card from Morocco* is smaller: the necessity, the awareness, the difficulties, and the effect of booze. The two central characters, the effete and pathetic Englishman, Lewis, and the brash, hard and antipathetic American, Slattery, share the same problem – the need to stop drinking. Shaw graphically illustrates the effects of booze, the listless, uncentred, unmotivated life, and uses it to get the men to speak, to divulge their innermost secrets to each other. But the secrets are meaningless. The medium is the message here. What is important is not the drunken ramblings, the endless and perfectly observed conversations of two men apparently pouring out their souls to each other, but their total failure to address, or even acknowledge, their dependence on booze. This is where the book achieves its success.

On the cover of the English hardback edition of the book, approved by Shaw, Lewis and Slattery are drawn as two faces sharing the same head, the idea being clearly, that they are two aspects of the same personality – just as it could be said of Connolly and Wilson in *The Hiding Place*. But whereas in *The Hiding Place* it is a quiet withdrawn Wilson who is artistic, trying to write his book, in *Card* it has become the loud-mouth braggart Slattery who has the artistic bent and paints and sculpts. It is difficult not to see these themes as autobiographical. The dichotomy in personality throughout Shaw's career, the quiet sensitive writer, against the flamboyant extrovert actor, had, in a sense, been resolved. The quiet writer had simply disappeared. What was left was the brashness of Slattery as an artist:

I have painted in shacks where there was so little room my ass was out of the door in the middle of winter. I couldn't block the window because of the light. Whatever you do, wherever you go, whoever you lay, that family of yours rubs off on ya! . . . to live with the naked mind . . . takes courage.

Shaw also uses Slattery to return to another autobiographical theme – the pain of his childhood. Slattery's character indulges in this pain, as Lewis points out, refusing to come to terms with it, to leave the past behind and become an adult, living instead, a rootless life, moving from country to country, stateless and childlike in his pursuit of immediate gratification through drink and casual sex.

Slattery makes an attempt to resolve his feelings towards his father. In Norway, trying to finish the book, Shaw had asked for a copy of *The Joke* to be sent out to him. In *The Joke* the resolution of Harry's relationship to his father is to turn a mock suicide into the real thing; in *Card from Morocco* the mock suicide is staged again for the father's benefit and for the same reason as in *The Joke* – that the father has ill-treated the mother. The 'joke' is the same.

The critics felt that *Card from Morocco* lacked the quality of Shaw's earlier work and this is undoubtedly true. Nevertheless it is a compelling book for, once again, Shaw manages to create two characters who are exquisitely drawn, who are struggling to find a meaning, in the religious sense, and whose conversations have, no doubt through an actor's ear for dialogue, an unerring ring of accuracy. The two men deal with the disaster of their lives in different ways: one by resignation and defeat and the other by raging against the storm. Shaw's talent for novel writing is clear: what is disappointing is his lack of concentration on giving the book the resonances of the other four novels. By repeating a device he had used 10 years earlier to achieve a resolution he was, in effect, demonstrating a casualness he had never adopted in writing before. For the first time he had allowed his writing to take second place to the other things in his life.

The dedications in Shaw's books were always important to him as a sentimental gesture. All his previous books had been dedicated to one person (his mother, Jennifer, Mary respectively) with the exception of *Glass Booth* (To Mary and Hannah Shaw). But *Card from Morocco*'s dedication is a catch-all: 'For Philip Yordan, Philip Broadley, Leo Vala, Jeremiah Slattery [Shaw loved to use friend's names as characters in his book] Donald Pleasence, Alex Davion, Alfred Rogoway, Irving Lerner, Laszlo Gombosh, Richard Hatton, my brother and my wife.' Such comprehensiveness may have been an indication that Shaw felt, unconsciously no doubt, that with the difficulties he had experienced in writing *Card*, he wanted to be sure to include everyone in his gesture of thanks, as there might not be another chance. He was never to write another novel.

It is not fanciful to assume that *Card from Morocco* reflected issues very much to the fore in Shaw's life at the time of writing, especially in relation to Slattery. Slattery's voice in the novel is Shaw's voice, anyone who knew him will recognise its rhythms and cadences ('Get the old man for Christ's sake and let's have a drink'). Whatever the complex symbolism of the mock suicide it is difficult not to conclude that in returning to a theme dealt with in *The Joke* and, in an entirely different way, in Halliday's obsession with his father's suicide in *The Sun Doctor* Shaw's feelings towards his own father and *his* suicide were very much on the agenda again. The other major theme in *Card from Morocco* was also close to home: booze.

In the early days, as his friends remember, Shaw was not a drinker. He would prefer a cup of tea to a whisky. But by the mid-60s heavy drinking had gone from being an occasional event – as on the night he met Mary Ure – to a regular compulsion. Offered tea by Noël Coleman, the actor who introduced him to Denham Golf Club, he'd set it aside, 'Come on, boy, get the whisky out, boy, know you've got a bottle in that cupboard.' Once he started to drink, as with everything else in his life, he did it seriously and the amount of alcohol that could be consumed in an evening became as much a competitive sport as a game of tennis. By the time of the BBC *Hamlet*, he was capable of drinking chalices of schnapps.

Shaw knew perfectly well that his father had been an alcoholic and that this had contributed to his suicide. Robert Hardy recalls he was chary of booze for that reason. But if he had a psychological resistance to it as a young man, by the mid-60s that resistance had disappeared. Mary, unfortunately for them both, was a drinker too. Perhaps in order to maintain her composure in the face of Osborne's affairs, or through a more profound psychological need, she had been drinking heavily during her first marriage and had continued with Shaw, though he never gave her any reason to doubt his fidelity in the early days of their relationship.

The problem stemmed from the fact that alcohol is not the stimulant it is assumed to be; after the initial boost it is actually a depressant. Whether it is the nature of the theatrical profession which attracts personalities who can easily become addicted to alcohol (or other drugs for that matter) is a matter of speculation but there is no doubt that in the '60s there were several major stars whose problem was booze (many of whom were known to the Shaws) – O'Toole, Laurence Harvey, Vivien Leigh, Peter Finch, Richard Harris, and

Richard Burton among them. At that time the idea that any of these people were alcoholics was not discussed. Booze was, so it appeared, a function of acting, of being in the public eye. It was a way of relieving the 'pressure'.

And 'pressure' there was. It is difficult to imagine that a man earning consistently, in Shaw's case, with income from investments, over half-a-million dollars a year has any real pressure, but worries about making ends meets had been replaced by other concerns and ones less easy to cope with. The erosive effect of being in the public eye has been well documented. Personal privacy becomes public property all too easily, the British press happy and eager to turn success into failure and delve into the darkest corners to illuminate areas that for most people would remain forever dark.

Shaw's concerns, the duality of his talent, and his relationship with his father, were scabs itching to be picked, to be opened and re-opened and never allowed to heal. The problem was time. It is little understood perhaps that the more successful an actor is the more time he has on his hands. It is not a life of nine to five with three weeks' holiday a year and seven Bank Holidays. Even making three films a year can amount to only 36 weeks' work. One film is only 12 weeks on average leaving 40 weeks off. This can be eaten into by a stage job or a publicity tour but in Shaw's case it is difficult to think of a year in which he had fewer than three months off and mostly it was six. It was an awful lot of time to kill.

In Shaw's case, it was time to write. But as his life became more complex, writing became more difficult and time away from acting, once valued, began to drag. He had time to sit in the attic room at Porch House and brood. Brood about his life, about his father, about things that might have been. Days would have no pattern, no routine. He had always been subject to depression, since school days, and when depression struck it was easy to turn to the bottle in an attempt to escape from the lowering clouds he imagined were drifting over his life. He would allow few people to see this side of his life. The bottle made matters worse, increasing the melancholia. The symptom had a way of becoming the disease.

His marriage to Mary had become a problem in direct proportion to the amount of booze consumed in the house. Mary's reaction to alcohol was very different from her husband's. It made her fly into violent rages, and it made her want to take off all her clothes. She would scream a litany of abuse. Shaw had taken all her money, destroyed her career, made her into a housekeeper. And, never one to refuse a challenge, Shaw would reply in kind, the resulting slanging match turning into, as Shaw remarked himself, a good imitation of

Who's Afraid of Virginia Woolf. But Mary's anger was more than drunken rage. It was an illness that her proclivity for alcohol was successfully masking.

In the *Omnibus* interview Shaw had insisted that *Card from Morocco* was actually about 'sexual insecurity' which was certainly graphically portrayed in the book. Whether this theme was also autobiographical it is impossible to know. Mary certainly never mentioned it but with the amount Shaw was drinking, physically it was certainly a possibility. It did not, however, prevent Mary becoming pregnant with her fourth child and Shaw's eighth, by the time filming started on *Figures in a Landscape*.

None of Mary's problems, either marital or personal, were confided to her friends. As Mary had been with Osborne, her loyalty to Shaw was absolute. She had no cause to complain of infidelity at this point in their relationship but other causes of dissatisfaction she kept strictly to herself. Only if a friend blundered into one of the 'Virginia Woolf' scenes was there any hint of what was going on under the surface. In public the couple appeared more than happy, apart from Shaw catching the sharp edge of Mary's very sharp tongue ('their interchange as husband and wife seems as self-consciously creative as their art,' noted Robert Thomas in the *New York Times*). With her sweet and beatific 'butter-wouldn't-melt-in-my-mouth' attitude, her white china-doll complexion, she was quite capable of uttering a string of 'cunts' and 'fucks', seemingly oblivious to the incongruity of such language from her lips. Over dinner on one occasion when Shaw was indulging his liking for discussing sex in detail over a meal, especially when there were female guests present – and better still if they were shockable – he complained that Mary would never let him bugger her. 'My first wife used to love it. But Mary says it hurts too much.' 'Robert,' Mary said firmly, 'you're such an arsehole why don't you bugger yourself?'

Shaw became aware, in the summer of 1969, on the filming of *Figures*, that as drink was a problem for Mary so was it for *him*. In the previous year one of his reasons for going to Norway to write was to get away from drink – he dutifully reported to Richard Hatton that in his first week he'd only had 'one glass of red wine'. But the depression caused by the reviews after the publication of *Card from Morocco* had made him reach for the 'crutch' again and during the filming he was drinking heavily. Fortunately for him it was a problem Joe Losey suffered from himself and was prepared to indulge.

In September 1968 Shaw had appeared on the Tonight Show in New York, where the host, substituting for Johnny Carson, had been David Frost, to talk about the opening of *The Man in the Glass Booth*.

Frost asked questions in relation to Shaw's attitude to religion and the Pope's declaration that the Jews were 'forgiven' for killing Christ, mentioned so prominently in the play, and Shaw, always happy to whip up controversy and enjoying the debate, began to criticise the Pope, calling him among other things 'a fool'. What right has this man to interfere in the lives of poor people by decreeing that they were not to use birth control? The Catholic Church wanted people not to exercise birth control because having excessive numbers of children made them, and kept them, poor and ignorant. They would, thus, remain loyal to the church. These sort of statements expressed, if not quite in the heart of American Catholicism, certainly in its head in New York, were bound to be provocative. The television switch-board was jammed with protesting viewers. To complete the interview Shaw had delivered a fair and unaccompanied rendition of Paul McCartney's *Yesterday*.

Among the television audience was a Broadway choreographer and director, Oona White. When in the summer of 1969 she had been hired to direct a stage musical based on the film *Elmer Gantry* (which had starred Burt Lancaster in the title role) she had thought of Robert Shaw based on his appearance that night. The musical was the idea of Joe Cates, who had previously presented Peter Nichols' *A Day in the Death of Joe Egg* on Broadway with Albert Finney and Zena Walker. But Cates had actually spent his life as an American television producer, firstly presenting the Russian State Circus (his family was from Russia) before graduating to the immensely popular Perry Como shows.

Figures in a Landscape had been an unusually long film in the making – 16 weeks – and physically arduous. But Shaw's primary motivation for accepting *Elmer Gantry* was that he knew that learning to sing and dance for the first time would involve a physical routine that would keep him off the booze. The deal was for $1,500 a week for rehearsals and out-of-town performances and $2,000 on Broadway against 10% on the box office gross, plus $1,500 expenses throughout. Rita Moreno, who had become a Broadway star on the back of the enormous success of *West Side Story*, was his co-star. Shaw left for New York at the end of September. He left Mary at home. She was expecting their fourth child in December.

The director of *Omnibus*, John Ingrams, had had to take over another *Omnibus* programme on George Robey when its director fell ill, so it happened that instead of filming the final interview with Shaw on his return to England from *Figures*, the programme followed him to New York where he was interviewed with his singing teacher and guru figure, Bert Knapp, sitting behind him at the piano. His mood, in contrast to the interview in Spain, was distinctly up-beat. Clearly his regimen allowed no time for drinking and the effect on his personality was remarkable. His 'energy' had returned. He talked of the excitement of learning a new skill and the pleasure of working with talented professionals: 'It's like being the star turn in a circus.'

The show opened on 15 February 1970 at the George Abbot Theatre. It was a Broadway-style flop and closed before the end of the week. Clive Barnes, continuing his admiration, wrote 'charisma is a quality hard to define but easy to recognise. Robert Shaw possesses charisma . . . He gives us as good a performance as you will find in this or any other season.' Otherwise, however, Barnes' review was disastrous for the play and, in conjunction with the fact that there were no other 'selling' reviews, Joe Cates took the decision to bring the show off immediately. It must be said, perhaps because of Barnes' review, the failure did little to dent Shaw's considerable reputation on Broadway.

Shaw returned to Porch House where his son Ian, born on 18 December 1969, was waiting for him, as was a new dark red Mercedes 600 which he had ordered before he left. The car cost £23,000. Also waiting for him was an urgent message from Laurence Olivier.

Chapter Ten

In 1969 Kenneth Tynan had suggested to Olivier that the National Theatre commission Robert Shaw to write a play. Tynan had approached Shaw and asked him if he had any ideas. Shaw, always a great reader, was in the middle of John Stanhope's account of the Cato Street Conspiracy and had replied with little thought that Cato Street would make a great subject for a play. With the National Theatre not reliant on commercial considerations, and with a large standing repertory company, it could also be a play with little restriction on the numbers in the cast. It could be an epic and that idea attracted Shaw.

The play was commissioned in January 1969 for delivery in September 1969 but by January 1970 very little had actually been written with the exception of a breakdown of Stanhope's book. Olivier was keen to see the play as he hoped to include it in the 1970 season at the National. There had been some criticism that the National was intent on pursuing a policy of being a 'museum' rather than a theatre and Olivier had decided to answer it by presenting new work. In February, on his return from New York, Shaw rang Olivier, presented his excuses and promised that as nothing else was on the horizon the play would be finished quickly.

It was perfectly true: 1970 was blank. It was at the end of 1969 that the once-buoyant, money-rich British film industry collapsed like a deflated balloon. The Americans had gone home. Most of the big American studios had had large production houses in London. MGM, had resident producers, writers, production designers, even production managers and construction supervisors on retainer working from their offices in Soho. Paramount, Universal and 20th Century Fox all had had similar operations. Naturally they were fearfully expensive and none of the English product made in the '60s had really justified the cost. Though, among the 50 All-Time Box Office Champions published in *Variety* in January 1970 eleven could be said to be British – *Thunderball* (the only one in the top ten), *Goldfinger, To Sir with Love, You Only Live Twice, Tom Jones, Bridge on the River Kwai, Lawrence of Arabia, 2001, Those Magnificent Men in their Flying Machines, Guns of Navarone,* and *A Man for All Seasons,* in order of gross earnings – only two in the list had relatively small budgets (*To Sir with Love* and *Tom Jones*) and the rest were still to re-coup their enormous costs.

MGM was the first to announce its withdrawal. The others rapidly followed. It was to be a period of retrenchment in the movie industry not only in England but worldwide. The decline of cinema-going, ultimately linked with the growth of television, had been a continual process. But 1970 was the watershed. The movie industry would not be able to reverse its decline.

With no offers of employment Shaw could concentrate on writing his play. But there was another subject on the agenda at the beginning of 1970 that was very rapidly coming to a head: tax. In spite of the arrangements Laszlo Gombosh had made in 1965 to try and avoid tax, initially on *The Battle of the Bulge* and subsequently on later films made abroad, it looked very much as though Shaw was going to have to face a huge tax bill.

In 1959 he had formed a company with his first wife to employ his services worldwide – River Enterprises. This was a common practice among high-earning performers; it makes it easier to claim deductions for cars, telephones, legal and accountancy bills and expenses of all sorts, and has some minor tax advantages in allowing a person to choose the amount they are voted in terms of salary and to set one year's earnings against another's. In fact Shaw's employment contract with River had lapsed in 1962, when it should have been renewed, but no one seemed to mind and the Revenue were quite happy to go on treating Shaw as an employee of River Enterprises.

However, if Shaw was going to take advantage of the tax loophole being used by so many of his contemporaries, River would have to be abandoned and an overseas company set up with an employment agreement for Shaw's services, so he could then benefit by being taxed only on the money he brought into the country (in tax-speak the money he 'remitted'). So Goddard's, Laszlo's firm, arranged for a company called Art Productions to be formed in Liechtenstein on 9 March 1965.

Unfortunately for Shaw, the urgency needed to get this company in place to take on *The Battle of the Bulge* contract, according to a subsequent counsel's opinion, led Goddard's to make mistakes that not only left them open to being sued by Shaw for negligence, but involved him in committing two criminal offences. Firstly, Shaw had started filming on *The Battle of the Bulge* in January under the auspices of River. The arrangements with Art Productions had not been set up before March, but subsequently the contract and monies were all paid to Art, which constituted a *criminal* offence not a civil one. It was illegal to transfer the business of a UK company to a non-UK company. The whole contract should have stayed with River (and, then, of course would have been subject to full UK tax). The only reason for the transfer was tax avoidance. Secondly, the Counsel, briefed by Shaw some years later to look into the question of Goddard's negligence, found that they had advised Shaw that it was perfectly all right to leave monies owned to him under his employment contract uncollected in Art Production in Liechtenstein. In fact, this was a criminal offence under the Exchange Control Act. The monies had to be paid immediately they were earned.

As ignorance of the law is no defence, Shaw was undoubtedly guilty. In effect, ignorance was a claim Shaw could fairly make. He could perhaps be accused of not asking enough questions, but the complexity of these matters, as can be seen, makes it extremely difficult to know what were the right questions to ask. Goddard's had instructed Counsel to pronounce on the efficiency of their scheme and his opinion was favourable (though it subsequently transpired that his opinion was based on information that was not entirely accurate). None of Shaw's other advisers made any objections. It is possible that had Shaw read the Counsel's opinion, provided by Goddard's, more carefully, he might have realised that there was a discrepancy in some of the assumptions on which it was based.

But Shaw trusted his advisers, he would trust such people in an almost childlike way all his life, and he was not interested in details. He was interested in money. He did not want to hear that he would have to pay tax on $350,000 at 90% because there was no time to set up proper tax arrangements – which was, in fact, the case. What he wanted to hear was that his advisers had done for him what had been done for his contemporaries – the other star actors whom the newspapers reported as avoiding tax in a cavalier manner – and succeeded in keeping large amounts of money out of the grasp of the tax man. It was in creating this atmosphere that Shaw bears final culpability.

But the effect of the new arrangements with Art Productions did not end there. They also, in due course, were to bring the spotlight of Revenue attention on to River Enterprises. If the employment contracts with Art Productions were questionable, by implication, the contracts with River might be equally suspect. As, in fact, Shaw's employment contract with River had lapsed, the Revenue could claim that all Shaw's income was from his profession as an actor, which they could then tax as a gross sum, as opposed to taxing the salaries and bonuses he received from River as their employee. This would mean that his total earnings since 1959 would be taxable as a gross amount.

The Revenue's investigation into the arrangements made in 1965 had become relentless, and on Shaw's return from New York, in February 1970, Richard Hatton had asked his own solicitor, and a director of his company, to look at Shaw's tax position in detail and come up with some objective advice.

Henry King, one of the brightest young solicitors of his day – whom Shaw would describe as looking like 'an English cricket captain' – took the documents from Goddard's and went over them. His prognosis was not what Shaw wanted to hear. The Revenue, he felt, unquestionably had a strong case against Shaw, and there was no doubt, in the worst case, that there would be a great deal to pay. Exactly how much it was not possible to say, but King's advice was unequivocal: leave England now and become non-resident. This would serve to protect his future earnings, in conjunction with a complete re-structuring of all the employment company arrangements both in England and in Liechtenstein.

At a meeting in Donald Bradley's office at the end of February Henry King and Ivan Paul explained the position to Shaw in detail. Shaw, with his usual bluster, reinforced by whisky from Bradley's well-stocked office cocktail cabinet, told King he had no intention of paying 'the bastards' a penny. If that were the case, King replied calmly, he would certainly advise him to take up residence abroad, and do so before the beginning of the next tax year, i.e. before April 1970. Of course this would not extinguish liabilities from the past, but in the event that the Revenue demanded more than he actually had – a distinct possibility, at least with his assets abroad – it would make recovery extremely complicated. King pointed out that should this dire eventuality arise Shaw would never be able to work in England again or even return to England. 'I don't give a shit about England,' Shaw continued in the same vein. The decision was made there and then, like most major decisions in Shaw's life, with little consideration and even less care.

From the financial point of view the decision was a success. In the remaining years of his life Shaw earned in excess of $4 million and paid no more than $250,000 in tax to various governments, mostly to England on pictures he made here which could not benefit from the remittance basis loophole. On a personal level it was a disaster. It was undoubtedly the single decision that most shaped the rest of his life. After leaving Porch House he never finished another piece of writing again. His drinking, at this point still under control, became chronic. His marriage, strained as it was, became a series of drunken brawls, where 'energy' permitted, punctuated by listless depression.

The casualness of his decision was matched only by his lack of self-awareness. Porch House represented stability and happiness in Shaw's life. He had undoubtedly had all his best times there, the happiest, and the most rewarding. In his study he had written his best novel and a great deal of other important work. He had wandered in the garden and through the orchard, and brought up his children there. He had played all his competitive sports there with his many friends. He had listened to test matches, and watched Wimbledon and the Five Nations Rugby Championship. It was a haven. It was a home. And he threw it away as casually as if it had been an empty pack of cigarettes.

Why? For money. Shaw's extravagance ('Live above your income') meant that though his earnings had been comparatively high – even if not in the top flight of film star earnings – he had spent a great deal of money. The Mercedes 600 was just the latest example. Should the Revenue succeed in their demands there was a good chance Shaw would be unable to pay. But in such cases in the past deals had been done, payments phased over the years. There could have been an alternative had Shaw wanted to explore it. From his attitude at the meeting it was clear to his advisers that he did not.

The real reason for his decision – and for the fact that after the meeting, unusually for him, he had no second thoughts – had more to do with Shaw's view of himself than with objective financial assessments. His career had not been as successful as he would have wished. For a time it had looked as though he might catch up with the Sean Connerys, the Michael Caines and the Peter O'Tooles. He did not. To most people he was enormously successful, but not to himself. His writing too, previously having won him the plaudits he craved, now provoked brickbats. His dissatisfaction with life was complete. It is difficult, against this background, not to see his decision to leave England as a gigantic V-sign, a fuck-you England, a gesture to show that he could not care less about losing what had been precious to him. It proved to be a gesture of self-destruction.

Returning to Porch House Shaw was scheduled to do the final interview for the *Omnibus* programme. The moroseness he had displayed in Spain was very much back in his mood as he sat in the same chair in which he had been interviewed almost a year earlier when the prospects facing him were very different. He talked of his unease at the interview, that he was being asked to examine himself in public when in fact it should be a strictly private business. Everyone, he complained, wanted a quick facile answer, an easy label. Above all, now, he wanted to do one 'lasting' book. He felt terribly insecure, if he didn't 'I wouldn't be pursuing pain so much . . . I long for applause . . . Everytime I know you're coming to see me again I feel I've got to fly in a plane and I hate flying in planes . . . You see such liars on television. How much should the artist confess? How much? What is the object of this whole exercise? I mean maybe I should never have done it. Probably shouldn't have. But I despise the writer who doesn't communicate. I see myself slacking off as an actor.' The latter remark was, of course, exactly the opposite of what he had said the previous year when he was going to work 'at the top' for 10 years and then return to writing. He did not mention that he was to leave Porch House and England but perhaps it is not fanciful to imagine a certain wistfulness as he wandered among the trees of his orchard, in the final shot of the programme.

Porch House was put on the market while Shaw worked on the Cato Street play for the National Theatre. In the tangle of copyright law Shaw wanted to make certain that the author of *The Cato Street Conspiracy*, John Stanhope, had no claim against him, as it was his book that was to be his main, and only, source. Tom Maschler, who had published the book at Jonathan Cape was contacted and after prolonged correspondence centring on a misunderstanding as to whether Shaw was 'adapting' the book or merely using it as source material, Stanhope was paid £100 against 5% of Shaw's gross earnings from the play up to a maximum of £1,000. Shaw's fee from the National was £200 against 5% of the first £400 of gross box office receipts per performance, 7½% of the next £300 and 10% of anything in excess of £700 (the daily basis rather than the usual weekly, determined by the fact that the National system was a repertoire of plays playing only two or three performances a week). The National would receive 20% of the gross receipts from a film sale of the rights and a further 20% if they mounted the production on Broadway.

At the end of March, Shaw delivered his play to Olivier. Shaw sent a copy off to Harold Pinter, who immediately pronounced it a 'masterpiece' and, remembering his conversation with Thornton Wilder in New York, Shaw dispatched it to Wilder too, with a letter asking for his candid opinion. The decision to become a tax exile meant not merely that Shaw would have to live abroad for the majority of the time. It was Henry King's advice that, in order to establish the firm intent to become a foreign resident in the eyes of the Revenue it was necessary to break contact with England for at least a year and that thereafter visits must be restricted to no more than 90 days in any one year. This meant that should the National go ahead with *Cato Street* – at this point called *Shadows in the Night* – in 1970 Shaw would not be able to attend rehearsals or see a performance. He appeared unconcerned and made no attempt to ask the National to delay production until the following year.

Before leaving Porch House for the last time, which he had to do by

Ten

5 April 1970, Shaw had been sent a copy of John le Carré's book, *A Small Town in Germany*, by the producer Robert 'Buzz' Berger. The book had been purchased by Warner Brothers for what was then a record amount of money for film rights. The story goes that Warners were so impressed with the deal that le Carré's agent in America, Dan Risner, had done with them, they offered the poacher the chance to turn gamekeeper and become head of production for them. David Cornwell (John le Carré) had written a script of his book but it was not to Warner Brothers taste. Risner had recently read *Card from Morocco* and had toyed with the idea of asking Shaw to write a screenplay of the book, when it occurred to him Shaw would be the right person to have a go at *A Small Town in Germany*. Buzz Berger sent the book to Porch House and Shaw packed it in his luggage before the furniture removal men came to take the contents of the house into storage.

Dan Risner was not the only person interested in *Card from Morocco*. Carl Foreman, the writer of *High Noon*, who had set up a production company in England after trouble with the Committee for Un-American Activities in Hollywood, and had subsequently produced and written *The Guns of Navarone*, was very impressed with the book too. Two days before Shaw left England Foreman took him for lunch at L'Écu de France across the street from his office and told him he was interested in the book and hoped he would be able to make an offer in due course.

Buzz Burger was offering $100,000 for Shaw to write the screenplay of *A Small Town in Germany*, $50,000 up front ($20,000 on signature and $30,000 when work began) then a possible cut-off and a further $50,000 if he was asked for a second draft. When Shaw read the book he was not particularly enthusiastic, though over the phone to Berger in New York he told him he knew just how to write the screenplay. Warming to his subject, totally off the top of his head and not based on any study of the book, Shaw gave Berger a brilliant analysis of what was wrong and what was right which he promptly forgot. But Berger was impressed.

Looking round the world for a place to live Shaw had settled on Ireland. He had been there a couple of times and had used it as a background in a section of *The Sun Doctor*. As he was not a sun-worshipper he did not care about the climate (it rains 2 days in every 3 whatever the season) and the beauty of the countryside was certainly exceptional. There was also a useful tax concession. In order to encourage Irish cultural life the Dublin government had introduced a policy by which artists could live tax-free. The definition of artists included poets, painters, sculptors and writers but excluded performers. Shaw, as the *Omnibus* interview had shown, was swinging erratically between the two poles of his talent and the decision for Ireland was made as the pendulum swung to writing. In addition the West Coast of Ireland was so thoroughly depopulated it was an ideal location for indulging in any tendency to isolationism. Ireland perfectly catered for one whole side of Shaw's personality. It did not cater for the other.

On the acting front things remained quiet. Shaw turned down the opportunity to play St John in NCB's *Jane Eyre* with George C. Scott as Rochester on the grounds that he should be playing Rochester. Mary Ure meantime, staying on in England to see to the packing up at Porch House, was offered a play for Yorkshire Television in a series they were doing under the general title of *The Ten Commandments*. Directed by Marc Miller the particular exemplar she accepted was *Honour Thy Father and Thy Mother*, with George Cole and Brenda de Banzie.

As Shaw started looking for a house in Ireland, Phil Yordan bounced back into his life, once again with material that Shaw would have been wiser to leave alone. Yordan's second picture with Benny Fisz in Spain was to be a Western with the apt title of *A Town Called Bastard* to be directed by Robert Parrish, an American director whose best-known picture was probably *Fire Down Below*.

Shaw was sent the script and spoke to Parrish on the phone. They both agreed – ritualistically perhaps – that the script needed a great deal of work to get it right. The state of the film business in Britain is clearly demonstrated by the deal. For *Figures in a Landscape* in June 1969 Shaw had got $326,000, while for *A Town Called Bastard* almost exactly one year later he received $75,000 plus $75,000 deferred to be paid from profits should there been any (there weren't). The film industry is a perfect example of what the economists call a 'perfect market': everyone in the market knows everything about everyone else, what is being offered and what is being accepted. The forces of supply and demand are therefore able to interact freely to settle a market price. As there was a plentiful supply of star actors and little demand for their services the price plummeted. Even his expenses were reduced from $1,500 a week to $1,000. Shaw's only condition before accepting the deal was that he wanted an assurance that Phil Yordan was going to come over to supervise filming and that the script was re-written. Yordan agreed.

Mary had joined Shaw in Dublin, where he was living in a hotel while looking for houses in the west, after completing her television play at the end of May 1970. They flew to Madrid on 5 June. No suitable houses had yet been found. John Huston's estate in Galway was 'too finished, too much a part of his life ever to become a part of mine', and a house in Tuam, owned by Lady Mary Cusack Smith, Europe's only official Mistress of the Hunt, had been overwhelming. Too grandiose. All those long, long draughty halls . . .' For the duration of *A Town Called Bastard* they had leased Orson Welles's villa in Madrid, Fincha Mi Gusto, in the Colonia Camerines, a very private enclave to the north of the city where the huge and heavily protected mansions had been the host to many fleeing South American dictators whose counties's budgets had been plundered to purchase these safe retreats against the day of the next coup. Ten-foot electrified wire fencing, Dobermanns and security guards armed with sub-machine guns were the rule rather than the exception.

With filming due to start on 16 June, any enthusiasm Shaw had conceived for *A Small Town in Germany* was waning fast. On 1 June he had been due to meet Buzz Berger in Bonn on a research trip. With Berger waiting at Dusseldorf Airport to meet his plane Shaw decided to cancel the trip. Berger had to be paged at the airport and told the news that his reluctant writer was unable to join him. Shaw had worked out what he thought to be a convincing excuse. As he was about to board the plane, his agent was told to explain, he'd realised it went to Dusseldorf via England and if he went to England even for 10 minutes, it would cost him £1 million in tax at the very least. Surprisingly, Berger remained co-operative. Shaw sent him a case of champagne 'as a token of Mr Shaw's regrets'.

Shaw's reluctance continued. In the draft contract it was stated that Berger should have the right to see 'work in progress'. Shaw refused and said he would do no more work until this was deleted and that it might be better if he did no more work in any event until the contracts were signed. He would have been only too delighted had something else gone wrong. Nothing did and Berger was able to ring him on 6 July to confirm everything had been signed, sealed and money paid. Shaw was trapped in a prison of his own devising.

His mood was not further improved by the work on *A Town Called Bastard*. If the previous Yordan projects had been bad, this was atrocious. Apart from the director, whom Shaw liked, and Telly Savalas whom Shaw could compete with at table tennis and arm wrestling, the picture had nothing to recommend it. Shaw's performance required little more than menacing grimaces and the promised improvements in the script had made very little differences in either Shaw's role or the film in general. If Yordan was a renowned script fixer this was not a job that was going to enhance his reputation.

Carl Foreman's expected offer from *Card from Morocco* came through in June too but it contained an unexpected element. Foreman had been greatly impressed with Shaw over lunch: Shaw's exposition of his book had been passionate, he had made the book come alive. So Foreman was offering Shaw the chance not only to write the screenplay of what he still referred to as his 'best book' but to star in it (as either Lewis or Slattery) and *direct* it. If Shaw was so convinced that the book would make a film, as he had been over lunch, then Foreman was prepared to let him prove it. Shaw found the idea literally stunning. He had never contemplated directing before. For once in his life he had no ready reply. Two days later he called Foreman and told him it was a great idea. He'd love to do it.

Foreman had explained that, since he was 'taking a flyer' he could not offer Shaw a great deal of money initially. The fee for writing was to be £10,000 plus £5,000 for 'expenses'. Shaw agreed. But over this project, for the first time in his life, a new element entered the calculation – fear. After Foreman's offer Shaw remained enthusiastic for a short time trying to convince himself it was a marvellous opportunity. Then, uncharacteristically, he confided to a friend that his main concern was that he would not be able to do it. If it was his screenplay, and his direction and his performance, there would be a great deal of attention focused on the film, and supposing it wasn't good? Wouldn't it be better, if he were to direct at all, to do it with someone else's material the first time round? Take the pressure off? Shaw was having a bad case of cold feet. Having talked up a storm with Foreman over lunch (as he had with Berger) he was beginning to wish he hadn't.

Working with Phil Yordan again Shaw was exposed to his charisma and his unending wheeling-and-dealing. At the beginning of the film Yordan approached Shaw with his latest concept. With Benny Fisz he'd like to set up a company to make two or three films (one a year) in Spain at and around the studios in Almeria. Instead of a fee Shaw would receive 25,000 shares in the company plus expenses. The film would be released theatrically if they could get a distribution deal but the budget would be kept small so that profits could be made from television sales alone. It would not be the last time such a deal was offered to Shaw by various producers. But having brought it up at the beginning of filming, Yordan never mentioned it again. Shaw's fixation with the man was beginning to wear thin and when, towards the end of filming, Yordan asked Shaw for a loan – in truth Yordan was a desperate man having spent all the money he had made – it was finally shattered. Nevertheless Shaw lent him the money.

Another figure to be finally degraded from mythic status in Shaw's life was Laszlo Gombosh. Henry King's firm, Denton Hall and Burgin, had taken over his tax affairs but Goddard's continued to be used for overseeing the film contracts including currently *A Small*

Town in Germany and *A Town Called Bastard* (as well as the play for the National). On 24 July Shaw, having had more than his usual amount to drink, spoke to Gombosh for the last time. Gombosh 'didn't like the way he spoke to me', at all. They were never to speak again. Mary, ever loyal to her husband, followed suit. Unfortunately it was not until 1974 that Shaw was advised that he could sue Goddard's for negligence, by which time it was largely too late.

Laurence Olivier had written to Shaw in Dublin in April thanking him for his play and apologising for what might be a delay in reading it as he was currently undertaking Shylock in *The Merchant of Venice*. The first reaction from the National came in June from Donald MacKechnie who was an associate director at the theatre and, at that point, Olivier's right-hand man. The play, he told Shaw, was 'precisely what we wanted. But . . .'. They were worried by the fact that he had changed Thistlewood, one of the main conspirators, into a woman (a worry he ascribed to Joan Plowright), that the part of Davidson ('the man of colour') had been written-up to such an extent that no negro actor at the National could play it, (and they did not think they could get Calvin Lockhart – the only 'negro' actor who they felt had the ability to play the part), and they were concerned about the role of Edwardes who turns out to have spied on the whole group concealing himself as a Frenchman – Monsieur Mabeuf. Overall, he wanted to emphasise, they were pleased. Robert Lang had read the part of Lord Sidmouth and was 'delighted with it'. However the title should be changed to *Cato Street*. The production was set to start rehearsing on 16 September 1970.

All seemed set fair. At the end of *A Town Called Bastard* in August, Shaw decided to lease the Madrid villa for a year and make occasional trips to Ireland to find a house. Sitting at a large Spanish table in Orson Welles's villa, placed immediately in front of a picture window neatly framing the swimming-pool, front garden, and ornate front gates of the house, with a good view of the rolling hills beyond, when the smog of Madrid allowed, Shaw may not have been able to contemplate a blossoming acting career. But his writing which, he had told his friends and the public in the *Omnibus* programme, was so important to him and which he always regarded as having to be subjugated to his acting for financial reasons, could now be central to his life. In *Omnibus* he had said that he'd earned more from his last film ($326,000 for *Figures in a Landscape*) than from all his novels put together, and it was perfectly true. Now, however, writing was no longer the poor cousin. A screenplay of *A Small Town in Germany* would earn him more than appearing in *A Town Called Bastard*, the adaptation of *Card from Morocco* would earn him further not inconsiderable sums and open up the possibility of a new career as a director, and his new play, with some changes, would be produced at the National Theatre whence – assuming he got it right – it could well transfer to the West End and Broadway bringing him further fame and fortune. Harcourt Bruce in America and Chatto & Windus were still anxious to publish the second novel in the trilogy started with *The Flag* and Clive Donner had rang to say he had interest in the possibility of filming *The Man in the Glass Booth* and if he could raise the money would Shaw like to write the screenplay? All he had to do was sit at his large table in the peace of Fincha mi Gusto, and write. As Noël Coward said, one must choose very carefully what one wants in life because one may well end up getting it.

Neither were there any further acting offers to distract him. There were approaches (but not offers) from Gordon Hessler with a re-make of *Murders on the Rue Morgue*, Guy Hamilton with a movie called *Five Against Capricorn* and Joe Shaftel for *The Trojan Women* which was to star Vanessa Redgrave, Katherine Hepburn and Irene Papas. But the problem now was that, with the sharp decline in the amount of finance available caused by the withdrawal of the American studios from European production, independent producers needed 'bankable' stars for their projects, stars that could be shown to produce results and inspire investor confidence by virtue of the financial success of the films they had made. Shaw was not 'bankable' in this sense, and though approaches were made, offers did not ensue.

He was also sent a book entitled *The Strange Voyage of Donald Crowhurst*. It was a fascinating story. Crowhurst had entered the Observer Single-Handed Round-the-World Yacht Race but instead of making for Cape Horn he had dawdled in the Roaring Forties radioing back false accounts of his position – so for a while it appeared he was leading the race – before disappearing. After a massive search in the wrong area his boat was found deserted, like the Marie Celèste, off the coast of a Caribbean island. On board were cassette tapes he had made documenting his descent into madness and indicating suicide. It would have provided a virtuoso role for Shaw, and he immediately signalled his interest. With the difficulty of writing a screenplay featuring only one character and the financing problems then current in the British film industry the project collapsed. The book was eventually made into a film by the French some 10 years later.

In August Laurence Olivier called Shaw in Madrid to ask if he would like to *act* at the National. Shaw explained that he was in self-imposed exile and could not return until after April 1971 and then for only 90 days. Olivier was not put off. 'I'd be happy to consider anything you want to play,' he told Shaw. Shaw thought about it not at all. It was a curious reaction from a man who had once dreamt of bestriding the stage at the Old Vic in the great Shakespearean roles. But the dream no longer had any significance for him. His primary concern with the National was to see his play produced there; the fact that he did not immediately leap at the chance to play Mark Antony – the obvious choice for him – was an indication that his priorities and his life had irrevocably changed.

None of this took up much time but far from using the opportunity to write he was thinking up reasons not to. Porch House had been sold at the beginning of September, so Miss Jay and Mary had to travel back to England to clear everything out and supervise the removal to storage. Three pantechnicons were needed to empty the house. There was an argument with the new owners as to whether they should pay extra for the lavish pine shelving in Shaw's study and recently planted rose trees in the garden. Shaw was insistent that they should.

Very untypically Shaw kept wanting to know the contractual details of negotiations on *Card from Morocco*. Once a deal was done Shaw usually had absolutely no interest in the small print and the seemingly endless re-wording of drafts for tax or other reasons. The *Card from Morocco* contracts were particularly complicated and, by now, they had been sent to Denton Hall & Burgin for comments, Laszlo Gombosh and Goddard's having been consigned to oblivion. There were, in fact, four contracts, one for Shaw to write the screenplay, one for his directing services, one for his acting services and one for the assignment of copyright in the original material. To complicate matters further, the rights in the novel were owned by River Enterprises while his writing and directing services had to be dealt with by his new Liechtenstein company International Actors and Pictures AG (I. A. P.) which had been formed to succeed the tainted Art Productions. The inter-relation of these contracts was complex and Shaw's questions in relation to them often difficult to answer. Was it possible that Open Road Films (Foreman's company) having acquired the rights to the book could reject his screenplay and get someone else to write a new screenplay? It was possible but Shaw had the right to buy back the book eight weeks after he was informed that the screenplay was not satisfactory. What would happen if he changed his mind about directing? What would happen if he didn't want to do revisions to the screenplay as requested by Foreman?

Shaw's cold feet were obviously beginning to turn to ice. In October, when Donald Bradley found a discrepancy between the deal agreed between himself and Foreman and the deal as expressed in the written contracts – a matter that could have been cleared up relatively quickly by calling Foreman direct – Shaw seized the opportunity, like a man with a rope round his neck being given a sharp knife, and walked, or more accurately, ran away from the deal. It was one bridge too far.

After the initial comments from the National, Donald MacKechnie had flown to Madrid at the beginning of August to discuss the *Cato Street* play further and tell Shaw rehearsals would start on schedule on 16 September. But by the beginning of September when Shaw's agent called to find out what was happening they were told that MacKechnie was on holiday, Olivier not available and the general manager, Tony Easterbrook, knew nothing about any production. Obviously the production had been cancelled, though no one had told Shaw. On 16 September MacKechnie, fresh from his holiday, called to say that 'they' – Tynan, Olivier and himself – felt that it was such an important work that they wanted to get it absolutely right and therefore it was essential for Shaw to be available to attend rehearsals. They knew full well this meant no production could be mounted before April 1971. This represented a distinct cooling of Olivier's ardent request for the play in January. Nor MacKechnie added, making no apology for the total lack of communication since his visit in August, and taking the temperature down still further, was it possible to guarantee a production at all, until they had seen the rewrites discussed in Madrid.

But Shaw was appeased and flattered. They were obviously taking the play seriously. He delivered the rewrites (plus two alternative titles 'An Evening Amongst Friends' or 'Oh Give Me Death or Liberty') which Tynan acknowledged on 20 October. The reaction to them was immediate. MacKechnie called at the beginning of November and told Shaw they were 'clever'. It had lost some of the essence of the original but generally speaking Olivier was 'delighted' and they would definitely do the play in April as soon as Shaw was available to attend rehearsals. Shaw had also received a long letter from Thornton Wilder in which he expressed his pleasure in the quality of Shaw's writing and made several suggestions for changes that he hoped might be helpful to Shaw. So pleased was Shaw with this letter that he had sent a copy to Olivier. Generally speaking Olivier felt Shaw had followed Wilder's advice and 'simplified' the play. But within a month further enquiries about the future of the play were met with another wall of silence, and though contracts were being drafted and there was vague talk of casting there were to be no further developments until February 1971.

Since July the director of *Omnibus* had been ringing Shaw to ask for help in obtaining clips from his various films for the programme. It was not as easy as it might seem. The clips provided by Columbia from *A Man for All Seasons* and by Benny Fisz from *A Town Called*

Bastard were not of suitable quality and in the end had to be substituted with clips from *The Battle of the Bulge* and *The Birthday Party*. Shaw had been anxious to help. There was no doubt the programme had assumed an importance in his mind, that he regarded it as some sort of statement – an address to the nation. As this was some time before the development of video recorders he actually never saw the pro-gramme, though Mary did at a specially arranged screening at the BBC. It was transmitted on Sunday 15 November following the Billy Cotton Band Show.

Meantime Shaw had to deliver the screenplay of *A Small Town in Germany*. Having cleared his desk of *Card from Morocco* and delivered revisions of *Cato Street* to the National, the only red spiral-bound exercise book that stared back at him from his desk bore the legend *Small Town* scribbled in Shaw's spidery handwriting on the first page. There was, of course, the second part of his trilogy of novels but the notes for that were in a suitcase that had not been unpacked and was stacked in the boiler room which was guarded night and day by a vicious 30-year-old parrot who would fly at the eyes of anyone who entered its domain. It had been named, whether aptly or not, Señor Welles.

Questions in relation to the novel were easy to deflect but Shaw had accepted $50,000 for *A Small Town in Germany* which gave Buzz Berger the perfect right to enquire how it was coming on. Unlike *Card from Morocco*, this was not an obligation that could be dismissed.

Mary's arrival back from England did not help matters. Shaw's decision to sell Porch House and move abroad had been taken with little reference to Mary. With no complaints to friends, she went along with the decision, packed up the house and started to tour Ireland looking for a new home. But her resentment was building to dangerous levels and, on returning from seeing Porch House for the last time, her mood was one far from equanimity. She began drinking heavily. Even Shaw, who was himself drinking more than writing, noticed that the mood-altering effects of alcohol on Mary were becoming more pronounced, and alarmingly so. Her compulsion to take off her clothes when drunk was embarrassing the two live-in servants – the gardener and his wife who acted as a housekeeper – and Shaw was in no condition to deal with her violence both to objects and people. Their rows escalated. It became a vicious circle, both of them drinking as a way of tolerating the way they were being treated by the other.

Shaw had always been fascinated by cassette recorders and radios. He had bought an expensive Zenith radio which could pick up signals on numerous wavelengths from all over the world, especially so as to listen to the BBC World Service for cricket and rugby news. He got through several cassette recorders and loved recording the conversations of others unbeknown to the participants (a feature noted in the plot of *The Joke*). One night at Fincha mi Gusto Mary had drunk herself into a stupor. Realising she was getting her period she managed to stagger, naked into the bathroom, but passed out before she could insert her tampon. She had not locked the bathroom door and her nine-year-old son Colin found her lying in a pool of blood on the white tiled floor. Naturally he ran screaming to his father.

But Shaw's reaction was less typical. He reached for his cassette recorder before following Colin up to the bathroom and recorded everything that followed as he and Colin cleaned Mary up and got her into bed. More extraordinary perhaps, Shaw would later tell this story and play the recording of his son's anguished reaction and his explanation of what actually was wrong with Mary, to anyone who cared to listen. He played it in his agent's office, for instance, rewinding the tape to play it again when someone entered who had missed it the first time round.

Neither of the Shaws was sleeping well either and any visitor was asked to bring out sleeping pills from the ever-helpful Dr Slattery, as well as supplies of aspirin and paracetamol for frequently complained-of headaches. Mary, after pill-induced sleep, would take to getting up in the middle of the night and walking naked out of the house. She would be found wandering the Colonia, among the barking Dobermanns and armed guards. In the morning she would remember nothing.

Then at 3.00 a.m. on 17 November the Madrid City Fire Brigade received an urgent call from Enrico, the gardener at Fincha Mi Gusto. The house was on fire. As the area paid a great deal in local taxes and housed some important people it was well served by the fire brigade and two engines were at the scene within 20 minutes. Smoke, though not fire, billowed from the first floor of the house, out of the window of Shaw's study and the sitting room opposite where the monumental fireplace from *Citizen Kane* had been shipped over from Hollywood and installed. The fire was brought rapidly under control. The house was safely evacuated with Mary no doubt remembering that this was the second dramatic occasion in her life that she had been awoken from a drug-induced sleep to be saved from a fire. On the first, on New Year's Day 1961, it had been her dachshund Snoopy that had aroused her and John Osborne; on the second it was Robert Shaw.

Accounts of the fire and the damage it caused varied depending on who was telling the story. According to Shaw the top part of the house was totally gutted destroying many of the *Citizen Kane* artifacts with which it had been furnished and the only remaining copy of Orson Welles's film *Too Much Johnson* (a record of his New York stage production). According to visitors to the house some days later the damage appeared to be relatively slight and certainly little major rebuilding had to be done. The cause of the fire was, of course, the diabolical Spanish wiring, or so Shaw would explain to anyone who asked. What other possible cause could there be?

Naturally, since the room in the house that sustained most of the damage was Shaw's study, the large wooden table he used as a desk was reduced to ashes and, so equally naturally, were the precious manuscripts neatly stacked on it. Only the blackened metal spiral bindings of the red exercise books remained. All Miss Jay's careful transcriptions of the handwritten pages too were gone. All the work Shaw had painstakingly undertaken on *A Small Town in Germany*, all the notes for *A Cure for Souls*, all the notes on the second volume, all burnt to a crisp. That was the official version.

Donald Bradley was called the next morning (the phone lines were apparently still intact) and given the news. He should call Berger and tell him what had happened and that Shaw was now just too disheartened to go on. It was a tragedy, that was the only word for it, but, said Shaw, what could he do? There was no way he could contemplate starting on the screenplay from scratch again. Bradley was to be sure and call Berger right away before he heard the news from another source.

The message was passed on to Berger, who, bearing in mind Shaw's conspicuous reluctance over the past months and his refusal to give Berger progress reports, drew his own conclusion though, with no proof, the laws of libel prevented him from publishing them. It did not take long for the rumours to spread, however, and Ann Rogers, Orson Welles's secretary, called on 19 November to say she had heard from the *Small Town* production office that it was Shaw's carelessness – meaning drunkenness – that had caused the fire and not any electrical fault.

The truth will never be known. How much he had written of the script is a matter of conjecture but on every other project he wrote he liked to discuss it at every state, reading large chunks over the phone to friends, and discussing plot intricacies. On *Small Town* he never wanted to talk to anyone about it, least of all Buzz Berger. The same can be said of the novel trilogy *A Cure for Souls*, which after some initial discussion with Nora Smallwood, and a reading of the opening pages to friends, had disappeared from view. On the night in question Shaw was alone in his study after everyone else had gone to bed. He discovered the fire and raised the alarm. If he started it, or at the very least threw his manuscripts into it, the result was the same – and the image of Shaw in his pyjamas gleefully throwing the manuscripts which he perceived to be the source of his deep depression into a bonfire of props from *Citizen Kane* has a certain resonance. Suddenly he was off the hook not only from *Small Town* but from anyone enquiring about *A Cure for Souls*, which students of his work did with irritating regularity. His relief was palpable. Warner Brothers made no attempt to reclaim the $50,000 they had paid him.

So with the arrival of a new table to replace the old in his study at Fincha Mi Gusto, Shaw could now sit gazing out of the picture windows at the smog-covered hills, unencumbered by recriminating exercise books. The only vague writing project on the distant horizon was that Clive Donner was still pursuing the idea of a film of *The Man in the Glass Booth* with George C. Scott to play Goldman. Donner was worried that Shaw would demur and insist on Pleasence. Actually Shaw was delighted with the idea though found it odd that Donner was planning to do the film in Israel, considering the subject matter (Israel had set up a series of tax shelters which suddenly made it attractive for film production). But this possibility was remote; effectively, at the moment, from having a desk full of writing projects, Shaw now had none.

Shaw's financial position might have been improved from the tax point of view by his move abroad but it was not improved from the point of view of cost. The treadmill of living expenses was now turning with blurring speed. At Porch House the children had been dispatched to their various schools with little or no trouble; now, every term and half-term most of them were picked up from school by car, taken to the airport and flown to Madrid. Debbie and Penny were at Wycombe Abbey, Kathy and Rachel at Maltman's Green and Colin at Walhampton, all expensive private schools. Shaw's cars, currently the Mercedes 600 and a Ford Country Esquire ten-seater American station wagon, had to be insured for Spain, and were both expensive to run and had to be returned for servicing in England. There was the rent of the villa to pay at $1050 a month, Jennifer's alimony (she now lived in Jamaica so children had to be flown out to her too), Miss Jay's wages, and endless air tickets for Miss Jay and Mary to go back to England on various chores, let alone the trips to Ireland to try and find a house there. It was an expensive life and to fund it, it looked as though Shaw was going to have to make the next Western that Benny Fisz had lined up, a film called *Captain Apache*, for which Fisz, now without Yordan's help, offered Shaw the same deal as *A Town Called Bastard*.

In England Columbia were opening *Figures in a Landscape* on 19

November. They had opened the film first in Switzerland and France, hoping, correctly, that the film would do better there than in England, where they had little faith that it would find an audience. The French reviews were excellent, as might have been expected from Losey's status as an *auteur* in France, but the English did not respond well at all and by 2 December the film was taken off. It was never released in America.

John Ingram had called Shaw too to report on the reaction to *Omnibus* which he felt was very positive. He had also approached the BBC with the idea of doing a drama-documentary on Tolstoy and thought that Shaw would be ideal for the part. Would Shaw be interested despite the fact that the money would not match his film fees? Shaw immediately called for a series of books on Tolstoy to be sent out to Spain.

But that was not likely to clash with *Captain Apache*, which loomed closer. Shaw was saved by a call from America. Since Shaw had been represented by Milton Goldman in New York, who worked for an agency then called Ashley Famous, his representation in Hollywood had devolved on to Ben Benjamin, the head of their Los Angeles office. Richard Hatton had long been associated with Ashley Famous and Benjamin looked after Sean Connery for Richard as well as Robert Shaw, Mary Ure and Leo McKern. Shaw, despite his appearances in films that purported to be American like *The Battle of the Bulge* and *Custer*, had never made a film there. John Gaines, one of the agents who worked under Benjamin, called out of the blue at the end of November to say that there was an offer for both Robert and Mary to appear in *The Daughter* for Columbia Pictures, to be directed by William Fraker and produced by Howard Jaffe. It would have had to have been a really appalling script for Shaw to turn it down, not only because of the prospect of working in Hollywood for the first time but to escape from *Captain Apache*.

The Daughter (later called *Labyrinth* and finally released as *Reflections of Fear*) was what was generically called a psychological thriller, the story of a schizoid young 'daughter' using her doll as a channel for the evil side of her personality. The daughter's condition had been created by her domineering mother (to be played by Mary Ure) and when her father arrived back in her life with a girlfriend in tow (Sally Kellerman) an increasing number of dead bodies were found littering the house. It was far from being a brilliant script but Shaw, considering the circumstances, was only too happy to accept. Once again the money was well down on previous rates but he was to receive $100,000 and 10% on the picture's profits for 10 weeks, as well as first position billing. Shaw's stand-in, Ned Lynch, whom he had worked with on his last three pictures, was also to be employed at the scale-rate and provided with economy class air tickets from London. Mary, however, was very much a subsidiary part of the deal. She was paid $10,000 for seven weeks with no expenses (Shaw receiving $1,000 a week) and no air fare. It was not a situation designed to improve her temperament or her feelings of resentment for her husband who was only too happy to point out, in the many moments of anger, that her employment depended on *him*. She accepted the money but insisted that Columbia bill her in the third position after Sally Kellerman, best known as 'Hot Lips' in the original film of M.A.S.H. If she didn't get it she would not do the film. Columbia agreed with little reluctance.

Shooting was to begin on 5 January 1971. Almost immediately the deal was concluded, Robert and Mary flew to Ireland to resume the search for a house. They then booked on the *SS Oronsay* which cruised from Lisbon to Los Angeles via the Panama Canal, and reserved a suite at the Lisbon Ritz before sailing. Shaw would take Colin on the boat with them despite the fact he would have to fly back to school almost immediately they arrived in America. Lizzie, Hannah and Ian would also go, of course, and be put into nursery school on arrival in California. Just to complete the expense Shaw decided to ship his Mercedes 600 out to Los Angeles on a fast freighter to arrive at the same time as the cruise boat. Shaw always had a peculiar logic when it came to spending money. The idea, which he expounded ardently, that shipping the Mercedes to LA would cost less than hiring limousines was a graphic example of how he liked to rationalise his extravagance. The Mercedes was Shaw's status symbol and his security blanket. In LA he would be a stranger, with no idea of his place in the pecking order, though suspecting it might be low. Taking the huge and expensive Mercedes, from what he had heard about Hollywood, insured he would be recognised as a star actor, even though few people might know his face.

At Los Angeles, John Gaines met them off the *Oronsay* and took them to their Belair Hotel until a suitable house was found. Gaines, from the IFA office, had virtually appointed himself as their agent and was determined to make a good impression on Shaw. He spent a lot of time with him, called him frequently and was only too happy to help him with domestic as well as business affairs. He was not the sort of agent Shaw was used to in London where the approach was altogether more staid. Shaw was suitably impressed and though, officially, it was Ben Benjamin who represented Shaw on the Coast, they rarely talked and Gaines became his willing proxy. He was good at making Shaw feel important and at the centre of things, he called him to tell him of all the movies he had 'put him up for' and was always optimistic about the possibilities of further work. He treated Shaw like a star.

Perhaps for this reason Shaw's spirits were high. He was also extremely careful, for the first time since leaving England, to watch his drinking. He had no intention of blotting his copybook on his first Hollywood picture. The filming went well and Shaw was impressed with the girl Billy Fraker had found to play his daughter, Sandra Locke (later to find fame and fortune as Clint Eastwood's co-star and co-habitant). Sally Kellerman, a generous, warm and funny woman, was also difficult not to like; altogether it was a happy picture. The director had been a lighting-cameraman with credits including *Bullitt*, *Rosemary's Baby* and *Paint Your Wagon*. *The Daughter* was only his second picture as a director and his last. He returned to photography and added *Close Encounter of the Third Kind* to his credits.

At the beginning of 1970 it had looked as though Shaw would spend his year writing. In fact he spent most of his time devising ways of avoiding the obligations to write. To his surprise and with no warning he found himself in Hollywood; acting, once again, asserted its dominance over writing. But worrying about the duality of his talent was the least of his concerns. There were other more pressing issues: the state of his marriage, the tax situation in England, finding a home, his drinking, and, at the end of January a call from his youngest sister Wendy.

Wendy was married to a Dutchman who, she told her brother, was now threatening to leave her and take her two children with him to Holland. She was desperate. Once in Holland it would be extremely difficult to get the children back into her custody. And she had no money of her own. Shaw told her to call Henry King, and, asking Henry to act for her and charge it to him, he also arranged for Wendy to be immediately sent funds to tide her over while things were sorted out. The next day Wendy's children were made wards of court, forestalling any attempt to take them abroad.

Not all problems were so easily solved. On 4 February in the Malibu house they had rented, the glasses started to shake, books fell from the shelves, the curtains on the windows swayed as though in a wind, the water in the swimming-pool started a wave action and a great crack appeared in the sitting room floor. Mary gathered the children and ran out on to the terrace. It was the worst earthquake Los Angeles had experienced for some years though, as Mary wrote, it 'left one feeling something more should have happened'. In the Shaws' life the rumblings were prophetic.

Chapter Eleven

After a silence of three months from the National Theatre Shaw now received a letter in Los Angeles from Laurence Olivier. After much discussion internally, they had decided to postpone the promised spring production of his play, he said. It was everyone's opinion that the play needed further work and to that end he had asked Kenneth Tynan to write a memo containing the view of his new associate directors Michael Blakemore and John Dexter. Tynan sent the memo on 11 February:

> The play is conceived with great vigour and theatrical daring. It opens and closes with some stunning scenes; the massacre at St. Peter's Fields and later the trial and the executions. Lord Sidmouth is characterised with melodramatic boldness that is a wholly appropriate counter to the revivalist fervour of the revolutionaries, and his appearance at the end of the first act provides a superb curtain. What criticisms I have were first voiced when I heard that the plan was to rewrite during rehearsals. I believe this to be a disastrous procedure with almost any play. Too many voices become involved, and the inevitable partiality of rehearsals makes detached judgments very hard to come by. On a bad day the play takes the blame when perhaps the fault lies with the actors or the director. The resulting insecurity, when even the words are there to be disputed, is usually destructive. I think I am right in saying that previous experience at the National, where the text has been shaped during rehearsals, point to this. It can work of course (as in *Oh, What a Lovely War*) when the director virtually usurps the writer's function, but I am assuming you would like to avoid this.
>
> My concern with *Cato Street* was some uncertainty about the way the narrative line of the play was clarified and sustained. Particularly in a work deriving from historical fact, where an audience come along expecting a story with a strong informational content, such clarity is most important, the more so when the writing and the characterisation is as highly coloured as in *Cato Street*. The case of Charles Wood's *H* illustrates this. Shortly before the play

opened, I saw the author on a 20-minute television programme in which he confined himself to a simple exposition of the historical events of his play; it was spell-binding. In performance narrative interest sank and vanished under the weight of his (frequently magnificent) writing. He knew the story so well himself that he seemed to be taking it for granted that we did too.

As the play stands at the moment, the narrative line seems to me to be missing a link. The radicals have met at the Crown and Anchor and violently disagreed. Up till now, the play had proceeded at a gallop. We now jump to the *Cato Street* loft, and settle down to a long scene in which as far as the story is concerned practically nothing happens. Grenades are prepared, gin is drunk, ideas and emotions are expressed and certain characters like Brunt are shown to us in greater detail. But they are not revealed through action as Susan, Davidson etc were in the opening scene; they simply explain themselves. Moreover how this group came to be in the loft, who initiated its formation, who spoke first to whom, most of this is left unexplained. It seems to me an extra scene telling us this part of the story would help to distribute the weight of new exposition that the play now requires . . .

We would see the conspirators at the beginning of their endeavours, fiery and enthusiastic. Later on at *Cato Street* we would see them disappointed and on the point of breaking up.

Not having researched the subject, I know no more about it than I have learnt from your play. But reading it the first time I had the feeling that certain rather interesting bits of story, simple facts if you like, were being denied me. Reading it a second time, I realised that in fact a great deal of information had been carefully structured in; but possibly the rhetoric of the dialogue had gone some way towards obscuring it . . .

All criticism is an impertinence, and I am well aware that where I have given your play a few hours of attention you have given it many, many months. I have harped on my reactions to a first reading, though, because I suspect that a first reading, in its very lack of total understanding, is not unlike the sort of awareness an audience brings into the theatre. And finally I have criticised your play only because I admire it, and want to see it not only *on* at the National but a considerable success there.

What had happened at the National was virtually a change of management. The 1970/71 season had been a critical and financial disaster for Olivier, and Michael Blakemore and John Dexter had been given the responsibility for creating some 'hits'. Quite clearly, from the postponement of the original September production, Olivier had had his own doubts about the viability of the play, now these were confirmed by his new team.

Shaw reacted angrily. He knew and disliked the waspish, high camp of John Dexter from the Royal Court and suspected his motives. Shaw had never been a member of the Dexter Appreciation Club. He was, he told Olivier in a letter delayed by a US postal strike, not prepared to do any further rewrites until a definite date was set for production. To his agents he said that if he did not get a definite date he would give the money back and take the play elsewhere. And if that happened he was going to write to *The Times* and cause Olivier maximum embarrassment. John Dexter and Michael Blakemore may not like it, he would say, but Harold Pinter thought it a masterpiece.

Olivier responded officially to Shaw's agent in a letter of 8 March after a disputatious call from Shaw on 25 February:

> I have since discussed this situation with my Associate Director and Literary Department and I would like to put on record our view.
>
> We are absolutely convinced that further work is needed on the text before the play can be accepted for performance. We are, however, prepared to guarantee a production date early in the financial year starting in April 1972 on condition that Robert Shaw should come over here for a period of one month, shortly after his return from the USA to continue working with us on the text.
>
> As you know we have gone to great trouble in the past because we do believe that this is a play of considerable importance. In view of this we want to ensure that the production should have the maximum possible chance of success. It is obviously in the interest of all of us to bring this about.
>
> Yours sincerely
> Laurence Olivier

But Donald MacKechnie, pushed sideways by the recent additions to the National staff, had other ideas. Knowing Vanessa Redgrave's political leanings he sent her an unrevised copy of the play. Her response was immediate; she too thought it was a masterpiece. She would be happy to play Susan Thistlewood but when? So the ball was back in MacKechnie's court. At a planning meeting he revealed the news of Vanessa's interest. Olivier, who had long wanted her to come to the National, saw this as an opportunity to offer her a line of parts to include Shaw's play as the icing on the cake. (He had not offered her the role himself because he was afraid it would offend Joan Plowright who had initially read the part.) But finding a line of parts for Vanessa would mean further delay.

By 13 March Shaw had been told nothing further and cabled Olivier: 'Please give me back my play. This eternal procrastination is deathly. Thank you.' Olivier's reply was immediate: 'Can't give you your play back. Strong possibility of doing it at the Young Vic in the autumn.' Vanessa Redgrave, far from wanting to do a line of parts at the National, wanted to do only Shaw's play. In a sense MacKechnie had been hoist on his own petard. Now they had not only Shaw wanting a date for the production but Redgrave. It was Frank Dunlop who suggested he might like to take the play to the Young Vic which had recently opened under his directorship as an adjunct to the National. The problem was money. *Cato Street* was an expensive play, a period drama with a large cast and the Young Vic's budget would certainly not stretch to it. Dunlop was hopeful, however, that with Shaw and Redgrave attached, the Arts Council might be persuaded to make a special grant.

Having been told all this, Shaw and Redgrave were placated. There was still the question of a director to be decided, especially as the play was now to be done outside the orbit of the National. The obvious choice was Harold Pinter. As he viewed the work so favourably (and had directed *The Man in the Glass Booth*), he might well be prepared to put his directorial services where his mouth was, though he had not volunteered, as he had on *Glass Booth*. Shaw was actually reluctant to tackle his friend directly, perhaps not wanting the embarrassment of a rejection. When Donald Bradley approached Pinter's agent, Jimmy Wax, he was told that Pinter was not available for the October dates that now looked most likely. But it transpired during the conversation that Pinter *was* free, technically free but not 'mentally' as Wax eventually put it. Wax was quite happy for Shaw to speak to Pinter direct and thought he could persuade him with a personal appeal. The best time to ring, he added, was before 12 as Pinter was directing Alan Bates in *Butley* and only rehearsed in the afternoon. Shaw never called, and Pinter – who must have been told about the conversation with Wax – never offered.

This was typical of the relationship between the two men. Shaw regarded Pinter as a friend but it was a very different friendship from those he had with Alex Davion, Philip Broadley and Leo Vala. With these men Shaw had a rough, jokey, physical relationship. With Pinter, though the friendship had lasted a long time, there was an element of reserve, there was always a line drawn which he knew he couldn't cross. When Pinter began his affair with Antonia Fraser, Shaw would joke with friends that Pinter had always wanted to be part of the aristocracy and this was the only way he could do it: but he would never share the joke with Pinter himself – which was uncharacteristic of a man who took delight in trying to needle others. Generally Shaw liked his friends to be either financially inferior, or, like Leo Vala and later Campbell Ingram, outside the business altogether. Equals he found difficult, especially as he had a sneaking feeling, for him heresy, that Pinter might actually be, in a way he could not define, superior.

The question of director was unresolved but Frank Dunlop added his two-pennyworth by saying that he would only want MacKechnie to direct if both Shaw and Redgrave stated they wanted him and even then he would insist on supervising. When Shaw pointed out that it was MacKechnie who interested Redgrave in the play and therefore they should both feel a certain loyalty to him, Dunlop replied it was Olivier who'd asked MacKechnie to contact Redgrave, because he hadn't wanted to do it for himself for fear that he would then become obligated, in her mind, to direct it. This was the second explanation as to why Olivier hadn't sent it to Redgrave himself. From this web of internecine theatre politics MacKechnie was thus eliminated as Frank Dunlop wished. Soon after he left the National and a year later was running the Pitlochry Festival.

Shaw returned from Los Angeles on 17 March and went straight to Ireland. Vanessa Redgrave suggested Peter Gill as a director and Frank Dunlop approved. Gill, another graduate of the Royal Court, was in Canada directing at Stratford, Ontario, but on hearing of the offer indicated that he would almost certainly accept, sight unseen. The play was dispatched to Canada and Gill duly cabled his acceptance. Shaw had been writing changes and was ready with a new version (and a new title, calculated to meet with Vanessa's approval: *Repression is the Order of the Day*). It looked as though all was set for October.

There was one more hurdle to jump. Frank Dunlop reported that the Arts Council was prepared to make a grant but that the Young Vic would still need a further investment of £2,000–£4,000 for production costs and £2,000 for actors. Just to complicate matters further the National had decided to cancel a production of *The Misanthrope* and were considering offering the resulting production dates back to Shaw's play. Shaw and Redgrave jointly declined this offer of an offer. Olivier was not heard from again.

The problem of financing *Cato Street* was solved a few weeks later when Michael White, who had produced a string of West End successes including *Oh Calcutta!*, *Saturday Night and Sunday Morning* and *Sleuth*, said he was very interested in the project. He had been sent the play by Donald Bradley and Laurie Evans – Vanessa's agent – and now suggested forming a production company in partnership with Shaw and Redgrave. A suitable 'shelf' company was found and duly named Thistlewood Productions. Each participant invested £1,500 initially. All that remained now was to finalise the dates at the Young Vic, have the National formally relinquish its rights to the play, and find a cast including an actor for the crucial role of Lord Sidmouth. The drama of *Cato Street* was not to end there.

While all this activity was taking place Donald Bradley had received a call from Carl Foreman a few days before the end of filming on *The Daughter*. Foreman wanted to offer Robert Shaw the part of Lord Randolph Churchill in a film he had been trying to set up for over two years, *Young Winston*, his own screenplay of Winston Churchill's autobiography *My Early Life*. Far from being put off by Shaw's sudden rejection of the *Card from Morocco* deal, Foreman rated his talent highly and he was the first to be cast for the film. As it happened, Foreman had been talking to Shaw's agent about the casting of Winston himself and was particularly interested in Malcolm McDowell who had joined Richard Hatton Ltd after *Figures in a Landscape*. Malcolm was very much a rising star in 1971. He had made only four films but their directors were impressive: Lindsay Anderson (*If . . .*), Bryan Forbes (*The Raging Moon*), Joe Losey, and Stanley Kubrick (*A Clockwork Orange*). It was the last of these, one of the most popular and controversial films of 1970, which had propelled McDowell into producers' calculations.

McDowell had many offers on the table by the time Carl Foreman came forward with the offer to play young Winston. Despite meetings with Foreman and considerable movement in price, McDowell decided to say no.

However, during these comings and goings Foreman had decided Shaw was the right actor to play Winston's father, Lord Randolph Churchill, and had made him an offer even before the McDowell situation was resolved. Shaw accepted the part the moment he read the script – subject as usual to money and billing. With Shaw and McDowell having the same agent and with McDowell currently enjoying the status of being 'hot', billing would have been a major problem since Shaw stated categorically he would not go second to McDowell or accept anything that looked like second place to 'the boy' from *Figures*. Fortunately the problem became academic, and in the final film, Shaw took first position to Anne Bancroft in Europe while she took first position to Shaw in America. Simon Ward, the actor finally cast as young Winston due to an uncanny physical resemblance, was given an 'introducing' billing as his name was not generally known.

Randolph Churchill was undoubtedly the best part in *Young Winston*. As written, and subsequently filmed, not only is it Winston's obsession with his father that provides the focus and theme of the film, but the scenes of Randolph's faltering speech in the House of Commons as his tertiary syphilis begins to develop, and of his shuffling uncertain walk while taking his son to the races, are the best in the film. Once again Shaw played a character whose impact in the film is out of all proportion to the actual size of the part on the screen.

In all, Shaw's involvement would amount to only four weeks, but because of the complexity of the schedule it would be spread over three months. Shaw's fee was agreed at $150,000 with no participation in profits. As usual Ned Lynch would be employed as his stand-in, and Shaw would be provided with his own car and driver whenever he was called to perform. Once again it was a Columbia picture, as were all Foreman's European films.

While the Mercedes 600 was shipped back from Los Angeles, Shaw read a review of the new 450SL Mercedes. He wanted one. After a great deal of research it was discovered that even buying the car direct from Stuttgart would take 18 months. But the article had woken his car-buying mania which had lain dormant for over two years. The confirmation of *Young Winston* encouraged his profligacy. He considered a Jensen Interceptor for £5838, a Lamborghini for £8958, a Maserati for £11,500 and a Ferrari for £9559.

Now into the new tax year, having spent his year abroad, Shaw could come into England again but wanted to save what became known as his 'tax days' in the event of another film in England. Any day spent in London from now on was to be crammed full before getting the last plane back to Dublin. On 7 May, for instance, he came over for his first day in England for 14 months. It started with breakfast at the Dorchester to discuss the tax case with Henry King and Ivan Paul, thence to the medical for *Winston* at noon (all films require the star actors to take a medical examination so that the film can purchase an insurance against completion) followed by lunch at L'Écu de France with Foreman and the newly appointed director Richard Attenborough, followed by a costume fitting at Bermans and a meeting with Vanessa Redgrave over dinner.

H.R. Owen, the car dealers, had a Volante Aston Martin convertible for £5950. From the breakfast Shaw phoned to ask if it had an electric hood and, if it did, could it be sent to Bermans in Leicester Square for him to inspect while he was fitted. Over lunch the maitre d' came up to the table where Attenborough and Foreman were discussing the film with an urgent message for Mr Shaw. 'Yes, sir, the Aston does have an electric hood.' Shaw grinned. It was exactly the sort of effect he loved to create. The car duly arrived. Shaw climbed down from the two volumes of the London telephone directory he was using to simulate the 'lifts' he always wore in his film shoes, went outside in half a morning-suit and bought the car on the spot.

It was not all that simple, however. Three different advisers had to be consulted. The new Irish lawyer Anthony Collins, brought in to sort out affairs in relation to his proposed residence in Ireland, was asked about import tax if the car were subsequently brought in to a house here; Henry King had to investigate the English tax consequences of having a car and which company should own it; and Ivan Paul was needed to confirm that River Enterprises could own it and provide the money to buy it.

The white Rolls Royce Silver Ghost that met him at the airport, paid for on this occasion and any other when the trip was directly related to work on *Young Winston* by Foreman's company Open Road Films, belonged to and was driven by Ted Talmadge, a film driver who had first met Shaw on *The Buccaneers*. Talmadge was to do all the Shaws' family driving – of which there was a great deal – from this point on, so impressed was Shaw by his efficiency. That night he was sent – at Open Road's expense – to bring Frank Dunlop to dinner with Vanessa Redgrave as a last-minute addition to the party.

Flying back and forth between Dublin and London for wig and costume fittings in order to save his 'tax days' Shaw would be met in Dublin by Miss Jay in the Ford station wagon and drive out to join Mary in the West where the search for a house continued. On 14 May 1971 they found what they were looking for – or at least as near to what they wanted as they had come to realise they were ever going to get in the West of Ireland. Just outside the small village of Tourmakeady, Co. Galway, the bishop of Tuam, le Poer Trench, had built a mansion in the early 1830's for his sister. At the bottom of a winding rhododendron-lined drive, alternately red and white in the flowering season, the house was built in the shape of a T in large granite blocks. From the drive it appeared as though it were only one storey but from the front it became apparent that there were two. It was not a pretty house, nor an example of a style commonly found elsewhere. It did have a certain Georgian neatness in proportion. Surrounded by 75 acres of land and with a lawn sloping down to the edge of Lough Mask – where a beach had been created by shipping in tons of sand and building a small wooden jetty – the house had not been lived in for years. It was going to need an immense amount of work, and money, to make it habitable, let alone luxurious, but the Shaw's decided, no doubt looking out from the sitting room at one of the finest views it is possible to imagine over the hills and valleys bisected by the Lough, that this was the house for them. They paid £75,000 for the house and the land.

So the saga began. The American novelist, Richard Condon, had bought a house in Ireland – induced by the tax incentives – and later wrote a book, not published in Ireland for reasons of libel, on the horrors of having a house re-built by Irish builders. The troubles the Shaws were to suffer from plasterers, plumbers, architects, surveyors and purveyors of almost every building trade would have made a similar account. The house was not to be ready for occupation until the summer of 1974 – three years after they bought it.

Shaw returned to Spain to await the beginning of filming on *Young Winston*. The low he had suffered in the last months of 1970 had been born away on the tide of fortune again. He had completed his first Hollywood film which had gone well and for which he had high hopes, encouraged by the director who had phoned to thank him for his work and tell him Columbia were pleased with the 'rough' cut (the first assemblage of the film). He was starring in the most prestigious production to be made in England in 1971, though in a 'character' role, and his play was being done with one of England's most respected actresses. Sitting in the study of Fincha Mi Gusto, the occasional whiff of charred wood still in the air, he would have been forgiven for thinking that the fire which had consumed his manuscripts had been mythic and that he had arisen from its ashes like a phoenix.

In this spirit he had an idea for a new novel and rang the Heywood Hill bookshop in London to ask them to send him everything they had on old people, old people's homes and the Inuit (Eskimos) Indians of North America. To add to his sense of well-being it looked as though *The Man in the Glass Booth* was going to be made into a film or at least a film for American television. In June, an American lawyer had called from New York to enquire whether the rights were available. He had a client who was looking for a straight role for the American comedy actor Sid Caesar and thought the play would be ideal. As nothing had come of Clive Donner's attempt to do it with the Israelis, the rights were available. Nothing further was heard until July when the lawyer called again. The position had changed substantially. It was no longer a project for Sid Caesar but the company, Dick Feldman Productions, were still interested. Meantime another contender had entered the ranks, the Ely Landau Organisation. They had a contract with NBC to film some 'major' contemporary plays for television and were interested in optioning *Glass Booth*. They had already bought a Pinter play and a Simon Gray. Their producer met Shaw at the Savoy during the shooting of *Young Winston* and agreed that he should have actor and director approval but Shaw made it clear he did not want to write the screenplay himself. A deal was made with a $500 option for one year against a purchase price of $30,000. A list of actors that Shaw approved was drawn up for convenience, to save having to ring him every time they considered a new possibility. He approved Marlon Brando, Nicol Williamson, George C. Scott, Richard Burton, Paul Scofield, Paul Newman, Jason Robards, Anthony Quayle and Donald Pleasence. He disapproved Topol, William Holden, Peter Finch, Melwyn Douglas and Alec Guinness. There was an option to release the film 'theatrically' (in cinemas) but no one believed it would ever play anything but television.

On one of the costume-fitting trips Shaw was booked into the Savoy by Open Road on 27 May for a fitting on the morning of the 28th. That night he called Harold Pinter and they went out to see *Butley* together with dinner afterwards. The dinner left Shaw so hungover the following morning that he missed the costume fitting and it had to be rearranged for the following week. Shaw had to pay for the flight and the hotel himself. Another such evening with Pinter was to have more fateful consequences in 1975.

Shaw was due to start filming on 29 June 1971. His new Aston Martin, complete with electric hood, had arrived in Spain a week or two earlier. On Sunday 20 June Miss Jay and Shaw set off in the car to visit a ceramics factory to look for tiles for the new house. Richardo Perez – a film driver Shaw had met on Phil Yordan's pictures whom he now used in Madrid on occasion – followed them in the Ford station wagon to provide cargo space should it be necessary. After a few miles the Aston was involved in a crash. The other car's driver was not hurt but Shaw panicked. Leaving Ricardo to deal with the police, Shaw took the Ford and Miss Jay and headed for the airport. Wearing only slacks and a short-sleeved shirt and open sandals Shaw raced to the ticket desk to get the first flight out of Spain. He had heard horrendous stories of foreigners thrown into Spanish jails for traffic offences. The richer they were the longer it took for them to see the light of day again, as more numerous bribes were required – or so he had been told. Having no intention of missing the first day's filming on *Young Winston* he took the first plane out – which happen to be to Copenhagen. Paying for the tickets in cash – Shaw never carried any sort of credit cards but always had a wad of cash in his pocket – they boarded the plane and escaped the clutches of the Spanish police.

The next morning, installed in the appropriately named Hotel d'Angleterre, the full army of advisers were swung into action: Henry King to recruit a Spanish lawyer in case Ricardo was in trouble with the police and to make certain Shaw would have no problem if he returned to Madrid; Ivan Paul to get a bank to send money to Copenhagen to pay the hotel bill and enable them to buy clothes (the wad having run out); the travel agents to book tickets out, the insurance brokers to deal with the damage to the car. Meantime Miss Jay showed Shaw the city where her son had been born. She left Shaw to call Mary, in Ireland, and tell her the news of the crash and explain why he had taken her with him on the plane.

Arriving at the Savoy on 26 June, Shaw was installed in a riverside suite. Ricardo, having been successfully extracted from the attention of the Spanish police, who were not at all happy at their 'star' witness having fled the scene, drove the Mercedes to England so it was available for Shaw's use during filming. Arrangements were made to have the battered Aston shipped back to England for repair. Unfortunately it was not as lucky as Ricardo, and it was seized at the Spanish border and impounded, the police wanting further details from their recalcitrant witness before they would agree to its release.

The night after his arrival in England Shaw got a call from Peter Hall. The RSC wanted to mount a Broadway production of *Old Times* by Harold Pinter which he had directed and which was currently running to packed houses in the repertoire at the Aldwych. Pinter had suggested Mary and Robert for two of the play's three roles. The American management, Dowling-Whitehead-Stevens, were enthusiastic. Mary was delighted: 'the part could have been made for me', she declared. Shaw was less pleased as he saw the man's role as distinctly smaller. Mary had also been approached, through John Gaines, to play a small role in a William Holden picture *The Revengers* that Columbia was making in Mexico with Daniel Mann directing. Mann had seen *The Daughter* and was keen for her to play the role and a deal had been done though, fortunately not finalised. Mary called Gaines and told him she had another offer. She told Milton Goldman in New York she would be happy to do *Old Times* but she must have 10% of the gross.

It had been made absolutely clear that the offer for Mary was independent of the offer for Shaw so his decision did not affect her employment. The production dates for what had now become known to everyone involved as *Cato Street* (Shaw's latest title *The West End Job* having been wisely rejected) had been set for October opening in November. The dates for *Old Times* were rehearsing for one week in London on 28 September and then going 'abroad' for two weeks, to save his tax days, and then back to London for two weeks before flying to New York for previews at the beginning of November. The two weeks abroad were necessary because, Shaw was running out of the 90 days he was allowed in the country. The dates were a direct clash with *Cato Street*. If he accepted not only was it likely that he would only be able to attend rehearsals of *Cato Street* on days when released by Peter Hall, which would be few, but also that he would miss the whole of the run of the play at the Young Vic and never see it performed.

It may seem odd therefore that he went ahead and accepted *Old Times*. Perhaps it was a decision made with boundless optimism that *Cato Street* would transfer to the West End. Perhaps he felt it would be better to be with, and support, Mary in New York. The money, $2,000 a week against 10% of the gross box office receipts, was good but hardly significant in Shaw's scale of things. Perhaps it was his loyalty to his friend's play above his own. Whatever the reason it was a curious decision, especially as the RSC were quite prepared to delay for a matter of weeks had they been pushed. It is tempting to think that he knew what the fate of *Cato Street* would be and accepted *Old Times* as a hostage against fortune.

Mary, of course, did not get her 10%. That went to her husband, the producers explaining they had only one such amount available. She was assured that Rosemary Harris, the actress playing the third role, was not getting a percentage either.

In August, Shaw appeared on the Michael Parkinson Show on BBC1 with Ringo Starr who had designed and was launching a series of fireplaces exhibited on the show. Though Shaw had availed himself of the BBC's hospitality, rather too lavishly, he did manage to remember to plug *Cato Street* and Vanessa Redgrave. He also, to the embarrassment of all concerned, and especially Ringo Starr, chose to repeat his unaccompanied rendition of *Yesterday*.

On the 12 September Shaw and Mary were flown out to Los Angeles to do 'looping' on *The Daughter*. Because a lot of the film had been made on a beach the natural sound was inaudible and it was therefore necessary to revoice the dialogue in a studio. The comings and goings on *Young Winston* – Shaw had flown in and out of the country more than 15 times to save his precious tax days – were brought to an end on the 24 September which was declared Shaw's last day of filming. He returned to Madrid.

The next problem with *Cato Street*, apart from its finances – the money needed had leapt from £4,000 to £8,000 to £10,000 – was the question of the opening night. The best night was thought to be 3 November but when this date was checked with the Society of West End Theatre Managers it was discovered that Lindsay Anderson's production of *The Changing Room* by David Storey opened on that night. Naturally when Shaw called Anderson for advice Lindsay told him it would be madness to split the first-string critics between the two productions. With much discussion it was finally agreed to preview from 3 November and hold the press night on 15 November, which was clear of any other major productions.

Shaw told Michael White that he was certain Irving Wardle would give him a bad notice but that Harold Hobson was a 'fan'. Shaw naïvely suggested taking him out to lunch and giving him a copy of the play. White thought the former idea would depend on whether Hobson would accept lunch but the latter was certainly a good idea. Hobson did not accept lunch. Neither did he review the play.

The casting of Lord Sidmouth remained an intractable problem. Olivier had decided that he did not want to play it from the moment he had read the play. Paul Scofield had turned it down. John Gielgud had expressed interest but turned it down on being sent the final rewrites. Shaw was asked if he thought Trevor Howard would be suitable and, in a fine illustration of the pot and the kettle, was enthusiastic provided that Howard could master his drink problem. The part was still not cast when rehearsals for the 'radicals' began on 20 September one week before the main rehearsals. The decision to cast John Arnatt had to be made by Peter Gill alone. When Gill wanted to discuss it with him, Shaw was on his way back from the looping in Los Angeles and his flight was delayed by fog and diverted to Frankfurt. It was not until 22 September that Shaw got to a phone whereupon Gill explained that he had no other choice but to go ahead. Rehearsals for the entire company began on 27 September. Shaw's own first rehearsal for *Old Times* was Tuesday 28 September.

On Tuesday 5 October he flew to Dublin having spent the previous day with *Cato Street* rehearsals. He had been scheduled to fly out on the 4th day but Hall and Pinter took pity on him and allowed him a day off knowing he would not be back in London until 18 October. Taking calls from Gill in his suite at the Hibernian Hotel, Shaw also used the time to consult with Michael Phillips, the architect, for the Tourmakeady house, Drimbawn, on his plans.

Back in London on 19 October Shaw had two weeks of his tax days left in England. He was booked on a flight to New York with Peter Hall and Mary on 2 November, one day before the first public preview of *Cato Street* at the Young Vic. After rehearsals on *Old Times* he would rush down to the rehearsal rooms, or failing that telephone Gill or Redgrave or Michael White to find out how it was going. He was desperate for a way of getting to see his show somehow once he'd opened in *Old Times*. He had had his travel agent investigate a flight leaving New York on Sunday evening and returning Tuesday morning – since Broadway theatres played Sunday nights and not Mondays – so that he could see *Cato Street* on Monday night. But, in the days before Concorde, Hall and the RSC pointed out that it was an unacceptable risk.

On 27 October, 6 days before the first preview, *Cato Street* was running four-and-a-half hours from curtain up to curtain down and the cast were deeply depressed. Cuts had to be made but the author had little time to make them. Given Monday 1 November off from *Old Times*, Shaw spent the whole day at the Young Vic working on the play. At 7.30 p.m. with Mary present, there was a run of the play at the end of which was further grim depression. Gill had assembled an impressive cast and among the 46 actors in the company were Bob Hoskins, Norman Beaton ('the man of colour'), Olivier Cotton, James Hazeldine and John Sharp, as well as Tom Kempinski and George Tovey, but there was no doubt the play was not working. Shaw returned to the Savoy with Mary, left instructions not to be disturbed before 10.00 a.m., took a sleeping pill and went to bed. There was nothing he could do.

On Tuesday morning, while Shaw slept, a meeting of ground crews at London Airport decided to go on indefinite strike until a pay claim was settled. All flights were cancelled, or, more accurately, all flights that had to be fuelled and serviced at Heathrow were cancelled. The 5.30 pm TWA flight to New York on which the Shaws and Peter Hall were booked was amongst them. Shaw's travel agents, aware of the urgency, called Shaw's agents at 9.30 a.m. with the news, but they were unable to persuade the Savoy switchboard to break their instructions so it was not until 10.01 a.m that Shaw was told what had happened. The travel agents were looking for an alternative flight possibly from Gatwick. Robert Shaw meantime dressed quickly and took a cab to the Young Vic.

Peter Hall's secretary called his agents too. She was trying to find a flight out but had been told it was impossible and the only thing to do was to go to Gatwick and get on anything that was going. But Shaw had no intention of doing that. Fate had handed him an opportunity which he was determined to grab with both hands. But there was not just the problem of getting to New York in time for the previews of *Old Times*. If Shaw did not leave by 4 November he would have exceeded his 90-day stay in England and his tax status as non-resident would be forfeit with obvious consequences on his tax liabilities. It was not a matter of calendar days. The 90 days were calculated in hours, minutes and seconds, from the arrival of flight in to the departure of the flight out. A careful record had to be kept, minutes totalled into hours, hours into days, and the 90 days would be up at 8.00 p.m. on 4 November. Shaw called Henry King for confirmation. Was there no way he could stay a couple of extra days? King replied firmly: 95 days would not be the end of the world this tax year but it would mean he could only spend 40 days in the following year and under present circumstances, with the current attitude of the Revenue to his affairs, it was 'not a risk . . . he ought to take.'

His room for manoeuvre was narrowing. Peter Hall's secretary had called again to say the French ferries were also on strike but that Peter would come around and pick them up and drive to Harwich where they could get a ferry to the Hook of Holland and then fly from Amsterdam. But Shaw, busy cutting slices from his play, had no intention of leaving, and, he told his agent, he decided he was not going to leave now until after the first public preview of his play the next day, 3 November, which effectively meant he would not go until 4 November, the absolute last minute in terms of his tax days.

Peter Hall kept calling desperate for news of his recalcitrant leading actor. Shaw's agents were instructed to tell him they couldn't find him. At the Young Vic, Shaw left instructions at the stage door that if Peter Hall called he was to be told Shaw wasn't there. Shaw spent the whole of that day, the 2nd, working on the play, but the run through that night, though shorter, had not substantially improved matters.

On the morning of the 3rd Peter Hall called again. He had got tickets on the KLM flight from Amsterdam that evening and they could go there by train. However, if flights could be *guaranteed* on the 4th then he'd be prepared to wait until then. There were certainly still no flights from Heathrow. Once again Shaw hid from Hall. A meeting with Donald Sartain, the Young Vic's manager, Michael White, Edward Burrell, White's company manager, together with Donald Bradley and his assistant John French was held at the Ivy Restaurant. Shaw arrived in a taxi during the lunch-break from rehearsals and the meeting got under way with the principle item on the agenda being whether it was advisable to sack Peter Gill as director. Redgrave had suggested the idea and was prepared to take over until Frank Dunlop returned from his holiday on Saturday. He would then work on the production for a week until it opened on 15 November. As there seemed to be no alternative, and the feeling was that *something* had to be done, the decision to sack Gill was taken. He was found and given the news over the telephone. Shaw would meantime continue to work on further cuts.

Peter Hall accepted the inevitable. They would go on any flight they could get the following day from Heathrow. Shaw's travel agents had got tickets on a Pan AM flight which was re-fuelling in Paris before departing from Heathrow and there was the possibility of an Air France flight on the same basis. Shaw went to see his play in front of a large audience at the Young Vic paying 40p a ticket. It ran three-and-a-half hours and was, generally speaking, a shambles.

He too accepted the inevitable. He ordered Ted Talmadge to pick him up at 11.30 a.m. at the Savoy and headed for the airport to catch the 1.30 p.m. Pan AM flight to New York. At the airport chaos reigned. It became quite clear that there was going to be no 1.30 p.m.

Pan AM flight to New York. Fortunately for Shaw the Savoy kept a personal representative at the airport who knew him well from the past. He had discovered that an Air India flight was expected in, re-fuelling in Paris, and therefore able to fly on to New York. The Savoy man changed Shaw's tickets and at 3.45 p.m. the Air India flight took off only 45 minutes later than scheduled. Shaw had seen one performance of his play and, escaped the jaws of the tax man by precisely four hours and fifteen minutes.

On 5 November Peter Gill called Shaw at the Algonquin. His friends, Gill said, blamed Shaw for his dismissal. Shaw assured him, with no hint of irony, that it was in fact Vanessa Redgrave's responsibility. Relaying this conversation to his agents in London Shaw added that the morale of the cast was very low and he expected Vanessa's performance, with which he was not at all happy, would deteriorate further now he had left. But he had now made the definitive cuts, he added. He had the version he wanted to have published and he was sending it over as *Plays and Players* had a contract to publish it in their first edition after the run at the Young Vic. The play was not subsequently published by either Chatto and Windus or Harcourt Brace, as *The Man in the Glass Booth* had been.

Dunlop's arrival steadied the boat. He cancelled the public perform-ances on Monday and Tuesday 8 and 9 November. On the 8th the assistant director, appointed by Shaw, reported that Gill had received flowers and telegrams of support and that Frank Dunlop had flu. Shaw's newest cuts were instituted and the production generally tidied up but the die had been cast. On 15 November *Cato Street* opened to the press. Irving Wardle did not disappoint Shaw's expectations of his review:

> where are the social injustices that underlie the clashes with authority? [there is] so much actual information . . . that would have held the attention better than any of the threadbare fictions supplied here.

On the subject of substituting a woman for a man as Thistlewood: 'apart from the most factitious theatrical reason I can think of no cause.' J.C. Trewin found the play 'noisily attractive, but that it ultimately 'leaves us cold'. The *Evening News* thought it 'not so much a play as a documentary of ideas bubbling to the surface at that time'. But the *Guardian* and *The Sunday Times* were kinder, Michael Billington liked the way play was staged by the 'unnamed director' (there was no directorial credit in the programme) and *The Sunday Times* (not Harold Hobson) admired it in general terms. Milton

Shulman was the most enthusiastic, 'its long arguments call for, and reward, close attention'.

None of the reviews could be called 'selling', but if anything they treated the play with undue kindness. There was a feeling that *Cato Street* represented the sort of play rarely tried by English playwrights, an epic historical piece, and for this reason it was given a very fair hearing. The subject matter certainly had areas that Shaw never managed to explore. What he presents us with is a naïve group who seem to have absolutely no idea how to go about revolution other than talking about injustice. There is no sense of political mechanism in the play nor a perspective which would at least examine their enormous self-delusion. The balance between their arguments and those of Sidmouth is finely wrought and so is the centre ground in the form of William Corbett – 'there is no principle, no precedent, no regulation . . . favourable to freedom, which is not to be found in the laws of England.'

In making Thistlewood a woman, however, Shaw created a problem within the play as well as one of historical accuracy – discussed in letters to the *Evening Standard* the week the play opened. As Corbett says, 'every *man* must have a vote'. But he is not saying that women should have it. The point is made that 'in England . . . they want gentlemen to lead': 'gentlemen' as opposed to commoners, not as opposed to women. But there is Susan Thistlewood doing just that. From the conversations with Olivier and the National in 1970 Shaw was aware of this criticism and answered it in a note printed in the script:

I have changed him [Thistlewood] into a woman because his wife Susan was, according to the historian E. P. Thompson, 'a spirited Jacobean in her own right,' and because I feel it is more interesting for the audience to have a woman to look at. The women of 1819 were active in the Radical movement . . . It was the Victorians who managed to put them down again.

He also defended himself against anyone who might read John Stanhope's book and be surprised to see whole chunks of his reported dialogue and monologues lifted word for word:

The language of the play may seem to some to be literary. I hope this is its strength. This is how those people spoke. There is very little dialogue in this play that somebody did not utter between 1810 and 1820.

Shaw called from New York on the morning of 16 November, having got up at 4.0 a.m., and was read every review over the phone. He repeated the process on Sunday 21 November but the Sunday papers had not come to the rescue of *Cato Street* as they had done with *The Man in the Glass Booth*. Michael White called him to say there was no way he felt that the production could be moved into the West End on the notices as they stood. The play ran until 27 November, and was never seen again.

But the one person who had not lost her faith in the play and its 'indictment of Tory governments' and their indifference to the people was Vanessa Redgrave. Susan Thistlewood, for her, expressed an attitude she could identify with: 'one generation passeth away and another generation cometh.' According to her autobiography it was *Cato Street* that made her at last hesitate no longer. She joined her brother Corin in the Workers' Revolutionary Party. It is not, therefore, a surprise she does not quote the lines immediately before, spoken from the scaffold:

> There are plenty of you present. Come up and cut us down. I say by Christ let those amongst you that have pluck come up and cut us down. Where there is no vision the people perish.

Of course Shaw's most immediate concern was *Old Times* which was to open at the Billy Rose Theatre on 16 November 1971, the day after *Cato Street* opened in London. Pinter had apparently been concerned that the play would not be a success. Critically he needn't have worried. 'Three superb performances . . . make *Old Times*, the rare, strange and powerful evening of theatre that it is.' William Reidy of Newhouse Newspapers wrote and Clive Barnes in the all-powerful *New York Times* agreed: 'a joyous wonderful play . . . nothing could be better'. Richard Watts in the *New York Post* added that Pinter was 'a stunningly skilful writer . . . [with an] ideal cast – it isn't possible to imagine three players more right for the trio of roles.'

This was a set of reviews that Shaw could certainly read with pleasure. Considering the circumstances of the rehearsals it was a considerable achievement in concentration. Shaw had proved again that he was an actor suited to the rhythms and cadences of Pinter's world and Mary, whose first Pinter role it was, had done the same. Surprisingly, the box office returns were disappointing despite the reviews and after an initial week in which the gross box office receipts were $46,000 they went down to $38,000 for 4 weeks and then dropped to $26,000 and continued at that level. The New York public did not appear to share its critics' enthusiasm for Pinter.

On the more mundane front, the Aston Martin had reached

England at last after endless wrangles with the Spanish police and was being repaired. With the Ford also back in England for repair after a minor accident in Madrid and service bills on the Mercedes 600 that made even Robert Shaw blanch, he was considering selling all the cars and starting again in Ireland, with Irish registered models, especially, as he thought he'd be in New York for six months in *Old Times*. On the family scene Debbie was about to go to university (having failed Cambridge she was going to Sussex) and a level for her allowance had to be set. Penny was only a year behind. Shaw took the problem very seriously. He did not want his children to grow up thinking that all they had to do when they got into financial difficulties was to get on the phone to daddy. On the other hand it was not realistic to pretend he didn't have money, and was unable to bail them out if necessary. Over the next years Shaw tried to tread a delicate line with his children's allowances. As each child reached the age where they might expect an allowance, he tried to arrive at a weekly sum that did not give them the impression that he was an endless fountain of wealth. This attitude, at least, encouraged ingenuity in his children. His agent, placed *in loco parentis* in this respect, was often presented with detailed reasons as to why the allowance they were getting was not enough and why they just had to have more. The discussion of money was not confined to weekly allowances either: the size of Christmas boxes was just as carefully weighed. At Christmas 1971 the calculation of the nuances between the children left Debbie receiving £17, Penny £16 and Rachel £12.

The plan to sell the cars fell through. H.R. Owen would only offer £4,000 for the Aston and £1,050 for the Ford. The Mercedes – according to them, 'the most expensive car in the world to maintain' – they would put in their showroom and try and sell for him but they would not take the risk of buying it themselves. Shaw decided not to sell. The problem with the cars was that they were all registered in England and would go to Spain or Ireland under normal 'green card' insurance. However, if Shaw was to go and live in Ireland it would be difficult to have three English cars belonging to an English company permanently at Tourmakeady. To import them to Ireland would cost a huge amount as import tax was the highest in Europe. To import the Ford valued at £1050 would cost £700. As Shaw regarded this sort of tax in the same way as he regarded income tax, which he was dedicated to avoiding, he was not prepared to pay and elected instead to try to cheat the system for as long as he could get away with it, despite the anxiety and inconvenience this added to his life.

The complications of the Shaws' domestic life were becoming ever more convoluted. They had a home in Madrid, a house being renovated in Ireland, and children at school in England while themselves living, for the time being, in New York. They needed money for domestic expenses in Madrid, Ireland, England and America, not to mention money for Jennifer's alimony in Jamaica. It was not just a question of ringing the bank and asking for the funds to be transferred. Each country had to be provided with money from appropriate foreign companies, in accordance with the all-important tax structure, instructions issued and, in some cases, permission sought from the Bank of England and later the Bank of Ireland to transfer funds abroad.

In these circumstances it was frequently the case that bills were not paid. This was probably Shaw's greatest source of irritation with his advisers. Having learnt the lesson from Phil Yordan, Shaw was a big tipper. He would give a doorman $10 and after awhile it would increase to $100. He would frequently tip room-service waiters £20 in England (then the highest domination note – multiply by ten to get a rough 1992 equivalent). If he took someone out to dinner and caviar was on the menu he was insistent they should have it and when the waiter came with the tin and carefully ladled out a small spoonful as one portion, he would tell him to leave the tin. He let his friends order the most expensive *grand cru* on the wine list. He enjoyed giving. He enjoyed being seen to have money. The idea therefore that anywhere in the world a bill addressed to him was not being paid was abhorrent to him. Calls from round the globe chasing up why a bill had not been paid became a routine of life.

The Irish situation was a major problem too. Trying to oversee the complete renovation of a house in one of the remotest spots in Western Europe from the Algonquin Hotel in New York through a lawyer in Dublin was a recipe for disaster and so it proved. In reconstructing the roof, for instance, the tarpaulin had been allowed to blow off and rain had poured into the house. Work had to be delayed while the house was dried out. As it was winter the house could not be dried properly until the arrival of warm weather.

At the end of January 1972 it was clear that *Old Times* would have to come off. It was decided to take it on a short tour before closing in the middle of March. Unfortunately the provincial audiences appeared no more enamoured of Pinter's obliqueness than those of New York.

In the middle of the chaos and confusion of the opening of *Cato Street*, in fact on 2 November, Trevor Nunn, then artistic director of the RSC, had called to offer Shaw the part of Antony in a production of *Antony and Cleopatra* he was planning for the next season at Stratford, and that he was to direct. Nunn knew about the 90-day restriction but had worked out precisely how Shaw could do the play,

rehearsing during the week, Monday to Friday, flying out every
weekend except the final week of rehearsal. This, he'd calculated,
would have 'spent' 45 days including the first performance. Then it
would play in repertorie for 50 performances, which including
matinées would only use up a further 25 days making 70 in all. It is
difficult to think of a Shakespearean role more suited to Shaw's
particular talents now that he was a mature actor.

Shaw had been tempted. The money, £150 a week, would hardly
pay for the enormous travelling costs the plan would entail but that
was not a consideration. The main problem was the actress playing
Cleopatra – Janet Suzman's career at the RSC had not been hindered
by the fact of her marriage to its director. She had been given a line of
parts in the recent productions which had been amply justified by the
appreciative reviews, but Shaw, in consultation with his theatre-
going friends (Shaw himself hated going to the theatre), was sceptical.
He turned the offer down on the grounds that it involved too much
travelling.

Trevor Nunn was not the only one to think that Shaw could make
the role of Antony his own. Michael Croft, the head of the National
Youth Theatre, had approached Vanessa Redgrave to ask her to help
raise funds for his theatre by appearing in a play. Why not *Antony and
Cleopatra* with Robert Shaw as Antony, she suggested? There is no
doubt that Vanessa had developed something of a crush on Shaw. It
had been evident during *Cato Street*. And it became equally evident
that it was something Shaw was keen to avoid. The peon of praise for
his writing in her autobiography – and her vivid imagination in
ascribing to him parts he never played – are testament to the impact he
made on her. In his presence she had often seemed to go distinctly
gooey. She had not realised that, compared to her deep convictions,
his socialism was more honoured in the breach than the observance,
though lack of socialist right-thinking had never been allowed to
interfere with her choice of men on previous occasions.

At the beginning of March 1972, as the Shaws packed to go to
Boston for a week in *Old Times*, Vanessa called to ask if he would be
interested. Shaw had got on well with her during *Cato Street* because
he needed to, but the idea of playing Antony to her Cleopatra frankly
appalled him. Being subjected to week after week of proselytising,
especially now she had become a full member of the WRP, was more
than he cared to contemplate. Nor was he unaware that such an
enterprise would offer her the opportunity to convert him to her other
designs. Not wishing to offend her, with vague talk of a US
production of *Cato Steeet* still in the air, he had to think of a good
excuse. In February he had torn the ligaments in his arm, in an arm-

wrestling contest with Burgess Meredith, the American actor whose house in Pomona they had rented after moving from the Algonquin. He had been to see two specialists for advice, as the arm seemed not to be healing and was giving him a great deal of pain. Seizing this as a convenient excuse and greatly exaggerating its effects, he was able to tell Vanessa it was clearly impossible for him to play Antony with a gammy arm.

The final rites were performed over Thistlewood Productions. An exhibition mounted in the foyer of the Young Vic during the run at a cost of £152.42 was, according to Michael White and Vanessa Redgrave, Shaw's responsibility and not that of Thistlewood as he had authorised it on his own. A cheque for £182.83 was received for Shaw's 5% royalty on the £3644.50 taken at the box office, and of the £4,500 each party put into the production each received back, eventually, £129.41. It had been an expensive exercise for all concerned.

Old Times had run for 18 weeks including the short tour of American provincial cities. Robert and Mary returned to Spain on the *SS Michelangelo*. Shaw had no immediate prospect of employment. Once again the roller-coaster ride of his career had hit bottom: he was out of work, and for the first time since the publication of *The Hiding Place* in 1959 this meant in writing as well as acting. After *Card from Morocco* neither Chatto and Windus or Harcourt Brace had commissioned another novel, though it is fair to say they had not been asked. He had already decided that his next book would be set in an old people's home in New York in the future, where old people were housed on an island which could be floated out to sea very much as the Inuit Indians put their old on an ice-floe to die. But he had written no more than the first couple of pages, which he changed again and again, reading the new versions to friends over the transatlantic telephone lines at 4.00 a.m. their time. *The Ice-Floe* was never finished.

As for acting, Shaw's fourth appearance in a leading role on Broadway had made little direct impact on his career other than enhancing his reputation there. But his hopes for *Young Winston*, which was to open in a blaze of publicity, were high. It was bound to be an international success and might well prove to be the elusive 'breakthrough' movie for Shaw or so he thought. It was not.

Chapter Twelve

While Shaw's expenses had gone through the roof, all too literally in the case of Drimbawn, his earnings had declined substantially since the heady days of Phil Yordan's Spanish extravaganzas. Between the beginning of 1970 and the end of 1972 he earned approximately $500,000, or an average of $166,000 per year, a mere half of his 1969 total. But expenses had quadrupled. Drimbawn was eating money and bills of over $30,000 were settled for the 1971 period alone. He had agreed to pay educational insurance policies on his brother Sandy's children, and in May agreed to a loan for his sister in Philadelphia of $3,500. Wendy, whose divorce costs Robert had met, now needed a new house and Shaw gave her a personal mortgage for the entire cost. He was planning a trip to the Munich Olympics and was determined to buy a new Mercedes 450SL as soon as one became available. Lizzie and Hannah were now ready to go to Maltman's Green School to join Kathy, while Rachel was old enough for Wycombe Abbey and Colin for a public school as yet to be decided. The Madrid house had to be rented for a further year, as Drimbawn was clearly not going to be ready and, as ever, therefore, the children had to be transported to and fro from Madrid or, in the case of Debbie, Penny, Rachel and Kathy, to Jamaica to stay with their mother whenever required. Miss Jay had been given a long-overdue pay rise in January. And added to the pay roll of professional advisers, which already included the English lawyer and accountant and a Swiss adviser, were an Irish lawyer and an Irish accountant to look after the tax affairs there.

Jennifer sent Shaw a series of letters complaining that money for her bills and her alimony was continually late. The problem was that Exchange Control permission had to be sought for all monies going from River Enterprises in England to Jamaica, and it sometimes took weeks. Shaw's accountants seemed to be incapable of working out a schedule that would regularise the permissions and therefore the payments, and Shaw was left to field Jennifer's complaints. He was anxious to meet her demands as he was afraid that she would decide to open up the question of the amount of alimony she was receiving, which had been fixed in the days before he was earning six-figure salaries.

But on his return from America it was Mary Ure, his second wife, who demanded his full attention. Mary, despite having 'rave' reviews in *Old Times,* was in a very bad way. She was drinking heavily and often continuously. Though she never missed a performance, it was a miracle that she did not. Shaw and Miss Jay had found bottles hidden throughout the house, wrapped in the brown-paper bags redolent of American liquor stores. But confronted with the evidence she would deny everything. The bottles belonged to Robert, she would tell Miss Jay.

Back in Madrid the situation did not improve. Shaw had a friend send for the Alcoholics Anonymous leaflets, in the hope that they might give some clue as to how to cope with Mary, but discarded them rapidly when he read the definition of an alcoholic as simply someone who had a drink every day. 'Then we're all alcoholics', he told a friend when the leaflets arrived. But alcoholism was not Mary's real problem. The symptom was masking the disease.

At the end of April the Shaws arranged a trip to England for Robert to see a doctor about his elbow, which was still painful, to go to Maltman's Green to fix up Hannah and Lizzie's school places – a prospect which terrified him, as he seemed to regard the Head-mistresses of both Wycombe Abbey and Maltman's Green as fire-eating dragons – and to test-drive the new Mercedes 450SL, as well as talking to Dr Slattery about Mary. He was then to take the Mercedes 600 on the Southampton ferry and drive them both back to Madrid.

Shaw explained Mary's behaviour to Slattery, who thought it would be a good idea if she went to see the gynaecologist, Dr Spicer, who had delivered all her children. Mary, he thought, trusted Spicer and would respect his opinion. An appointment was arranged and Spicer, in turn, recommended her to see a Dr Benaim. While Robert drove the 450SL to Maltman's Green in Buckinghamshire to meet the Headmistress, a rather longer test drive than H.R. Owen might have envisaged, Mary did the rounds of the doctors.

On their return to Madrid, Shaw called Benaim privately and was told that Mary needed to be hospitalised for tests. In one mood, he told Benaim that would not be a problem, she would be perfectly reasonable and agree, but in another she would tell him that he was a cunt and should go fuck himself. In the event, they returned to England on 8 May and Mary went to see Spicer and Benaim again. Benaim told her he would like to book her into a nursing home for tests. On 14 May Mary was admitted to Greenways in Fellows Road, Swiss Cottage.

The next day Shaw was booked on the 5.15 p.m. flight to Madrid. He called Mary three times during the day, each time being told she

was under sedation and that he was not allowed to speak to her. At
3.00 p.m. Mary called Slattery. Her behaviour on the phone was so
alarming the hospital staff sedated her again. Slattery called Shaw
before he left. No one knows, he said, what effect the damage done to
the liver by drinking can subsequently have on the brain. He had
talked to Benaim who was working on the theory that she had
received some brain damage as a child. It might not be possible to keep
her in Greenways, he said, if she became too difficult.

Mary woke the following day, Tuesday, in a lucid mood. She had
read a review of Al Alvarez's book on (*The Savage God*) suicide and
wanted a copy sent round. The book begun with a quote from Sylvia
Plath:

> Dying
> Is an art like everything else
> I do it exceptionally well
> I do it so it feels real
> I guess you could say I've a call.

Mary appeared to have caught her husband's fascination with the
subject though her mood was far from suicidal. Before leaving for
Madrid in April she had left a copy of some poems she had been
working on with her agent, and was eager to talk about them now as
she lay in the nursing home. Though they were by no means skilfully
crafted they had a moving simplicity and a remarkable ability to
express emotion:

THE BABY NEW YORK 1970

I lay curled up to my husband crying for my mother
Sobbing with his arms around me
'Quiet' he whispered
'Only if I have my baby with me'
And he fetched the crying baby
And I put him to the breast that had no milk
And he was calm

THIRD LOVE POEM

We ate badly at the round Regency Table
And talked and went to bed
He loved me gently as new lovers do
But I said no
I threw the cap across the room and said

I want your child – your child
And never stopped crying

DEPRESSION

I could not move, I only saw the grey
I could not move to pick
The note book from the table
By my bed

The children came and brought me flowers
They only made me cry
I wished I could have said
How beautiful they were
And smiled – but how?

I lay and turned my head
And wept until all energy was spent
And there was nothing else
But only greyness.

John French went to see her in the nursing home. She looked weak and worn, fragile, terribly ill. She made an attempt to make up her eyes and put on a face but gave up after a few minutes. The following day she got up, dressed and went to see Zsuzsi Roboz at her studio for lunch. Zsuzsi too was shocked by what she saw.

Shaw rang from Madrid to tell Benaim he had discovered that Mary had nearly died of measles when she was eighteen months old. Could this be the brain damage he suspected? Shaw planned to go to Tourmakeady at the end of May taking Miss Jay with him. The children would then spend their summer holidays in Ireland. He called Penny and Debbie and asked them to go and see their step-mother.

Michael Phillips, the Irish architect, had heard from Mary who had changed all the colours on the plan for the house. Mary asked for Sean Connery's number. She called Lindsay Anderson for the home. She called Dickie Goulden, Alison Leggatt and Lyndon Brook, all old friends. And she called her husband and told him she knew he was having an affair with Miss Jay. She knew when it had started and where. Miss Jay, who she had taken into her home with an infant child, had betrayed her. 'Is it any wonder,' she screamed 'that I'm ill?' She slammed the phone down before her husband could answer.

Later Shaw told his wife he would come to see her on his way to Ireland on 26 May. His flight was due to arrive at 11.50 a.m. and he was booked on the 3.35pm to Dublin, which gave him two-and-a-half hours to get from Heathrow to the nursing home on the other side of

London and back to Heathrow again in time for the flight. Ted
Talmadge and the white Rolls Royce were booked to await his arrival.
Dr Slattery too, anxious that Shaw should see Mary, was told of the plan.

By 12.30 p.m. Ted Talmadge couldn't find out where the flight was
and could get no information from BEA. At 1.30 p.m. Shaw finally
cleared Customs. He had clearly been drinking. There was obviously
going to be no time to see Mary and catch the flight to Dublin. He
could, of course, cancel the Dublin flight and stay overnight giving
him plenty of time to see his wife. The option was never considered.
Instead he asked his agent to ring his wife and tell her his flight had
been delayed and he would not have time to see her. He did not, he
said, think it wise to call her himself. He boarded the Dublin flight.
Shaw never saw his wife in hospital.

Mary checked herself out of Greenways on the following Monday
and flew to Madrid. Shaw joined her there leaving Miss Jay, tactfully
perhaps, in Ireland. The problem was not solved but shelved. Shaw
told Benaim that Mary had sworn to him on the life of her children
that she was not drinking. When Miss Jay arrived back in Madrid she
was greeted with icy indifference, but there was no confrontation.

While domestic dramas had taken centre stage there was little that
might indicate Shaw would soon be gainfully employed. In New
York Paul Rosen, an agent with IFA (Ashley Famous had been taken
over and become the International Famous Agency), had taken Sidney
Lumet to see *Old Times* in the hope of getting him to offer Shaw a role
in the picture he was doing with Sean Connery. Connery had agreed,
in 1971, to return to the part of James Bond, after the disastrous failure
of George Lazenby in the first Bond picture made without Connery.
But the price he demanded for appearing in *Diamonds Are Forever* was
massive. His fee would be $1¼ million, all of which would be donated
to a charity he was to set up, plus a 12½% cut of the gross of the film,
increased percentages of the gross earnings on all the previous Bond
films he had done, plus the guarantee from United Artists that they
would finance two $1 million budget films chosen by Connery that he
would star in, direct or produce, or all three. At that time it was the
biggest deal ever done for an actor to play a part in a film.

The first of these two pictures was to be *This Story of Yours* (released
under the title of *The Offence*) by John Hopkins, the play that Terence
Baker had persuaded Glasshouse Productions to back for a West End
run. Though Hopkins and Connery were both represented by
Richard Hatton Ltd in London, as was Shaw, the idea that Shaw
should be used had not been mooted. Nor did Paul Rosen's
intervention in New York produce an offer from Sidney Lumet. The
part was played by Ian Bannen.

When Shaw heard of the Connery deal, it occurred to him that the project he still owned, the John Hopkins script of *The Mayor of Casterbridge*, might be resurrected. As Joe Losey had expressed an interest in the past he rang him with the idea. But Losey was discouraging. There was no way that *The Mayor of Casterbridge* could be made on a budget of $1 million, he told Shaw emphatically. In the end it would be made for a great deal less, though not as a feature film.

It happened that both the plays that Glasshouse Productions backed, *The Man in The Glass Booth* and *This Story of Yours*, were made into films. The contracts for both plays stated that Glasshouse was entitled to a percentage of the film rights for as long as they continued to present the play and for one year thereafter. During this period Glasshouse should receive 20% of any money the writer received in respect of film rights. In the case of John Hopkins there had been a small payment to him during the period but as it only amounted a sum of £230 due to Glasshouse the matter was dropped. In the case of *Glass Booth* the rights had clearly lapsed as Glasshouse had not presented the play since the Broadway production, but in a complication that would no doubt delight lawyers, the contract between Glasshouse and the American co-producer Ivor David Balding gave the later entitlement to 50% of what Glasshouse received from the film rights, irrespective of presenting the play, for a period of five years. What it amounted to was that Ivor David Balding could sue Glasshouse for the money for the film rights that it, in turn, had no right to receive. This tangle of contractual niceties (known by lawyers as 'limping' contracts) was resolved by Shaw paying nothing and hoping Ivor David Balding would not sue. It worked.

This mess had a further consequence. Investors in the original production, including Dirk Bogarde and the producer of *This Sporting Life* Julian Wintle, were entitled to payment from the sale of the film rights too. Unfortunately the contracts relating to the original production were lost and it was impossible to discover who owed what to whom. The play was caught in a legal quagmire.

There had been a number of offers and enquiries for Shaw over the months but nothing that proved tangible. There was talk of a re-make of *Lost Horizons* with Shaw in the Ronald Coleman role and Philip Saville offered him the part of Hector in a film of *Troilus and Cressida*, which he was setting up with Geoffrey Nethercote producing. Shaw turned this down on grounds of its size. Charles Schneer offered him the part of Koura in *Sinbad's Golden Voyage* which he turned down on the grounds that he would prefer to play Sinbad. Eric Shepherd, yet another agent at IFA in New York, told Shaw that Hal Prince would be interested to meet him for a musical he was working on with

Stephen Sondheim to be based on the Ingmar Bergman film *Smiles on a Summer Night*. The meeting never took place. John Ingrams, the director of *Omnibus*, also called to say that the scripts for the BBC Tolstoy were in but the budget had gone from £30,000 to £60,000 and the BBC could not proceed without a co-producer. And to complete the negatives on the work front, when Shaw asked Donald Bradley to find out who was going to play the role of the Jackal in *The Day of the Jackal*, which Fred Zinnermann was to direct, Bradley was told that Zinnermann was looking for someone 'rather nimble and willowy'.

Faced with such bleak prospects Shaw had joked that if he didn't get a 'decent' film sooner he would have to find another agency. Since he had joined Richard Hatton in 1954 he had actually only had to make one decision in relation to his agents and that was whether to accept Donald Bradley in 1969. His association with Milton Goldman in New York had never been a conscious decision on his part: it was rather a sort of osmosis; Milton simply absorbed British stars on Broadway. That had begun Shaw's association with Ashley Famous (subsequently IFA), but it was very much Richard Hatton's decision to allow him to be represented by Ben Benjamin and their West Coast office. Now Shaw received a letter from Benjamin's associate, John Gaines, telling him that Gaines was joining an agency called APA (Agency for the Performing Arts), and asking Shaw if he could take over his representation on the Coast. Shaw, who had liked Gaines and the attention he had lavished on him during the filming of *The Daughter*, immediately said he would – another major decision taken with little thought. But Shaw also wanted Milton Goldman to continue to represent him for the theatre in New York. Ben Benjamin blamed himself: 'I felt badly because in a sense I sort of abdicated my relationship with Robert when John [Gaines] took over . . . but I assure you that if Robert stays with us I will give him the kind of attention that I know he needs and wants.' But Benjamin, always the gentleman, added in his letter, 'I cannot criticise John Gaines. As an agent, he is damn good . . .' Had IFA told Shaw that they were not prepared for the anomalous situation in which he was represented by one agency on the West Coast and another on the East then they might have got Shaw to change his mind. As they did not play this card Shaw stuck to his decision and was henceforth represented by Gaines, as was Mary.

For the first time Shaw had an agent independent, in a sense, of Richard Hatton Ltd and not appointed by them. It would only be a matter of weeks before Donald Bradley would be writing his first letter of complaint to Gaines, who had called Shaw directly about getting him a role in *Abdication*, a picture Anthony Harvey was to direct starring Vanessa Redgrave. In future there would always be conflict between the two agencies especially as Shaw earned more: it was a conflict that Shaw did nothing to discourage. His love of competitive sports extended to watching them too.

Ben Benjamin had also tried to get Shaw into *Abdication* as a sort of *quid pro quo* for staying with IFA, and Donald Bradley had spoken to Bob Solo at Warners in London. As it happened George C. Scott was Harvey's first choice but Shaw was sent a script in any event. As soon as he read it he pronounced it 'terrible', so everyone's efforts had been wasted.

Mary had received several offers too. She had turned down a small part in *Hammersmith is Out* with Elizabeth Taylor and a television play for Granada to be directed by their *enfant terrible* Michael Apted. Michael Rudman had sent her a play she found 'unconvincing' and Mark Miller wanted her to do another television play with him. But she was more concerned with her poems. She had sent them to Harold Pinter in the hope that he might suggest a publisher. But Pinter did not like them, and told her so.

The next event on the agenda was the opening of *Young Winston* on 20 July with a double première at two cinemas in Leicester Square – a nightmare of protocol as it was a Royal Première and everyone wanted to go to the cinema attended by the senior royal. Columbia also informed Shaw that *The Daughter*, now called *Reflections of Fear*, would open in America in October. Hopefully one of these two films would revive interest in Shaw's work. Neither did. The lavish première of *Young Winston* was attended by show business figures and politicians alike along with Churchill's remaining family, of whom there were many. Despite the massive publicity the picture was not the success, either critically or commercially, that Carl Foreman had hoped for. This may have been because the story was treated like an old-fashioned Hollywood bio-pic, with a 'voice-over' narration by the young man himself explaining, rather unnecessarily, his feelings and emotions, and because of Attenborough's rather leaden direction or the inexperience of Simon Ward, whose likeness to Winston Churchill was not matched by his ability to establish a rapport with the film audience. Foreman had been delighted, however, with Shaw's contribution, and there had been talk of an Oscar nomination before the film was released. But there had always been doubts about the film, and no one was happy with its ending. How many versions were shot or cut together it is impossible to establish but the final version, with the ghostly presence of the father addressing the son as he never did in life, is clearly wildly unsatisfactory.

The film was not to be a breakthrough in Shaw's career. It did him no harm, and, as *Figures in a Landscape* and *A Town Called Bastard* – his last two films seen in Britain – had made little impact, *Young Winston* probably re-established him in the public eye after what might have been perceived to a considerable period of absence. But that was all.

Reflections of Fear did not improve matters. William Fraker had not managed to disguise the obviousness of the plot. The cause of the growing number of bodies that proceed to litter the film is patent and the word 'psychological' used to preface 'thriller' in the publicity material was clearly Columbia's way of telling their audience not to expect any surprises. In effect the film was dated, belonging to a brief genre of films that had a vogue in the early '60s (the first being *What Ever Happened to Baby Jane?*) The picture was savagely attacked by the US press and Columbia did not attempt to release the film in America as a whole or in Europe at all.

In July Charles Schneer rang Shaw direct at Fincha mi Gusto. He was making *The Golden Voyage of Sinbad* in studios in Madrid and would like Shaw to play the part of the Oracle which would take one day and for which Schneer would pay Shaw $5,000, literally cash in hand. In the script the Oracle was to appear in a haze, never to be seen as more than a ghostly presence. Shaw agreed provided that he was given no credit whatsoever and not mentioned in the cast list. On 5 August Ricardo drove Shaw to the studios and back at the end of the day with the money stuffed into his pocket. It was unlikely that anyone would recognise his face, so obscured was it and his voice was electronically altered by the sound engineer.

The ongoing tax case in England had taught Shaw a lesson. Instead of pocketing the money, Shaw called Henry King and told him what had happened and asked him what he should do. It was an awkward tax problem, agreements with I.A.P. in Liechtenstein had to be drawn up and the receipt Shaw had signed replaced with proper documents. A whole set of papers had to be signed in relation to Shaw receiving an advance in cash against salary. By the time the arrangements for the $5,000 had been made and correctly dealt with, from an international tax point of view, the legal fees had taken a good chunk of it. But Shaw was determined he was not going to be caught out again.

Though there was a possibility of a picture with Irving Lerner for Paramount in Argentina where the studio were unable to export their 'frozen' currency, it looked most likely that, once again in his career, it would be Benny Fisz to the rescue. He had a script which Don Sharp was set to direct, which was quite as awful as its title, *The Beast Must Die*, suggested. Shaw attached his name to the package but Fisz was still having trouble with the financing and the prospects for a film in 1972 seemed bleak.

In August the Olympics beckoned. Never one to cancel extravagance, Shaw drove the Mercedes 600 to Munich and was installed in the Hotel Königshof. After badgering the British Olympic Association with endless phone-calls, and offering his services for any presentation they might want to arrange, Shaw had succeeded in getting tickets for all the major athletic events of the tournament. The massacre of the Israeli athletes at their hotel – 'I heard the shots, submachine guns', Shaw reported – cast a pall over the games, however, and Shaw, in common with the other spectators, found it hard to relish the finals. After the car crash they had witnessed at the Mexico Olympics in 1968 Shaw's visits to the Games had not been short of incident.

Immediately on his return from Munich the Shaws de-camped to Westport, the nearest town to the village of Tourmakeady. They had found a large Victorian house, Rosbeg, to rent and began the process of moving their personal effect from Fincha mi Gusto to Ireland. Among the consignment shipped over was a large number of books removed from Orson Welles's library at the Spanish house. Future guests at Drimbawn, browsing in the shelves of books there, would often be curious as to why so many of the volumes bore a little green sticker on the inside fly-leaf proclaiming 'PROPERTY OF ORSON WELLES'.

It was not until October that Shaw received a definite offer of employment. Terence Baker, erstwhile literary agent with Richard Hatton Ltd, had turned from theatrical producer to film producer. Shaw had invested in his first theatrical venture, the David Mercer play *Flint*, which had starred Michael Horden and Harold Pinter's then-wife Vivien Merchant. It had not done well, but now Baker returned the favour by offering Shaw the title role in a Wolf Mankowitz adaptation of a L.P. Hartley novel *The Hireling*, which at that point Otto Preminger was set to direct. L.P. Hartley was very much in vogue after the success of the Joe Losey film *The Go-Between* scripted by Pinter. Luckily for Shaw he had used up very few of his 'tax days' since the new tax year in April, as the whole picture was to be made on location in England. It had to be a condition of the contract that Shaw could not work in England for longer than 70 days come what may. Unluckily for Shaw, as the film involved work in England he would be taxed on it in the traditional way, as he had been already on *Young Winston*.

The fee of $100,000 was agreed with no argument but the billing was more problematic. Sarah Miles had been cast as the other lead and was not prepared to take second billing to Shaw. Shaw was not prepared to take second billing to Sarah Miles, so there was deadlock.

Eventually it was agreed that Shaw would go on the left above the title and Miles on the right but with her name half-a-line higher. This inelegant solution, meaningless in all probability to the general public, was to be used over and over again to settle billing disputes. 'Stepped' billing, whenever it occurs, is always a sign of two or more actors deeply concerned about the position they are perceived to have in relation to each other.

By the time filming began on 27 November the director had become Alan Bridges, who had largely worked on television, though he had made a sci-fi film *Invasion* in the '60s. The complications of Shaw's tax affairs made it essential to consult his advisers as to where he should stay during the film. Ivan Paul expressed his preference for a hotel – as on *Young Winston* – but Henry King felt a service apartment within a hotel would be satisfactory: it would be cheaper and Shaw said he would prefer it. It was not possible for Shaw to take a house or flat, however, or have someone else rent one for him which would be 'available for his use'. This would be seen as establishing residency again which at all costs, and they had been great so far, had to be avoided.

Robert and Mary moved into a service apartment at the White House Hotel near Regent's Park and filming began. On *The Hireling* Shaw's expenses had been further reduced from the dizzy heights of $1,500 in 1969 to $500 a week which certainly would not have covered living at the Savoy. For once Shaw was concerned with economy and conscious of his financial situation. They were spending £100 a week on food, he told a friend. No doubt 'food' included drink. It was quite clear to anyone who visited the apartment that they were both drinking to excess. During the filming there was more than one day when shooting on Shaw would have been impossible had it not been for the fact that his part, for long sequences, was composed of meaningful looks rather than intricate dialogue. Where dialogue was required Shaw was quite capable of making up his own apparently with no detriment to the film.

Shaw's moods were liable to violent swings. *The Hireling* was worthy but it was not going to change his career, nor would it help his financial situation as the fee would be subject to a hefty tax. The Inland Revenue were continuing to press their case against his past liabilities and were anxious to interview Shaw personally which Ivan Paul was heavily resisting, suspecting, correctly, that such an interview would be a disaster for Shaw. Over lunch, to test this proposition, on a visit to the location at Sutton Place, he asked Shaw a few questions which the Revenue would pose. Who decides what films you should do? 'I do,' replied Shaw. Wrong. Paul advised him to do as few press interviews as possible so hopefully the film would be over and he would be gone before the Revenue got wind that he had been here.

On Christmas Eve 1972 just as the office was closing for business Shaw's agents got a call from Paul Newman. Newman had been in England on location making *The Mackintosh Man*, an uninspired spy story loosely based on the George Blake escape, when he had been sent a script of *The Sting* by Richard Zanuck and David Brown and Universal Pictures. In the story Newman is required to play a character called Mr Shaw and in reading it, the name had made him think of Robert Shaw for the part of the 'mark', Lonnegan, in the film. Newman was about to leave for New York but sent the David S. Ward script over to The White House by car, and said he would do all he could to row Shaw into the film.

Shaw recognised it for what it was, a superb piece of writing. He called John Gaines in Lost Angeles and told him to do all he could to get him *The Sting*. But Newman was as good as his word and on 12 January 1972 an offer came in from Universal for $150,000 for eight weeks work with one week's rehearsal prior to shooting. Shaw was jubilant and, for once, had no qualms in accepting billing in the third position. When it emerged, however, that Universal wanted to bill him under the title, not above with Newman and Redford he was adamant. He would not do the film unless he went above the title. For two or three days matters hung in the balance. Shaw paced the floors of Rosbeg long into the night waiting for the calls from L.A. Finally on 15 January it came. Universal had agreed to put him above the title. The film was on.

Actually it was a considerable coup in terms of billing. Shaw's career to date in films hardly justified his position in relation to Newman and Redford. Julia Phillips, who produced the film for Zanuck and Brown, later wrote in her book *You'll Never Eat Lunch in This Town Again*, that his agent's insistence – it was, of course, Shaw's – on above-the-title billing had cost him an Oscar nomination for Best Supporting Actor. This may or may not have been true at the time, but Sean Connery won an Oscar for Best Supporting Actor in *The Untouchables* with billing that was more or less identical some years later. In the end, Universal had the last laugh. Shaw's billing clause specified the use of his name not his 'likeness'. In the final poster for *The Sting* Shaw's name is above the title as it should have been contractually but it is the 'likenesses' of Newman and Redford that dominate the poster.

It was odd that Shaw was so enthusiastic about *The Sting* since Lonnegan was very much a character part. It was a key role in the way that Grant, Henry VIII and Randolph Churchill had been, but nevertheless it was a small role and a loser, a part Shaw normally shied away from as much in films as in life. Actually Shaw's enthusiasm came from being, however uncharacteristically, star-struck. This was a major Hollywood picture, if not *the* major Hollywood picture of 1973, with one of Hollywood's most respected directors and, at that time, *both* Hollywood's biggest stars. Surely in touching the cloak of greatness some of the threads had to rub off on him?

Meanwhile Mary was developing plans of her own. A great friend of hers, the novelist Olivia Manning, had suggested she should read the recently republished Jean Rhys book *Good Morning Midnight*. She saw immediately that the central character would be an ideal part for her. Her agent approached Jean Rhys's agent, Peggy Ramsay, to find out if the rights were available. They were not and the producer who owned them already had a star, the ubiquitous Vanessa Redgrave, a writer, Arthur Hopcraft, the *éminence grise* of British television drama, to do the screenplay, and a director, Michael Apted, fresh from Granada Television where he had directed some of their most notable plays (*Slattery's Mounted Foot*, *Another Saturday and Sweet F. A.*) and his first feature film (*Triple Echo*). For the time being, apart from Ms Ramsay assuring Mary she would mention her interest to the producer Graham Cottle, that was that.

At the end of January 1973 the Shaw household flew out to Los Angeles and were installed in a house in Malibu, on the Pacific Coast Highway, where they already knew the necessary nursery schools. Shaw was on his best behaviour again. He swam and played tennis every day to get himself 'into shape' – in theory at least. And, the week before rehearsals began, he agreed to play a game of volley ball after his tennis match at the Beverly Hills Racquet Ball Club. On one corner of the court a drain had been blocked and there was some surface water on the artificial Astroturf. Reaching for a ball in his usual all-out way, Shaw slipped on the wet surface and strained the ligaments in his knee. That day he could barely walk. The next was not much better. Filming his first scenes was eleven days away and rehearsals only seven.

There was no way to hide the news from the director of *The Sting*, George Roy Hill. Universal immediately sent round their doctor and the next day Shaw was despatched to a specialist who told him he could have physiotherapy but would not be able to walk without a pronounced limp. A quick production meeting was held and Doyle Lonnegan became a character with a stick and a gammy leg. By the fourth week of filming Shaw's natural limp had gone though the leg was still painful. The Beverly Hills Racquet Ball Club were sued, in the customary American manner, and settled out of court for $20,000.

What they would have had to pay if the limp had resulted in Shaw losing the film is the Racquet Ball Club insurance company's nightmare.

In Chicago, where *The Sting* filmed for two weeks on location, Shaw was fond of telling his friends that the National Guard had to be called out to restrain the crowds trying to catch a glimpse of Redford and Newman or both. Redford kept himself very much to himself, but Newman and Shaw stayed in the same hotel and one night Shaw suggested they go out for a drink instead of being stuck in the hotel. Newman agreed. Instead of taking the limousines they called a cab and asked the driver if he knew a good quiet bar. Newman began his accustomed litany of dirty jokes, which Shaw did not enjoy – Shaw didn't like laughing at other people's stories – and talk of cars, which Shaw did. The first bar they went to the owner recognised Newman at once and, assuming he wanted privacy, seated the party at the back out of sight of the main room. After a few minutes Newman decided he wanted to go somewhere else. In a second bar the same thing happened and again Newman wanted to go elsewhere. At the third bar there was no private booth. Within twenty minutes Newman had been recognised and asked for his autograph. 'It always happens,' he complained, 'everywhere I go.' The stay in the last bar was much longer.

The Ely Landau organisation, who had taken the option on *The Man in The Glass Booth*, were currently filming Harold Pinter's production of *Butley* by Simon Gray. Both its producer, Otto Plaschkes, and Harold Pinter wanted Mary to play the part of Anne. Not having seen the play, she asked for a script to be sent over. Mary was horrified to discover that the part was not more than one speech. She turned it down instantly, furious with Pinter that after playing a major role on Broadway for him, and getting rave reviews, he had offered her such a part. His attempt to persuade her by phone the following day did not improve her mood.

Mary did work in Los Angeles, however, doing an episode of *Ironside* in five days, earning the Shaw coffers $25,000 in the process and, for the first time, using cue cards – 'idiot boards' – as there was no time to learn the script.

Shaw's knee injury continued to be painful and two American specialists advised him to have surgery. Dr Slattery, however, whom Shaw consulted from Los Angeles, was totally against it. All Americans, he said, were 'knife-happy'. If Shaw could hang on until he got back to England he'd organise an English specialist. He was right. Shaw did not need an operation. The knee could be added to the other list of complaints that Shaw recounted to anyone who would listen. As a nascent hypochondriac he liked to examine and magnify the slightest pain into the onset of something serious, and like a child playing Snap, would match any visitor's malady with his own 'I'm sure I've got that.' Real injuries gave him greater scope for elaboration.

The knee had another important role to play. Vanessa Redgrave had not given up her desire to play Cleopatra to Shaw's Antony. This time the charity to benefit was to be Sam Wanamaker's Globe Theatre Trust. Originally Shaw had replied to Wanamaker by telling him that he wasn't going to be available but, not taking no for an answer, Wanamaker had discovered that *The Sting* finished in April in plenty of time for his May production. So the knee came to the rescue just as the elbow had done a year before; he didn't think, he told Wanamaker, that Antony could be played with a limp.

The Shaws returned to Ireland in April. Graham Cottle, the producer who owned the rights to Jean Rhys's *Good Morning Midnight*, had called Mary to say that it now looked as if Vanessa Redgrave was going to do another film after *Antony and Cleopatra*, and therefore the part was open again. Mary was delighted and flew to England to meet Michael Apted for lunch at the Savoy. Apted was impressed and Cottle took the project off to the Cannes Film Festival. On 18 May he told Mary that he could not get the money on her name and had been 'forced' to go with Glenda Jackson.

Cannes was also going to be the destination for *The Hireling* which was to be the official British entry. It was the first film Shaw had ever been in that had featured in the competition but he showed no interest in attending. That was left to Sarah Miles who was besieged by the popular press since it was her first appearance in public since the death, in mysterious circumstances, of her 'manager' David Whiting. Whiting had died in her caravan on location in California while she had been filming *Cat Dancing* with Burt Reynolds in February 1973. What the press at that time did not know, and would have given a great deal to find out, was that Miles's estranged husband, Robert Bolt, had immediately flown to Los Angeles to be with her, staying with the man he had liked and befriended on *A Man for All Seasons*. Bolt spent a week at Pacific Coast Highway with the Shaws, dodging the press and helping his wife deal with the police questioning into Whiting's death. Shaw's discretion was absolute. He told no one who was not a close friend.

Fielding questions on this subject four months later in Cannes with a smile and silence, Sarah Miles described *The Hireling* as 'a tragedy of incomprehension'. The film shared the Grand Prix at the Festival with an American film, *Scarecrow*.

Columbia Films picked up *The Hireling* for distribution and on the back of the success in Cannes opened the film on 11 June in New York. Though one or two critics found the film sensitive, in the main the view was 'stereotypical symbolism' and Vincent Canby in the *New York Times* wrote:

> by effectively reducing the conflicts within the English social order to a misunderstanding it becomes not only silly but grossly misleading.

But when the picture opened in England the following month it received a much better press. Dilys Powell found Shaw's performance 'superb . . . every gesture . . . has a kind of contained sexual drive'. The *Sunday Telegraph* thought it 'exceptional' and the *Observer* 'worthwhile and perceptive'. But despite the critical acclaim the film was never destined to find a popular audience. There is no doubt about the quality of Shaw's performance which relies heavily on his ability to establish a hypnotic relationship with the camera. In close-up his talent for suggesting a barely controlled violence and a profound sexuality is transmitted with the minimum of effort and with the maximum effect.

Back in Tourmakedy, Drimbawn was ready to have the lights and carpets fitted. These were extracted from storage and sent over to Ireland. Though there was a great deal to do on the domestic front, including arrangements for doctors to see the knee, and preparations for Jennifer who had decided she needed 'a two-bedroom flat near the park' for a year in London, while she did a teaching course, there was almost no activity on the work front. After the excitement of *The Sting* things had once more gone quiet.

Shaw's next offer of employment was not to come until July. Yorkshire Television had arranged a co-production with an American company of a play by William Fairchild, *The Break*, which David Cuncliffe was directing. He offered Robert and Mary the two leading roles. The script had little to recommend it. Two madmen who turn out to be policemen, torturing a civil servant into confessing he had an affair but was also a spy. ('It amazes me that anyone would want to fabricate, or a producer to put on, a play like *The Break*', *Sunday Times*.) Though the money for the American transmission was guaranteed, £11,000 for Shaw and £2,400 for Mary, for one UK transmission and two in America, it was not a great deal in comparison to his movie fees and would be taxable in England. But Shaw accepted. With such an obviously terrible script it was an odd decision. Actually, Shaw was bored. He wanted to come to London and see his friends, be surrounded by people again. The isolation of Tourmakeady and Madrid was beginning to pall. At least when Drimbawn was ready he would be able to have friends to stay.

The play rehearsed in London, where Shaw stayed at the Savoy, making a large dent in the fee, and recorded for three days in Leeds. Originally, conscious of economy for the second time, Shaw had told his agents not to book the Savoy ('I'll stay in a pub round the corner from the rehearsal rooms') but his resolution did not last. A television studio in Leeds is a long way from the back-lot of Universal Pictures in Hollywood with Robert Redford and Paul Newman, but that was where Shaw found himself five months after finishing *The Sting*.

The television play took up most of August 1973 during which time Shaw also met with Counsel to discuss the continuing Revenue assault on his fortunes. Any effect this might have had on his spirits was off-set by a cable from Zanuck and Brown:

> We had extraordinary preview and exhibition of *The Sting* and your performance was received with special delight and interest. Warmest regards.

A few days later the Shaws sat up late in their suite at the Savoy and watched Richard Nixon resign the Presidency of the United States.

Shaw also took the opportunity, while in London, to visit the Savile Row tailors Huntsman at Ned Lynch's behest, to be fitted for two suits. Shaw proudly told journalists that he 'never spent money on clothes', and it was almost true. Most of the time he was scruffy, in slacks and a check shirt and sweater. But Lynch had persuaded him he should have at least two decent suits and took him along for fittings. With the extra pair of trousers provided by a judicious tip to the cutter they were the only tailored clothes Shaw ever owned, with the exception of the jacket the Jewish tailor in New York had made him.

While they were at the Savoy, David Hare had wanted to send Mary Ure a play he was directing at the Royal Court Theatre Upstairs. Not wanting to send it to her agents, he had found out her address in Ireland and sent it off to her there. The Shaws' mail was being re-directed to their Irish lawyer Anthony Collins who had read the play and pronounced it 'crummy'. This circuitous route took four weeks. Mr Hare had also written Mary a letter congratulating her on her performance in a Charles Wood play at the Royal Court the previous year (Mary had not set foot in the Royal Court since 1961). It was not the ideal way to entice an actress to play a part.

Rather like *The Sting*, Shaw's next film also came out of the blue. At the beginning of October John Gaines called to say he had an offer for

Shaw in a film to be made entirely on location in New York *The Taking of Pelham 1–2–3* (Pelham 1–2–3 is the destination of a New York subway route), to be directed by Joe Sargant and starring Walter Matthau. The script was sent off and Shaw accepted immediately. It was a good, well-plotted thriller, with Matthau as the lugubrious Transit Authority cop and Shaw the leader of a gang whose plan is to high-jack a New York subway train, taking hostages and demanding a large ransom in return for their release. It had a wealth of other well-drawn characters and it was quite clear that it would make a commercial film, perhaps a *very* commercial film. There used to be a Hollywood dictum for star actors who wished to remain star actors: never play a part where the character is killed or, if he gets killed, it must be in the last few minutes of the film. Shaw's part in *Pelham* qualified on the latter grounds.

The deal was agreed quickly at $120,000, an approvement on *The Hireling*, with expenses of $1,000 per week. The film was to be shot in a disused subway station and surrounding lines in Brooklyn (Court Street Station) which the Transit Authority kept open specifically for the use of film crews – a good business for them considering the number of films that feature subway scenes. For once, Shaw did not argue the billing and was prepared to go second to Matthau.

Leaving lists of instructions for the architect, giving up the lease on Rosbeg in the hope that Drimbawn would at least be fit for human habitation on their return and asking for large quantities of sleeping pills from Dr Slattery, the Shaws asked Milton Goldman to find them an apartment in New York though Milton had nothing to do with the film and would receive no commission. He found them a service apartment at the Volnay on 74th Street without complaint. The Shaws arrived in New York on 12 November.

The Taking of Pelham 1–2–3, though made in the heart of New York, was one of the most uncomfortable films Shaw ever had to make, working on the subway train outside the station and on the track. The line was filthy, there were rats everywhere and every time someone jumped from the train, or tripped over the lines, clouds of black dust rose into the air, making it impossible to shoot until it had settled. It was stiflingly hot and the noise from the frequent trains braking on the approach to the nearby Hoyt-Schermerhorn Station was deafening. At the end of a day's work actors and crew alike emerged looking as though they had been mining for coal.

On the Court Street Station platform itself some semblance of civilisation had been created with cubicles for actors' dressing rooms, catering and a full-sized table-tennis table in what had been the main station concourse. Shaw got on well with Matthau. 'My wife thinks you're the sexiest Jewish actor around,' Shaw said when they met. 'How does she know I'm Jewish?' Matthau asked. 'Because she's anti-Semitic,' Shaw replied, laughing. Fortunately Matthau laughed too.

Whether Richard Burton would have classed Walter Matthau as an 'aging actor' or not, Robert Shaw was certainly 'consigned' to playing ping-pong with him. Matthau won.

The one advantage of Brooklyn was Gage & Tolner's a long-established restaurant – the waiters wore a star for every 10 years of service and some had five stars – which served oysters, little neck clams and 'surf and turf'. Shaw and Matthau lunched there if filming permitted. It was an interesting contrast of personality, Matthau very much at home with himself full of homely aphorisms; Shaw, bright, intelligent but ultimately restless and uneasy about his place in the scheme of things. Matthau told Shaw quite seriously that after he'd seen *Deep Throat*, the Linda Lovelace porn film which had broken all box-office records in the US for a film of its type, he had not been able to sleep with his wife for a week. Shaw, on the other hand, was fascinated by the New York FM radio show where people phoned in with their sex problems and discussed the most intimate details on air. On the limousine ride back to Manhattan he always had the chauffeur tune to that station. There was nothing as daring in England.

Shaw's inability to beat Matthau, a man seven years his senior, at table tennis, was an indication that, once again, booze was playing a central role in his life. Long before the fire in Madrid in 1970 drinking had been a constant factor, sometimes well under control, sometimes totally out of control, but always a subject for discussion. There were few conversations when booze was not mentioned, the number of drinks he'd had or not had, the type of drinks, what was best for a hang-over, what he had tried and hated, what he had always hated, what drinks he really loved. There seemed to be no obvious correlation between the times when it got out of control and the onset of particular difficulties in his private or professional life. The only correlation was that he drank when he was depressed, and depression, profound depression, came and went for no apparent reason throughout his life. In these dark moods life would seem impossible, the bubbling cauldron of the things in his life that were unresolved and painful – his inability to find time to write was a current theme in 1973 – used as a stick to beat his psyche. None of these feelings were rational by definition. Nor, therefore, could they be cured by rational means. It was absolutely no good pointing out that Shaw was in a privileged and fortunate position. The competitor etched deep in his soul by the endless games he had played told him he was running second or even third best. Wanting always to win was a recipe for unhappiness. For all his intelligence Shaw would never look back ('never look back' as he'd screamed at his son Colin), take stock, weigh what had been achieved; he could only see the white tape on the finishing line ahead of him that seemed, on a bad day, to be moving away from him as fast as he approached it.

At the end of 1973 Shaw had another major decision to make. The Richard Hatton agency had changed in the last years. In 1972 Richard Hatton had decided to give up and concentrate on other interests, leaving Donald Bradley as the sole senior partner. During 1973 Sean Connery and Leo McKern had left the agency and at the end of 1973 Donald Bradley too decided he had had enough of being an agent. John French, Donald's assistant since 1970, given the choice between unemployment and setting up his own business, opted for the latter course. In fact he had been acting as Mary Ure's agent for the past two years, since an incident when Mary – in an alcohol-inspired rage – had screamed abuse at Donald for paying no attention to her career. Now he asked Mary and Robert if they would join him as clients of his new agency. He was 28 years old with only three years' experience in the business. Shaw agreed immediately, again a decision taken without the slightest contemplation.

John French had looked after the Shaw's domestic problems, the children's transportation to their various schools, their flights out to their father wherever he happened to be, buying, selling and servicing of the cars, arranging for bills to be paid and all the other minutiae of detail that the Shaws' complicated life entailed. Now he took over Shaw's career too. Knowing French had little money, Shaw invited him to come over to New York to stay with him at the Volnay during the final days of shooting in January 1974. And Mary, congratulating him on his new business, in a letter, wrote a prophetic warning in relation to John Gaines whom she did not like: 'I have several warnings to you about Gaines – a very good hustler but a hustler. I've made you out to be just as smart (smarter) than he thinks he is.'

In December 1973 *The Sting* opened on both sides of the Atlantic in time for Christmas business. The film about conmen that itself 'conned' the audience with its remarkable finale, and started a revival of interest in the music of Scott Joplin, was an immediate and huge success. It went straight into the Variety Top Grossers' Chart where, by January it was in sixth position. The manager of the Odeon Leicester Square told George Melly, then film critic of the *Observer*, that it was doing better business than *The Godfather*. And Shaw's role as the villain was very much recognised as one of the film's strengths in America and England:

> As characters, the two Americans may leave Robert Shaw standing in the deft process of making him a million illicit dollars poorer, but as performers they have nothing to teach him. One glare from those ice-cold eyes speaks volumes of treachery (*Daily Mail*).

But more important than the critical acclaim, Shaw had greatly impressed Richard Zanuck and David Brown. *The Sting* was seminal to the rest of his film career.

At the end of January 1974 Milton Goldman had an offer for Shaw from Joe Papp who was producing the *Dance of Death* by August Strindberg at the Lincoln Centre in New York with Joanne Woodward to be directed by A.J. Antoon. The play was to preview in Philadelphia and then play the Lincoln Centre for four weeks closing on 5 May. Shaw was perfect casting for the showy, exhibitionist role of Edgar, a part that Olivier had played at Chichester in the '60s to ecstatic reviews, and he did not hesitate to accept. Money was agreed at $1,000 a week (well below commercial Broadway rates) with $500 a week expenses. Billing was not a problem as Papp's productions were all billed alphabetically. The Shaws would continue to live at the Volnay in the meantime, sending Miss Jay back to Ireland to supervise the completion of Drimbawn and the arrival of the furniture from England.

During the first week of rehearsal it was clear that Joanne Woodward and Robert Shaw were not going to be compatible. At the end of the week Ms Woodward left the production to be replaced by Zoe Caldwell, who had played Isabella in the 1961 production of *The Changeling* at the Royal Court with Mary Ure and Robert Shaw, and was very much a Royal Court graduate. She had lived and worked in New York for some years. To their credit neither Shaw nor Joanne Woodward made any rash press statements on events and the matter did not become a Broadway *cause célèbre*. Privately Shaw told friends that she had been nervous of appearing on the stage after a long spell away, but she may have been more nervous at Shaw's insistence on drinking before, during and after rehearsals.

It was the biggest role Shaw had ever played on stage, the most demanding in terms of concentration and effort but also a role that could have been written for him. Strindberg's misogyny is amply illustrated by the Captain's character, Shaw taking delight in the constant suspicion of women – which echoed his own – as well as the strutting physicality and the opportunity for vocal brilliance and surprise. The temptation to overdo the exuberance was well under control, however: what made this such an exciting performance was that behind the charismatic role-playing that the part demanded there was a realism that his experience in Pinter had instilled as a necessity. In comparison to Olivier, behind whose bombast and infinitely calculated gestures there appeared to be little, it was the depth of pain that Shaw revealed in the character that made it such a mesmeric performance.

Once again Shaw's extraordinary ability to produce results under the most trying circumstances was clearly demonstrated. His home life with Mary at the Volnay was simply a nightmare: he was not sleeping, and he would often drink from morning to evening and all through a performance. Performing drunk was like playing Russian roulette. He wanted to test himself, to see how far he could go. Amazingly the drink did not prevent him from delivering his astonishing performance, at least not on the press night, and apparently not on many others.

The New York critics were unanimous in their praise. Clive Barnes, long an admirer of Shaw, wrote a rapturous review which was thrust into Shaw's hands, hot from the presses, at the Sardi's first-night party – the printing presses are actually round the corner from Sardi's which explains the papers' rapid arrival and their heat. 'It is a performance of triumph rather than tragedy. From its catatonic trances to its galvanic Othello-style collapses, it is a performance both of explosive energy and steely restraint.' The short run was packed.

Shaw's career had blossomed as his personal life withered. His performance in *The Sting* had given him a new profile in the eyes of Hollywood producers. He had justified his extravagant billing. His performance in *The Dance of Death* in New York, had confirmed his status as a major stage actor capable of comparison with any of the other great stage actors of his, or earlier, generations. His career was poised to take off. But the runway was littered with obstacles that had nothing to do with any professional impediments: the obstacles were all of his own making.

Chapter Thirteen

Mary Ure was in a deep decline. Whether she had been drinking heavily because of Robert or Robert had been drinking heavily because of Mary was immaterial; both partners were locked into a daily liturgy of drink. And New York was a drinker's paradise. Wall-to-wall booze, 24-hour bars and 24-hour liquor stores which, for no extra cost, would deliver 'fifths' to the door within 20 minutes of a telephone call.

It is difficult to know what demons haunted Mary. Her mother's death had obviously affected her badly but she seemed to have gone through a normal grieving process.

> MOTHER
> I made coffee in my mother's room
> Where she lay dying
> I tried so hard to warm the milk.
> The best china, embroidered tray-cloth.
>
> I handed her the cup
> She shouted out; the drip of coffee
> on the cloth and how it tasted.
>
> Little did I know of her endless suffering,
> Her living death and her knowledge of it.

After her hospitalisation in the summer of 1972 Dr Benaim had told her that there was some sort of 'salt' deficiency in her brain and that was causing her wild and erratic mood changes. A chemical antidote had met with little success. She was now dependent on drugs for any sleep (as was her husband). She was drinking each and every day and had an uncanny ability to conceal the fact, until one drink too many would take her over the edge and all hell would break loose. She would become violent, battering whoever – usually Shaw – or whatever got in her way. At the Savoy on one occasion she had actually torn a door off its hinges. And she would, as before, take her clothes off. On two separate occasions during their stay in New York

Shaw would wake in the middle of the night to find Mary gone. On the first he got up to walk the streets to find her – a dangerous occupation in New York. He found her three blocks away walking naked along the edge of Central Park. It was January and it was snowing. On the second occasion the doorbell woke him. The police had found Mary at the stage door of the Billy Rose Theatre, where they had played *Old Times* in 1971, completely naked again. She had walked thirty blocks in the middle of the night with temperatures below freezing. In the morning she had absolutely no recollection of either incident.

To the world at large the Shaws appeared a normal married couple. The fact that both were intelligent, witty people gave the marital banter a touch more spice and venom than normal but Mary's beauty and grace and Shaw's rather shambolic, unco-ordinated appearance seemed to fit into the pattern of a successful and well-adjusted marriage. The presence, inevitable, of one or more of the eight children added to the picture of unaffected normality. And they were both good hosts, keen to look after any guest. But underneath this surface affability the two were tearing each other apart.

It was impossible to say whether the chemical imbalance Dr Benaim had suggested was responsible for Mary's decline but it was undoubtedly true that Shaw's effect on her had become disastrous. Though she knew full well that he had no interest in philandering with *other* women, she still suspected, she 'knew', he was having an affair with Miss Jay, which was a great deal worse since it was carried out, presumably, in her own home. She 'knew' he had deliberately destroyed her career, and had no respect for her talent or her intellect. For most of the time she accepted these sights, whether true or imagined, just as she had accepted the affairs of John Osborne, suppressing her anger and rage behind an icy smile. Perhaps psychoanalysis would have helped to release this bottled-up resentment but she had dismissed the idea and so, in the same discussion, had Shaw. 'You're too intelligent for any bloody analyst I've ever met,' he told her, and added, 'So am I'.

Richard Zanuck and David Brown, riding high on the success of *The Sting*, had now lined up their next film. They had brought the film rights to *Jaws* by Peter Benchley on reading the galley proofs and had commissioned him to write a screenplay with the help of Carl Gottlieb. Their telegram to Shaw after the first preview of *The Sting* had not been the usual industrial grease: they had actually been extremely impressed with the way he had made Lonnegan into a substantial and interesting character rather than the standard 'heavy' portrayed in the script. And it was obvious to them both that *Jaws* contained a character which Shaw could equally make his own. In the middle of April they sent a copy of the book, which had immediately become a best-seller in hardback, to the Volnay and a promise of the first draft script as soon as it was complete. With hindsight it is difficult to imagine now, but Shaw, in common with Universal Pictures who had put up the money for the film, was very unsure about whether the book would work as a film. It was, after all, about a fish. After the success of *The Sting*, Shaw felt that it was more than likely that *The Taking of Pelham 1–2–3* would also be a successful film and, as he played the lead, albeit the lead villain, it might prove to be the breakthrough in his film career. *Jaws*, therefore, appeared to be a risk, especially as it was only the second feature film of its proposed director – 28-year-old Steven Spielberg – whose first film, *Sugerland Express* with Goldie Hawn (also produced by Zanuck and Brown) could not be described as a hit. (He had also directed a film for television, *Duel*, with Dennis Weaver, which had been the subject of critical acclaim and had something of a cult following.) Shaw, however, could see the potential of the part he was being offered. Quint, a small role overall, but crucially important in the story, could have been played by any number of American character actors. Shaw would give the part a different status, as he had Lonnegan in *The Sting*, turning a character role into a leading part, with those 'ice-cold eyes', and the mesmeric relationship he had been able to perfect with the lenses of a 35mm Panavision camera. Shaw expressed his interest and waited for the script.

While Shaw finished off the run in New York Miss Jay returned to Tourmakeady to help supervise the unloading of the three pantechnicons bringing the furniture from storage – plus a newly acquired sofa from Heal's – into Drimbawn. Not that the problems of the house were over.

Mary stayed in New York at the beginning of April rather than return to Ireland because she too had a new project – to learn to sing. Bert Knapp, Shaw's singing coach from *Elmer Gantry*, had suggested to Mary that she audition for Hal Prince, who was looking for an actress to play Glynis John's part, Desirée Armfeldt, in the London production of *A Little Night Music*. The idea, Bert had suggested, might act as an effective therapy. From that point of view it did not work. Mary was adroit at compartmentalising her private and professional lives, but at least in the short term it did give her an immediate aim, and she threw herself into it with a will. She had never attempted to sing before but after lessons from Bert her version of 'Send in the Clowns' was a masterful combination of power and vulnerability and the song, if not the part, had echoes of her own life that made her efforts the more poignant and moving. Knapp knew the Broadway scene better than anyone, and for her audition with Prince hired a Cadillac limousine to take her to the theatre. Wearing an artfully chosen red velvet dress, with her best fur coat worn over her shoulders, she walked on stage, the presentation of a star. Bert plucked the fur away and handed the annotated music to the surprised pianist, who had played 'Send in the Clowns' 40 times that day already. But Bert wanted it played *his* way, the way he had coached Mary, and a 50-dollar bill was clipped to the music. The artifice did not work. Mary was extremely nervous and only got through the song on the second attempt. She did not get the job but had made a lasting impression on Hal Prince, the *auteur* of Broadway.

As Mary prepared for her audition Shaw was now free from *The Dance of Death* and returned to Ireland on 6 May. Despite assurances from all concerned that Drimbawn would be habitable after almost three years of renovation, it was not. Feeling in an extravagant mood, buoyed by the offer from Zanuck and Brown, Shaw booked into Ashford Castle, a few miles from Tourmakeady, where an elaborate Victorian 'folly' had been built on the banks of Lough Corrib, a lough of 365 islands, one for each day of the year. Away from Mary and back in the quiet of the Irish countryside with Miss Jay, Shaw played golf on the hotel's own course and seemed, for once, genuinely relaxed. His drinking had not stopped but it became, for a short time, an enjoyment rather than a necessity.

Another offer awaited him on his return to Ireland. Lew Grade had formed an association with the Italian producer Carlo Ponti who was looking for roles for his wife Sophia Loren, an actress who had fallen out of favour with film producers since her hey-day in the '60s. In order to revive her sagging career he was quite happy to provide finance for films to the tune of several million dollars provided they guaranteed a role for Sophia. Lew Grade wanted to re-make *Brief Encounters*, the classic Trevor Howard-Celia Johnson weepie of 1946, and when Ponti suggested a co-production starring his wife, Grade agreed, though it is difficult to think of an actress less suited to the part. While he was casting the Trevor Howard part, a letter just arrived on Grade's desk about Shaw's availability, and surprisingly too perhaps, Grade – who had given Robert Shaw his first break in *The Buccaneers* – thought that Shaw would be excellent casting. Back in Ireland, Shaw was sent the script. He was enthralled by the idea. Almost everything he had been offered, or ever played had been a role full of violence or the threat of violence. He had played roles that required a certain sexuality, like *The Hireling* but in his entire career he had played only one love scene in the true sense (with Sally Kellerman in *The Daughter/Reflections of Fear*.) Shaw had always been offered character roles, villains or 'heavies'. In fact, he saw himself as a leading man, as James Bond not the blond killer, as Thomas More not Henry VIII. Of course this was an expression of his competitiveness as much as any artistic preference. Leading meant *leading*. Now he was being offered the chance to play a thoroughgoing romantic lead, and though Grade would not agree to more than $50,000, a considerable drop in salary which he would never have considered under normal circumstances, and would have to accept 'stepped' billing to Sophia Loren, he did not hesitate.

There was, however, one problem. The script for *Jaws* had arrived in Ireland and it completely fulfilled the promise of the book. The deal was for $100,000, lower than *The Taking of Pelham 1–2–3*, but for only 4 weeks' work. There was a difficulty over billing in relation to Roy Scheider (Richard Dreyfuss was then only on his second film and therefore not a problem) but it was solved in the same way it had been on *The Hireling* though the positions were reversed, Roy Scheider going on the left and Robert Shaw on the right and a line higher. Any reservations Shaw may have had disappeared, as always, once the money was on the table.

Lew Grade was undaunted. *Jaws* was due to start on 28 May 1974 and finish on 25 June. *Brief Encounter*, with Alan Bridges now set as its director, was scheduled to start on 8 July for a week's rehearsal with principal photography starting on 15 July. There was therefore no reason why Shaw could not do both films as long as Lew Grade was prepared to accept the proviso that Shaw could not enter into a contractual commitment on *Brief Encounter* until he got a 'stop-date' on *Jaws*. And he was.

An actor's role on a movie is always open-ended. A film role starts on a given day and is set for a number of weeks in the contract but may continue at the producer's discretion for as long as he is prepared to pay the actor 'overage' i.e. a weekly salary calculated by dividing his fee by the number of weeks specified in the original contract (in Shaw's case on *Jaws* $100,000 divided by 4 = £25,000 per week). It is rumoured that Robert Mitchum earned $2 million on 'overage' in the 8 months he waited on call in Ireland for the right wave to arrive to film the storm sequence in David Lean's *Ryan's Daughter*. Only the production manager gives the actor his formal 'stop date': from thence the film is no longer entitled to his services.

Shaw had been working continuously from 12 November 1973 until 5 May 1974. He was due to leave for *Jaws* on May 18 giving him only two weeks in Ireland. On 18 May he was needed to shoot one scene before his main part began on 28 May. It was Shaw's longest period of continuous employment. And it was to be much longer than he'd imagined.

While Shaw waited for his 'call' from Martha's Vineyard where *Jaws* was to be made, he called a site meeting at Drimbawn to discuss the problems that had still to be sorted out, and there were many, primarily that the well dug to provide water for the house didn't work. It was going to be necessary to dig another well or pipe water from a reservoir in the hills. All the toilets in the house were 'backed-up' and it had been discovered that the main drainage pipes had been laid the wrong way round. Shaw had ordered wooden toilet seats for every toilet in the house. He hated sitting down on cold plastic. None of these had yet been fitted. The American-style shower stall that Shaw wanted off the main bedroom, with shower jets from both sides, was another major headache: however they tried, the combined intelligence of architects, quantity surveyors and plumbers could not produce more than a concerted trickle from either of the expensive German shower heads.

It had been planned that Charles and Colin would spend their half-term in Ireland with Miss Jay. On 20 May the Birmingham pub bombings and the enormous public outrage that followed significantly raked up the tension between the English and the Irish. Shaw decided the plans should be changed and the children were sent to Miss Jay's parents instead, where the rift caused by her illegitimate child had healed sufficiently for her to be allowed to darken their door once more. The bombings brought home another lesson to Shaw, however. He was a rich and well-known Englishman living in the heart of Ireland in a very remote area in a very secluded house (when Irish builders finally permitted). It was not difficult to see him as a target. He had always been careful in what he said to the press about the IRA, so as not to attract undue attention, but many friends asked him if he thought he wasn't running a substantial risk. The truth was that since Shaw bought Drimbawn he had alone revitalised the economy of Tourmakeady. He would eventually employ two full-time gardeners, a cleaner and local building firms. His orders supported several small shopkeepers – especially liquor suppliers – and garages, and his custom helped local pubs. It is difficult to imagine that the local community would have allowed the IRA to do anything to kill the goose that was consistently laying golden eggs.

That is not to say Shaw didn't take the danger seriously. He locked up every night. He talked of getting a shot-gun licence (though never did). Many nights in the isolated house suspicious noises were investigated, especially if there were guests in the house who could be scared easily. In addition, when Binkie Drum, the surveyor, suggested delaying payment to the builders because of unfinished work Shaw did not think that was a good idea. He did not want to make any enemies in the area.

With the confirmation of *Jaws*, and money, at least in theory, to spend, Shaw's eyes turned to the car market again. A Range Rover seemed the logical choice for his country house, and for the first time he decided to buy a car in Ireland. Naturally he wanted white but the only colour available in the Republic was gold. The price of a Range Rover in England was then £2,000; in Ireland it was £3,800.

Because of the tax Shaw had ordered the Mercedes 450SL, for which he had hankered for so long, in England. But as River Enterprises was being wound up as part of the rationalisation of his tax structure, a new company had to be formed, Markgate Ltd, specifically for the purpose of owning the new Mercedes. Meantime the Mercedes 600 and the Ford station wagon were used with the hope that the Irish Customs and Excise would not come and investigate the fact that they carried English plates and were permanently in Ireland.

There were two further developments on Shaw's plays before he left for *Jaws*. Debbie Shaw, now a leading light of Sussex University Drama Society, wanted to know if her father would let her do *Cato Street* at Sussex in the autumn (where Penny was now at University too). He agreed happily but as the rights were owned by Thistlewood both Michael White and Vanessa Redgrave would have to be consulted. They consented, but the plan never materialised. On *The Man in the Glass Booth* there was news too. The Ely Landau Organisation had taken up their option on the play at the beginning of the year and were now setting up the production. As Shaw had director and title role approval, Henry Weinstein, the designated producer, rang to ask if he'd now accept Peter Finch, whom he had originally rejected, and Arthur Hiller as director. The script – by Edward Anhalt, the writer of the book on *Elmer Gantry* – was now ready and Weinstein would have it sent to Martha's Vineyard to await Shaw's arrival. Shaw agreed to both names. Two days later Weinstein called again. Would Shaw approve Maximilian Schell? Privately Shaw was bemused by the choice of Hiller, and Schell seemed to him an even stranger option but he did not feel strongly enough to disapprove.

It was to be an omen of things to come on *Jaws* that Shaw's original first day was postponed three times and it was 22 May before he finally got on a plane from Shannon to Boston (Aer Lingus flew more flights to Boston than to New York) where a light aircraft took him to Edgartown. A short car journey over the famous Chappaquiddick bridge – where Edward Kennedy's presidential aspirations found a watery grave – and he was at a traditional Cape Cod white clapboard house that had been hired for his use. Mary, packing up the flat in New York, joined him there. Miss Jay remained in Ireland dealing with the problems of the house.

The Man in the Glass Booth script awaited him. His reaction was instant and categorical. He hated it. He would fight it tooth and nail, he declared. The dialogue was appalling and the whole complex moral dilemma had been lost. But though Shaw had approval of the director and the actor he did not have approval of the script and, in effect, there was very little he could do about it. Weinstein agreed to go to Martha's Vineyard to discuss the matter, however, and try to work out an acceptable script. On 28 May he arrived and took the Shaws out to dinner promising by the end of the meal to take account of all Shaw's criticisms.

By 6 June *Jaws* was already 14 days behind schedule. The weather had been appalling, making it impossible to film at sea, and the mechanical shark refused to work. The production manager was fired on the principle of shooting the messenger bearing bad news. Unless the weather improved Shaw was not going to be able to get to Pinewood for 15 July and *Brief Encounter*. But he had another problem to worry about if the filming went over the allotted 4 weeks in his contract. He had been in the US since November 1973 apart from three weeks in Ireland in May. Anybody who spent more than 183 days in the US during any tax year could be deemed resident and therefore liable to US income tax. And this was not – as Shaw was currently enjoying in Ireland – on a remittance basis but on total worldwide income. So Shaw was faced with a familiar scenario, flying out of America to save 'tax days'.

As the looping on *The Taking of Pelham 1–2–3* required his attention, and there were several loops to do due to the difficulty of sound recording in the subway tunnels with extraneous noise from distant trains bouncing off the walls, he flew out to Toronto for a long weekend and waited there to be called back, completing the looping at the same time. In the following weeks he flew to Barbados, Bermuda and Montreal, only spending the minimum of time necessary in the US when he was called to film.

It was becoming increasingly obvious that he was not going to be able to do *Brief Encounter*. Cecil Clarke, the producer, who called every couple of days for updates on the situation, decided to rejig the schedule, mainly due to Lew Grade's insistence that if it was at all possible he wanted to keep Shaw. Instead of shooting the interiors in Pinewood in the first week they would do this at the end of filming thus not requiring their leading actor until 23 July. The latest script was sent out to Martha's Vineyard. On 14 June Shaw reported that it

looked as though they would send him out of the country for two
weeks to return on 1 July when hopefully the shark would work and
he could then finish by 22 July. He duly flew to Montreal but by 25
June there had been another development. American Equity had
called an actors' strike to begin on 30 June. Universal Pictures were
faced with a major decision to shut down production for the time
being or cancel the picture altogether. Steven Spielberg was called
back to Hollywood to meet Sydney Sheinburg, the Head of
Universal, who, so the story goes, kept him waiting for two hours,
and then asked him why he shouldn't cancel the picture. Spielberg
convinced him by the end of the meeting that it was worth continuing
even if the strike forced a postponement. (A Head of Studios would
never keep Spielberg waiting again!)

It didn't. The strike was called off after a ballot of members. Shaw
resumed work but not without further delays. Cecil Clark now
planned to do all the scenes at the railway station, which were at the
beginning of the schedule, with Sophia Loren on her own, filming the
'reverses' – the close-up reactions to what she was saying – when Shaw
arrived. On 9 July Zanuck told him Shaw might just make it by the
new start date of 29 July. But by 16 July the shark had broken down
again and it was clear Shaw was not destined to play his first romantic
lead. At the same time Roy Scheider became ill. *Brief Encounter* could
not wait any longer and Richard Burton was brought in to play the
part. Three weeks later an article appeared in *The Spectator* saying that
the reason Shaw was not doing *Brief Encounter* was that he and Sophia
Loren had not got on. The truth was that they had never met.

The problem on *Jaws* continued. By 17 July only 96 shots had been
filmed and another rumour that Universal was about to cancel the
picture was rife. The lease on the house in Martha's Vineyard was up
at the end of July and another house was taken until the end of August
doing something to allay the rumour. On 25 July the mechanical
shark, needed for filming Shaw's death, was put into the water – and
worked. But five days later the towing boat sunk, damaging the shark
in the process. It was the eleventh week of what was supposed to be a
four-week engagement. Shaw was earning $25,000 a week in overage.
It was not until August 5 that the shark was actually filmed in action
and there was, at last, only 3 weeks' work left to do.

While Mary had been at her husband's side in Martha's Vineyard,
Eric Shepherd from IFA in New York had called to say that Hal Prince
was going to do two plays, *Love for Love* and Pirandello's *The Rules of
the Game* in repertoire for the Phoenix Theatre Company starting in
Philadelphia before moving to New York. He had been very
interested in Mary Ure at her audition for *A Little Night Music*. The

situation was that Glynis Johns had first refusal on the parts but if she dropped out he would like Mary. The money was agreed at $1,250 a week plus $250 a week expenses with Mary Ure in the first position for billing with John McMartin in the second. Rehearsals for *Love for Love* would begin in New York on 16 September with the first performance in Philadelphia on 16 October. Rehearsals for the Pirandello would begin towards the end of November. The entire engagement would last until April 1975 with a short tour at the end of the New York run. Mary was keen to work again. After an anxious two-week wait Shepherd was told that Ms Johns had decided that she did not want to join the Phoenix Theatre Company so Mary was confirmed.

The problems at Drimbawn were rapidly turning into an Irish farce, with too many players and not enough doors. A quantity surveyor, Binkie Drum, had been brought in to try to sort out the problems as the Shaws' confidence in the architect was waning fast. Campbell Ingram, a retired surveyor, and Dick Gandy, another neighbour, were also on hand to help. Plumbers and electricians plied their trade trying to find the mystery 'noise' in the central heating system, establish a permanent rather than an intermittent water supply, replace the boiler and get the washing machines in the utility room to work – a necessity with nine children to cope with. In all the comings and goings the wardrobes had been damaged, the wooden toilet seats were still not fitted and some of the light fittings refused to work. As it was impossible for Shaw to get to Ireland to sort things out it was decided Mary should go before returning to New York to start on *Love for Love*. Her visit made little impact. The problems remained.

Once again Shaw's expenses were horrendous. His brother had called asking for new educational insurance policies, Jennifer wanted a holiday and the children were currently being flown in and out of America for school breaks. Donald Pleasence had called Shaw and asked him for a large loan which Shaw, with typical generosity, agreed to. Shaw's attempt to avoid residential qualification for income tax in the States had cost him a small fortune in hotel bills and first class air tickets. And what is more it had failed, so, to add to the Swiss banker, the English lawyer and accountant, the Irish lawyer and accountant, Shaw now had to hire an American lawyer – soon followed by an accountant – to file an American tax return, and hopefully persuade the I. R. S. (Internal Revenue Service) to treat him with leniency. The happy news from England was that the tax inspector dealing with his case had returned from holiday, no doubt refreshed, and was now getting ready with another round of questions. And finally the two gardeners who worked for Shaw at

Drimbawn, clearing the land and beginning work on his garden, wanted a rise in line with forestry workers in Ireland.

With the new Mercedes 450SL arriving in London the old Mercedes 600 was finally sold for £1,400. A few weeks later on the arrival of the Range Rover, the Ford station wagon was taken to England and sold for £100 which included its unique numberplate – URE 2. Curiously, with all his fascination for cars Shaw himself drove very little. He preferred Miss Jay to drive or anyone else who was available. It may have been a realisation that for most of the time his blood alcohol level would have made it unwise.

The new script of *The Man in the Glass Booth* arrived and Shaw was still unimpressed. He had made up his mind not to like it long before he received it and his cursory glances at the new version did nothing to change his opinion. He told Henry Weinstein he wanted his name removed from the credits, actually a fairly fruitless gesture as it would still be called *The Man in the Glass Booth*, and there was only one play of that name. Added to which he was not legally entitled, under the contract, so to do. After some heated discussion, when Shaw threatened he would go to the press over the matter, just as he'd threatened Olivier over *Cato Street*, Weinstein agreed, provided Shaw made no press statement on the matter. *The Man in the Glass Booth* was filmed with no reference to who its author might be.

On 9 September Shaw had still not finished on *Jaws*. They had filmed his death but were waiting for good weather on another shot and asked him whether, if they were to go into another week by just one day, he would accept $5,000 for the one day rather than the full $25,000 to which, under the strict provisions of the contract, he was entitled.

As his relationship with Zanuck and Brown was so good, (he was forever telling them that the picture would turn out right and be a hit, he agreed. On 11 September a fine day dawned and, by the end of it) he was officially released. A job that was supposed to last 4 weeks and earn him $100,000 had lasted 16½ weeks and earned him $322,000. The budget of the film had increased by 100%. It was a worthwhile investment.

Shaw returned to London as Mary flew to New York. He was anxious to see Dr Slattery. He had been experiencing acute stomach pains. He had visited an American doctor who had told him it was nothing serious but he was not so sure and Slattery booked him into a specialist. Shaw had been drinking all through the filming of *Jaws* and had been saved embarrassment on one or two occasions only by the fact he had so little to say by way of dialogue. When he had a big speech, like the character's introduction at the town meeting (the first shot in which he is seen) and the long speech about the sinking of the *USS Philadelphia*, the ship returning from taking the two atomic bombs to Hawaii – which he had written himself to give Quint some depth – he had been careful. His food intake was erratic too, alcohol frequently destroying appetite (in fact sclerosis of the liver, the alcoholic's complaint, is a form of malnutrition). The English doctor told him he did not have ulcers, which is what he suspected, and he had a large drink in celebration. The pains disappeared, though his hypochondria didn't.

Before he left London to return to Drimbawn, Shaw was invited to lunch by Harold Pinter at Odin's on 23 September. Pinter had a very definite agenda. Swearing Shaw to absolute secrecy and tentatively at first – bearing in mind the Shaws had known and liked his wife Vivien Merchant quite as long as they had him – told his friend that he had taken a lover. 'Is it someone I know?' Shaw asked. 'Antonia Fraser,' came the reply. With growing enthusiasm Pinter regaled him with stories of the Lady's virtues and how he was totally and completely smitten with her, 'like a 16-year old'. Shaw said nothing and listened. The following morning from Drimbawn, where he had spent his first night in the house over three years since he'd bought it, he was obviously bound by his vow of secrecy to call every friend he could lay his hands on and tell them the story. 'I could have caught flies with my mouth,' he said, bursting into helpless giggling until he managed to control himself enough to repeat, 'Antonia Fraser, it's Antonia Fraser.'

A new theme entered Shaw's life at this point. In *The Hiding Place* Connolly has a presentment of death which is very vividly written; in the *Omnibus* programme Shaw says casually during one of the interviews, 'I probably only have a few more years', and Philip Broadley speaks of him frequently saying that he would not see old age. Such dire prophecies are only remembered in the event that they are fulfilled and have little importance except to illustrate the point that Shaw was undoubtedly preoccupied with death in general, and as his work demonstrates, suicide in particular. When Henry King in September 1974 casually suggested to Shaw that he should make a will, the idea seized Shaw like a child suddenly given the gift of a fascinating new toy. It appealed to all his worst instincts. He could have arranged a meeting with Henry and told him what he wanted, had it signed privately and never mentioned again. But that was not to be his way. The Will became a living thing, an expandable instrument of torture, a sword of Damocles hanging over errant heads. It was to be the device by which the delight he took in creating confusion and conflict in life could be carried on after his death. But for the good sense of Miss Jay, it would have succeeded.

He told everyone how they were going to be treated in The Will. He solemnly told Charles Jansen, Miss Jay's son, that he was going to be included in The Will as though he was his own son, equal with his children, the 11-year old boy having little idea of what he was being told. He discussed everything about The Will with everybody, from the gardeners to his agents, all his lawyers and all his accountants and his children and mother and brother. He discussed what he was going to do and what he wasn't. He changed details over and over again. It was rare for a conversation with his agent or Henry King not to include some reference to The Will from that time on. There was no doubting his absolute fascination at what would happen to his wealth after his death, always assuming it had not all been spent.

Back at Drimbawn Shaw began showering his friends, whom he had not been able to entertain since 1969, with invitations to come and stay now that the house was, at least in theory, habitable. He ordered sets of boules from Harrods, outdoor driving mats for golf practice and a golf net, and he joined Westport Golf Club. At last Drimbawn could be turned into the centre for sports that Porch House had once been. At last, after three stateless years, Shaw had a home. And somewhere to write.

If the view from his attic study in Porch House had been beautiful over the fields of rural Buckinghamshire, the view from the small narrow study that had been built next to the sitting room at Drimbawn was breathtaking. Outside the window a stone terrace gave way to a lawn which sloped down alarmingly at first, and then more gently, to the artificial beach and the little wooden jetty at the edge of Lough Mask. Everywhere beyond was mountains, often shrouded in mist, or topped with cloud, the loch itself reflecting the sun with different iridescence according to the time of day. Since it rains in Ireland constantly, rainbows stretching across the water were a common sight, as was a lone man in a row boat fishing, or a flight of great crested grebes. The quality of the light was different too, unaffected by industrial pollution, a very clear but creamy light so often diffused by the soft rain of Ireland.

In the design that the Shaws had approved for the reconstruction of the house there were two big flaws. The first was that on one side of the house 'the ground' floor was below ground level, the top of the windows being the same height as the driveway. Allowing the architect to site the kitchen on this side of the house meant that the room most likely to be used by a large family, had the air of a cellar, so dark the overhead lights had to be on all the time, even on the brightest of summer days. The second was that Shaw's study, far from being isolated as it had been at Porch House, in Drimbawn was squeezed between the main sitting room and the dining room and was off the main entrance hall. It was not an ideal place in which to concentrate.

Shaw, sitting at the same drop-leaf desk he had used at Porch House now without the black leatherette swivel chair, had not written anything since the rewrites of *Cato Street* in 1971. He had thought of writing a book set in the Spanish Civil War after reading Ronald Fraser's account of the life of Manuel Cortes, *In Hiding*, published in 1972. The story of a man who, having fought on the Communist side in the Civil War had been forced to hide in his own house for 30 years, afraid that his neighbours would denounce him to the authorities, until the amnesty for civil war offences was announced in 1969, very much appealed to Shaw. As he was getting nowhere with *The Ice Floe*, he started reading every book he could lay his hands on about the Civil War. Knowing Spain as well as he did was an extra bonus. But the reading never crystallised into an idea. In a television interview his frustration was clear: 'I'm bored with writing novels. As I get older it's increasingly more tiring, more difficult, in fact it's depressing, I get despaired [his word]. Plays are short, they don't take so long, the rewards are much greater, much more fame, if you write one good play in your life time you can live on it in terms of temporary fame.'

Shaw and Miss Jay were alone in the house; Mary was in New York rehearsing with Hal Prince and due to open in Philadelphia on 16 October. One of the first guests was George Roy Hill whose visit coincided with Philip Broadley's. It had been some years since Broadley had seen Shaw and he was surprised at how much he was drinking. The kitchen at Drimbawn, though subterranean, was huge with a table at one end capable of sitting 30 people. It was quite a walk to get to the drinks at one end. After dinner Shaw asked Broadley to fill George Roy Hill's brandy glass; by the time Broadley had returned the bottle to the drinks cabinet the glass was empty again and Shaw chided him for not looking after his guests: 'Thought you were going to help me, boy.' The pantomime was repeated several times to everyone's delight. Every refill Broadley gave Hill was matched by one for Shaw's glass.

Donald Pleasence visited too with a young Israeli wife who Shaw had not met. Pleasance was the least *sportif* of Shaw's friends but was prepared to indulge Shaw's more scatological interests. Over dinner, where once again brandy had been liberally distributed, the discussion turned to whether it was possible to pee while having intercourse with a woman. Pleasence's wife stormed out in disgust while Shaw claimed, naturally, that it was a feat he had accomplished many times and Pleasence that it was a physical impossibility. Later in the evening Shaw reminded his friend about the money he'd loaned him: 'When do I get it back, boy, that's the point?'

A few days later, one of the children ran up from the playroom, which was sited directly under the sitting room, to ask Shaw why smoke was billowing from around the edges of the playroom ceiling. He dashed down into the playroom calling for Miss Jay and sure enough it was true. Most of the smoke was coming from a spot directly underneath the sitting room hearth where a large log fire had been burning every day. Rushing upstairs again, Shaw and Miss Jay poured buckets and bowls of water on to the fire, and called the fire brigade. Soon water was dripping on to the playroom floor. The fire was out before the fire brigade arrived. The Irish builders, instead of laying the new fireplace on steel girders had used wood. It had only taken a few weeks for the cement to crack and the wood supporting it to be exposed to more or less direct heat whenever the fire was lit. Had the Shaws left the fire at night unattended the consequences might have been much worse. As it was the whole fireplace had to be rebuilt and much of the playroom replastered. This time no manuscripts were lost.

The sports centre activities returned with the guests. If they played golf they were taken off to Westport Golf Club, if tennis then a court had been built for that purpose. There was a plan to build an indoor swimming pool and a squash court in one of the barns. But when there were no guests, and even sometimes when there were, the melancholia would set in and no amount of competition in sport could overcome it. The usual exterior problems were blamed, his inability to write, his wasting his talent in 'pieces of shit'. 'Boredom' became a favourite phrase in interviews of the period, boredom with writing, boredom with acting. On the evidence of his previous work, the constant image of suicide and death that pervaded it, particularly in *The Sun Doctor*, *The Joke* and *Card from Morocco*, it is not fanciful to believe that he was using writing to try to come to terms with the death of his father. The fact that he now found that, for whatever reason, this form of 'therapy' was no longer available to him may have explained some of the emotional difficulties he was experiencing. Broadley saw him sitting on the edge of his bed, fighting back his tears; he touched his shoulder but Shaw waved him away. Robert Shaw was not a happy man. None of the quite obvious delights of his wealth made any real impression: his love of sport which, in his 20s had been a passion, appeared now as a ritual comfort, the effects of which, like a drug, wore off all too quickly.

At the beginning of October Irving Kershner, the director of *The Luck of Ginger Coffey*, rang Shaw to say that he was associated with two Hollywood producers on a Frederich Dürrenmatt project. Shaw had to explain his hoot of derisive laughter when Kershner told him it

was *The Judge and his Hangman*. The rights had long since reverted to
Dürrenmatt who had taken it to another Swiss-German, Maximilian
Schell, to help him write a screenplay of his own novel. Schell had just
finished filming *The Man in the Glass Booth* and was now in Zurich
preparing to direct *Hangman*, now called *The End of the Game*, and had
already cast Jon Voight, Jacqueline Bisset and the American film
director Martin Ritt, who was going to play Barlach. Kershner had
been enlisted to call Shaw, no doubt – rather than going through more
formal channels – because though he was obvious casting for
Gasmann, whose sexuality and violence were combined with a
brooding presence throughout the film, the actual part was as small as
it had been in Shaw's own version. It was hoped Shaw's friendship
with Kershner might be used to persuade him.

The producers Arlene Sellers and Alex Winitsky arrived at the
Dorchester Hotel where they took up residence in the Oliver Messel
suite. They hired Ben Arbeid, the line producer of *The Hireling*,
whom Shaw liked and trusted and a deal was struck. The problem was
that the film's financing was extremely complicated. Twentieth
Century Fox had agreed to put up a third, with the Film Funding
Corporation, Robert Hagiag and Maximilian Schell himself provided
the rest – a total budget of $1.6 million. They could not afford Shaw's
asking price of $100,000 nor Jon Voight's $150,000 so what had been
agreed with Voight, and what they hoped Shaw would accept, was
half the normal fee, with the other half deferred until six months after
the first showing or one year after the first day of principal
photography whichever was the sooner. Shaw agreed. He also agreed
to a special credit 'With Robert Shaw as Gasmann' – what used to be
called on Music Hall posters 'Full Bottom'.

The decision followed what had settled into a pattern, the rush to
take work whenever it was offered. Shaw would hum and haw
endlessly about films that were mere possibilities, but when the
money was on the table, provided the billing was right, he would
usually accept anything. It is particularly difficult to understand why
he agreed to be in *The End of the Game*. The part was small and
undemanding, the sort of character role he had played many times, the
money was low and the billing poor. *The Taking of Pelham 1–2–3* was
about to be released, *The Sting* continued to make an impact and
though no one knew about *Jaws*, Shaw himself had felt it would be a
hit. He accepted *The End of the Game* rather as he had accepted *The
Break* after *The Sting*. It was ultimately perhaps a desire to do
something rather than nothing; to stop himself sitting round
Drimbawn thinking too much.

At the same time as negotiations for *The End of the Game* were concluded Menahem Golan called Shaw to offer him the lead in an Israeli picture he was directing called *Diamonds*. Golan, later to become the head of an enormous film empire (Cannon) which, still later, crashed, was at this point an Israeli director who had not made an international film. He had the script of what was called a 'caper' picture which he wanted to cast with international names in the hope of getting distribution beyond Israel. In Hollywood he had approached John Gaines about Shaw, and Gaines, after reading the script, had suggested Richard Roundtree (who had played the title role in *Shaft*) and Barbara Hersey, who were among his clients, for the other two lead roles. Currently, Golan was thinking of English actors, David Hemmings or Michael York, for the other male lead, though he was interested in Barbara Hersey.

The script was dreadful, the story of twin brothers –- both to be played by Shaw – and the obsession of one to outdo the other, who happens to be the designer of security systems. One of his systems protects the Israeli diamond exchange – the second biggest in the world next to Amsterdam. With an elaborate and totally ridiculous plan this brother breaks into the vaults, steals the diamonds and then forces his not unnaturally reluctant partners in crime to give them all back. Any excitement that might have been generated in the raid on the vault, which is the set piece of the film, is dissipated by the feeling of the total implausibility of the whole exercise. *Rififi* it was not. Neither had the writer made any attempt to establish a psychological truth between the two brothers, or any motivation as to why their relationship was so fraught, nor worked out how this unlikely affair would in any way help to resolve the relationship, a lack that effectively meant that the end of the film, with one Shaw smiling knowingly at his brother, has no *raison d'être*.

But the money was on the table, this time $150,000 with $1,000 a week in expenses and billing in the first position, and once again Shaw accepted the part – or parts. He extracted promises of script rewrites, as he had on *A Town Called Bastard* – the script whose awfulness best compares with *Diamonds* – but no end of changes would ever have solved the basic problems and he knew it. There were financial pressures, of course, and despite the overage on *Jaws* his financial position was, as ever, precarious. He certainly *felt* he needed money and told people so. And at least this role was a leading man, and even – to stretch a point, in that *Diamonds* contained an entirely gratuitous suggestion that the leading lady was the subject of a *ménage à trois* – a romantic leading man. But once again it is difficult to feel these factors actually decided him to accept the film. More likely it was terminal restlessness.

The feeling that it was a backward step was mitigated slightly by the reception of *The Taking of Pelham 1–2–3* when it opened in New York and subsequently in London. Though the film did good business it was by no means a hit. If there was an obvious fault in the film it was a lack of exposition of character and especially of Shaw's character, who is given no background, no interior monologue and no motivation other than to acquire money. The audience is never allowed to know him. The same is true of Matthau's role, though Matthau's bear-like persona carries with it more easily identifiable characteristics for an audience to grasp and sympathise with. Whatever the problems the critical response – which rated the film as a good thriller but no more and praised Shaw as effective but not more – gave the film no impetus. It was given a general release in the UK, but did not do well.

Interestingly enough, the film was particularly badly received in Ireland. There was, and is, a feeling that Ireland can somehow skip the 20th century. The Irish like to imagine that the problems of drugs and violence and sex heavily affecting the rest of the world, have been by-passed in their cultural idyll. The overt violence of *Pelham 1–2–3*, particularly the cold-blooded killing of one of the train passengers, was criticised by the *Irish Times*. Shaw had become Irish property, and his involvement in films which were met with blank disapproval was not appreciated.

The decision to accept *Diamonds* presented the usual tax problems for Shaw's advisers. Israel did not have a double taxation treaty with Ireland (an Irish company Moonstone Productions was now providing Shaw's services through another agreement with I. A. P. in Liechtenstein) which meant that any payments made would be subject to withholding tax. A double taxation treaty is an agreement between two countries that its citizens will not be taxed twice, once in each country; if no such agreement exists any payments made to an 'alien' are subject to a tax, usually 30%, which can then be set off against income tax in the alien's homeland. As Robert Shaw did not pay income tax in any homeland, the deduction represented a straight tax on his earnings. Obviously, in his world of tax avoidance, this was a problem.

Menachem Golan had the answer. His finance was from Switzerland so he could arrange for the money to be paid, not from Israel, where it would be subject to withholding tax, but from Switzerland where it would not. However he was not prepared to be so obliging for nothing. He required a discount on Shaw's fee. 10% was finally agreed, Shaw refusing 15% point blank. A start date of 12 January 1975 was set.

At the end of October Shaw flew to Zurich to begin work on *The*

End of the Game. Though he got on well with the veteran director Martin Ritt and was able to beat Jon Voight at table tennis ('it's not like a war with him'), he took an instant and abiding dislike to Maximilian Schell. Schell started on the wrong foot by defending the film version of *Glass Booth*, which did not endear him to Shaw, and as filming progressed it became obvious that the two men were diametrically opposed to their approach to life and work. Schell, according to Shaw, was a clock-watcher, a marionette, and a pocket Hitler. He had no sensitivity to actors' needs, a remark provoked when Schell criticised his performance in one scene. In a sequence where Shaw had to drive through the streets of Zurich, Schell, in the camera car had driven too fast and Shaw – never liking to drive anyway – was unable to keep up. This loss of face infuriated him more. 'He thinks he's so English,' he sneered.

On 13 November, in Philadelphia, Hal Prince fired Mary Ure from *Love for Love*. She had had no intimations of impending disaster. On 7 November she had called her agent to tell him how well it was going and how good Hal Prince had been. She was already looking at the part in the Pirandello which was due to start rehearsals once *Love for Love* had opened in New York. Hal Prince had given his reasons to the press. Ms Ure, he said was 'unable to communicate with the audience'. Mary was incensed. Clive Barnes who had travelled from New York to see the show, had given her a good notice and none of the other critics had raised so much as an eyebrow. It was outrageous. When the manager of the theatre made a statement saying that her 'psychiatric and neurotic disorder brought gloom into the company' she was determined to sue for defamation. Calling Shaw in Zurich he agreed that she should stay and fight it out.

The truth was, that Mary was ill. It was an illness that came and went, leaving her capable of performing as well as she had in front of the press on the first night in Philadelphia while, on the next evening, she would have the rest of the cast wondering whether she was going to make it to the end of the show. She had been separated from Robert since leaving Martha's Vineyard at the beginning of September and his absence had undoubtedly taken some pressure off her. She had, after all, got through long rehearsals and two weeks of performances. But whatever her illness was, if it was salt deficiency, in the end it was its unpredictability that made it difficult to cope with. Her mood changes could be dramatic and abrupt. In the restaurant of the Barclay Hotel in Philadelphia, having been charm itself to the restaurant 'Captain' at the end of the meal when her dinner guest asked for cheese and a triangle of Camembert wrapped in silver foil and almost frozen solid was presented, Mary insisted on calling the Captain to the table and

lambasting his pretentious pseudo-European restaurant. The astonishment of the Captain was only matched by that of the other diners in
the vast dining room, all of whom could hear Mary's theatrically
trained voice.

None of this negated the necessity to challenge Prince's pre-
emptory dismissal and lawyers' letters were exchanged, with Clive
Barnes volunteering to testify on Mary's behalf. On Broadway
rumours were spreading and sides were being taken. Aside from the
question of competence, there was also the financial question. Under
her contract Mary could have expected to earn $1,250 a week for 26
weeks. The Phoenix were offering no monetary compensation. Mary
stayed for four weeks to fight her corner. It was finally agreed that
there would be an arbitration of the whole matter in February. Mary
came home to Ireland.

While Shaw had been away, chaos, particularly in the plumbing
department, had resumed at Drimbawn. All the bathrooms were
flooded again and when Miss Jay was sent back from Zurich to
investigate she discovered that none of the list of remaining jobs had
been done. In the shower stall not only were the jets still not working
but tiles were beginning to peel off the wall and the whole lot would
have to be stripped and replaced. Binkie Drum advised, at long last,
that the builder should be dismissed from the contract and no response
made to his version of the final account. Shaw agreed now regardless
of local opinion. And he thought it should be the architect who would
bear the responsibility and be sent a stiff solicitor's letter. Worst of all
there was a proposal to build a filling-station adjacent to Shaw's land.
Shaw was anxious to try to stop it. The garage, he thought, would
greatly increase the flow of traffic on the main and tiny road to
Drimbawn, and the noise might drift the quarter-of-a-mile down to
the house.

Though the completion of *Jaws* had left him a good deal richer, its
potential impact on his career still remained to be seen. Until it opened
Shaw's forward progress appeared temporarily becalmed. The omens
were good, but producers apparently wanted hard evidence before
they would re-cast Shaw in the manner of a fully-fledged Hollywood
leading man. Rather than relax in the rural bliss of Drimbawn, for the
first time in three years a place he could call *home*, he chose instead to
rush into the first jobs that were offered regardless of their quality.
The drop-leaf desk in his study overlooking the glories of the lough
offered a rebuke perhaps, rather than an invitation.

Chapter Fourteen

Mary returned to Drimbawn from New York on 12 December and Shaw from Zurich on 13 December, filming having been slightly delayed. At Zurich airport he had bought an American newspaper which was predicting the outbreak of war in the Middle East. From Drimbawn he called Golan, who was optimistic. There will be no war, he told Shaw.

He had now confirmed the casting and had accepted John Gaines's suggestions of Richard Roundtree and Barbara Hersey (once in the '60s she had changed her name to Barbara Seagull for symbolic reasons), and they had delayed the start of filming, at Shaw's request, until 21 January to obviate the need to take his children to Israel for the school holidays.

Back in Ireland, offers for employment were coming in a dribble rather than a flood. Ben Arbeid had given Shaw the script of *Bleak House* which John Briley (later to win an Oscar for his screenplay of *Gandhi*) had adapted from the Dickens novel. Shaw thought it a marvellous piece of work and agreed immediately to play Tulkinghorn, whom he described as an 'elegant, tough lawyer'. But Arbeid had yet to raise the finance for the film. He was offered *Camelot* in Los Angeles which he turned down because he was not 'particularly attracted to the role' and Jack Levin offered him a role in *The Lonely Passion of Judith Hearne*, a Brian Friel screenplay originally written for Katherine Hepburn but which currently had Anne Bancroft attached. Once again Shaw liked the script, though it was certainly not a commercial film. And once again Levin was having trouble raising the finance. (The film was made 14 years later with Maggie Smith and Bob Hoskins – producers need persistence.)

The long saga of Shaw's ownership of the rights in *The Mayor of Casterbridge* finally ended when Martin Lisemore, a producer at the BBC approached Shaw to ask him if he would sell the rights for a television production. Shaw agreed. Alan Bates was cast in the title role. Of the £2,000 the BBC paid for the rights £1,000 had to go straight to the Hardy estate. It had not been a profitable investment.

An altogether different kind of offer came from Joe Cates, the producer of *Elmer Gantry*. Cates's main business had always been in producing television 'specials' for the American networks. He had been thinking about Shaw and had worked out that with all the re-runs of Shaw's films due on American television he would be very acceptable to the networks in drama specials. He proposed to form a company with Shaw specifically to use this kudos to attract network programme buyers to buy shows with Shaw attached. He had just made *The Cantonville Ghost* with David Niven in co-production with HTV in Wales, which, he said, illustrated the networks' desire for such material. He had a George MacDonald Fraser book in development and wanted to start with a Sherlock Holmes story followed by Alexander Dumas's *Prince of Outlaws*.

Cates was entertained royally at Drimbawn. Shaw had always liked him and accepted what he had to say. But there was a difficulty. In England actors moved between media freely but in America there was a distinct feeling that appearing as a 'star' on television hampered and impeded a film career. Television was for 'has beens' or 'might have beens'. The cross-over that occurs now in American television with actors like Ten Dansen, Shelley Long and Tom Selleck did not happen then. It was fair enough for an actor to get his training in television – Clint Eastwood, Robert Redford – but for a film star to chose to appear on network television was an admission that he had failed in films. Very many star actors in Hollywood were out of work and in financial problems but would not accept television roles for this reason. It was an attitude Shaw was well aware of. He saw the sense in what Cates was proposing and certainly did not give a categorical 'no'. But he wanted to stay in films.

None of these offers represented tangible work for tangible reward and financial worries were pressing in each day. The largest and latest expense was that Jennifer Shaw, still unmarried 13 years after her divorce from Robert Shaw, wanted a house in Jamaica. She had found one with a beautiful view of the Blue Mountains: £31,250. She also wanted a car, a Volvo: £2,300. Two acres of land had become available next to Drimbawn and was snapped up by Shaw at a doubtless inflated price: £750. The new Mercedes 450SL was delivered: £9,000. The Range Rover arrived: £3,890. He sent his mother money: £1,000. There was, whatever the result of the various disputes with builders at Drimbawn, at least £24,500 still to be paid, not including £6,000 for plumbers. The Irish accountants bill was £1,700 and the Irish solicitors wanted £1,350.

Worse than this, counsel who had been briefed to advise on the English tax case had delivered an opinion stating that the British Revenue might well come to the conclusion that the scheme set up by

Goddard's was 'an arrangement to avoid tax' and Shaw would therefore be liable to tax on his gross earnings up to 1970 when he moved abroad, in other words on his highest earning period. There was also the American tax situation caused by the overrun on *Jaws*. He was definitely liable to pay something, but no one was prepared to guess what. To make matters worse, Shaw had given an interview with the *Irish Times* stating that Ireland was now his home and he wanted to live and *die* there. The morning after this interview was published his Irish accountant, Liam Flynn, was on the phone with warnings of dire consequences. The Irish Revenue were already beginning to ask questions about Shaw's 'remittances' into Ireland. If Shaw was not only going to be resident in Ireland but *domiciled* there (for some reason the definition of domiciled for tax purposes is perversely the place in which you intend to die) then the remittance basis would not apply and they would treat Shaw as an Irish citizen for tax purposes liable to pay tax on his worldwide income – except the income from his writing which, ironically as it was now virtually nil, was tax-free.

Added to these worries was his insistence on buying the new Mercedes in England rather than Ireland. Ireland was about to clamp down on the use of foreign cars by residents, which was apparently a thriving pursuit in order to avoid the large import tax on cars. The Ford and the Mercedes 600 had attracted attention and suspicion quite correctly; now the arrival of the new English-registered Mercedes with English numberplates might well provoke a visit from the excise man. The tax on importing it into Ireland officially would have been nearly £7,000. Rather than pay this price Shaw behaved like a fugitive whenever any unexpected visitors knocked at the front door, refusing to answer and remaining hidden until they had gone.

Coming to England immediately after Christmas for wig. and costume fittings for *Diamonds*, Shaw arranged to take his mother to lunch at the Empress Restaurant in Berkeley Street. She had not seen her son for some time. The lunch was cordial but restrained. Any warmth that either party felt for the other was well disguised. Shaw returned to Ireland and was drunk for two days.

The children were used to seeing their father in the throes of drink. Often at Drimbawn he would collapse on the carpet in the hall, or on the stairs. They would step over him and largely ignore it. Occasionally they would make an effort to rouse him. 'Come on dad, please, get up dad, come on.' But they would soon give up again and go back to play. Only the older children appeared upset by it because they understood what was happening and could not understand why.

On 20 January 1975, having despatched the children from Shannon to their various schools, Shaw travelled to Jerusalem with Mary, Ian and Miss Jay. The next day he was working on a scene with Shelley Winters. The 'loops' necessary for *Jaws* had not been ready in time for Shaw to do them in London so they were flown out to a sound studio in Tel-Aviv and completed the following weekend. The opening of *Jaws*, it was assumed, would be the next major event in the Shaw calendar.

The day after the Shaws left Drimbawn, Dick Gandy, the neighbour left in charge of the house, reported that two ceilings in the corridors had fallen down and two more were bulging and about to fall. Major replastering was needed. Binkie Drum was called in and a debate ensued as to whether the plaster had been put on too thickly or the wrong mixture used. The result was the same. More builders traipsed through Drimbawn. The saga continued.

When Mary arrived back in London on the way to New York for the arbitration on *Love for Love* on 22 February there was an offer waiting for her. Don Taylor (the director of *The Winter's Tale* that Shaw had done in 1962) had written a television play for Christmas 1973, which had been described as a 'Marxist ghost story'. *The Exorcism* (not to be confused with the film *The Exorcist*) had enjoyed a critical success and he had been encouraged to turn it into a stage play which a little-known producer, Frederick Granville, had taken up. The play, a four-hander, was to be directed by Peter Coe, who offered Mary the part of Rachel. Mary liked the play and Coe, and, more to the point, had something to prove. By the time she got back from the arbitration she was committed: rehearsals beginning on 3 March and the play opening on 2 April with previews from 24 March. She would be paid £250 a week and 5% of the gross box office receipts, and be billed second to Honor Blackman whom Granville regarded as his biggest 'draw'. It would be almost exactly 14 years since Mary's last appearance on the London stage in *The Changeling*.

In Israel, Shaw was delighted with the news. He was finding life difficult enough without the added complication of Mary's problems. Another enforced moratorium of hostilities was welcome. He was regretting his decision to do *Diamonds*. As a 'piece of shit' it had less to recommend it than other examples of the genre he had undertaken and it required little or no effort on his part in terms of acting. The only compensation was his son Ian, in whom he took great delight, and Miss Jay, who had spent more time with him than Mary since the summer of 1974.

Shaw, for the first time in his life, was becoming acutely aware of his financial problems. When John French had taken over as his agent he had asked him to try and find out exactly what he was worth financially. He had no idea how much he had and where it was. No one had ever presented him with an accurate statement of his total financial position worldwide. The legendary Swiss discretion over banking matters seemed to extend to their own clients, judging from the reluctance with which statements of account were supplied.

Drimbawn, positioned where it was in the back of beyond, was not, and never would be, a good investment. The thousands of pounds Shaw had poured into it and was continuing to pour into it would never be recouped. Had he kept Porch House, by 1975 it would have been worth well over £250,000. Drimbawn would be lucky to fetch £100,000 assuming a buyer could be found. All in all, it was finally calculated that before the money from *Diamonds* was earned, Shaw had no more than £90,000 left. Adding *Diamonds* the total would be £140,000 (the dollar sterling rate then 2.5). It was not a lot to show for almost exactly 10 years – since *The Battle of the Bulge* – of relatively highly-paid films. Had most of the money not gone to Switzerland, whose currency had appreciated from eight francs to the pound to nearly three, the position would have been a great deal worse. As it was, he knew the whole amount could be wiped out by the British tax case and more besides.

Shaw actually began to think of economies. At the Sheraton in Tel-Aviv the suite had a kitchen and Shaw sent Miss Jay out to buy food rather than have it sent up, expensively, by room service. On one occasion Barbara Hersey's son Free (she had abandoned her own 'symbolic' name but not that of her son) was deposited in the suite to spend the day with Ian Shaw when she and Shaw were required to go out into the desert for one particular sequence. The two boys were left in charge of Ned Lynch, Shaw's faithful and no-nonsense stand-in. He prepared hamburgers and chips and tomato ketchup, which was consumed with relish. Free asked for more. There were no more hamburgers so Lynch offered sausages which the boy also devoured greedily. On returning Barbara asked Ned if her son had eaten anything as he usually has a very poor appetite. Ned was astonished as the boy had eaten everything in sight. Only when he told her precisely what the boy had eaten did it dawn on her that she had forgotten to tell Ned her son was a vegetarian.

In London rehearsals for *The Exorcism* began on schedule with Brian Blessed and Ronald Hines making up the cast. Mary, initially, was on good form. She had found a service apartment at 56 Curzon Street, which though small and overheated was handy for the Comedy Theatre where the play was due to open. Mary turned down an offer to play Roxeanne to Keith Michell's *Cyrano* at the Chichester Festival, but the proposal further boosted her confidence.

She bought a cassette recorder to help her learn her lines. She also gave an interview to *The Observer* which, the moment it was over, she declared 'terrible'. So it proved. The piece, with reference to her 'false eyelashes' and 'too vivid make-up' and 'dark glasses' gave the impression that Mary was vacuous in the extreme. Mary's mood was broken. She was late for rehearsals and had a stand-up fight with the producer over the Thea Porter dress she had 'no intention of wearing'. But on the first preview on 26 March she gave a better than competent performance, bringing a spark of life to a rather dull character.

On 24 March Miss Jay had arrived back from Israel. Originally it had been planned that she should have a week off to visit her parents before going to Drimbawn but the week had been cut to three days and on 26 March she departed for Ireland to have the children for the Easter holidays.

Shaw himself arrived back from Israel on Easter Monday 31 March with Colin, who had been flown out to Israel for a week before returning with his father. Shaw had taken at least two calls from anxious mutual friends asking him not to go to Curzon Street and stay with Mary. She was dreading his return, they told him, because all she wanted to do was concentrate on the play. The flat was too small for either of them to escape each other – there would be barely room for the luggage – and Colin would have to sleep on the couch as there was only one bedroom. But Shaw ignored the advice. His major concern now was economy. He wasn't going to spend a fortune at the Savoy when he could sleep with his wife. An argument ensued as soon as he walked through the door. Both took their usual sleeping pills to get to sleep with Shaw's supplies from Israel added to the quantities Mary had already got from Dr Slattery.

On Tuesday 1 April Mary struggled to rehearsals in the afternoon and Shaw called Harold Pinter to arrange dinner that evening. A cable arrived from Zanuck and Brown, the first news of *Jaws* since he'd completed the looping:

> We have now previewed *Jaws* twice in Dallas and once in Long Beach to enormous praise and excitement. Your predictions regarding this film seem likely to be fulfilled. You were always our most confident one. We thank you for your brilliant and mesmerising performance which will set audiences afire the world over. What a joy it has been for us to be associated with you on two films of which we are enormously proud.

Mary's performance that evening was shaky. She was clearly ill. When she got back to Curzon Street she took a sleeping pill and went straight to bed. Shaw arrived after his dinner with Pinter at 3.00 a.m. Though he knew the play opened to the press that night he woke her. He was drunk and she was drugged. Did she know, he told her, they were completely broke. She had organised a party after her first night with family and friends. Didn't she know they couldn't afford it?

Late that Wednesday morning, with Shaw off filming the first of two days locations in London on *Diamonds* to complete the film, Christine Ure, Mary's stepmother. came round to the flat and was distressed to find the state Mary was in. Since Shaw had woken her she had been awake for the rest of the night. She was crying and told her stepmother that Shaw had insisted she cancel her first night party for the family who, like Christine, had flown in from Scotland, and friends, but that she was not going to do it. Christine called Mary's agent to express her misgiving and to say perhaps it would be better to cancel the party and arrange something on the spot after the show. She also told him that she had no idea how Mary was going to get through the show that night.

At 2.00 p.m. Shaw arrived back from work and the argument resumed as if it had never stopped. Mary was not going to cancel her party, she told her husband: if it had been *his* first night the question would never have arisen. If it had been his first night, he replied, he'd have been earning a proper salary. Mary, called for rehearsal at 3.00 p.m. tried to get her make-up on and get dressed. At 2.30 p.m. John French arrived alarmed by what Christine Ure had told him. He was shocked at Mary's condition. She was trembling from head to toe and was having the greatest trouble getting into her clothes. Shaw sat impassively in an armchair, ignoring her screams of 'cunt' every time she passed him. As he got up from the chair she turned on him, caught him by the lapels of his jacket and screamed abuse at him so loud the words bounced off the walls of the room. How could he have done this to her? Drinking all night. Him and his fucking friend Pinter. Pinter knew. He knew. You selfish cunt, cunt, cunt. Her voice was hoarse with the effort. At 3.00 p.m. she slammed out of the flat refusing offers to help her get a cab.

The two men were left alone to talk. Shaw made no attempt to justify his position but, taking large glasses of whisky one after another and sitting on the edge of the double bed, said he had to get a divorce, that there was no way he could go on, that the marriage could not go on like this. It would be better for both of them. The lack of concern for his wife was palpable. It did not seem to occur to him that in four hours she was going to have to face an audience, with no sleep, in an emotional rage and with her voice damaged by effort. It was as if he had divorced her already, as if something else dominated his mind.

And something else did. The first thing he had done on arriving in England was to go and see Harold Pinter. The last time he had seen Pinter it was to be told he was having an affair with Antonia Fraser. Now the boot was on the other foot. He had to see Pinter to tell him that he was having an affair with Miss Jay, and what is more, that she was pregnant.

Fortunately Colin Shaw had been taken out by his step-grand-mother but was returned to the flat in time to help his father change into a suit and tie. Shaw's mind was still thinking of economies. He called John French at 6.00 p.m. to say he was going to send Charles, Ian, Elizabeth and Hannah to Irish school (but not Colin). Not only would the fees be cheaper but it would cut down on the cost of flying them in and out of Ireland every term and half-term. And, he wanted to know, had Donald Pleasence paid his loan back yet?

Mary Ure's first night performance could hardly be described as a triumph. Considering what she had been through that day it was remarkable that she managed to give a performance at all. But she did. There were one or two fluffs but apart from these she succeeded in reaching the end of the play without a major mishap, though her voice did show signs of giving out. The concentration required for this feat left little room for characterisation. As it was a new play her inadequacies were not as noticeable as they might have been in a classic. However, after such a long absence from the London stage, and considering her previous celebrity and the reviews she had received in the '50s, the critics were curious to see what had become of her.

For once Robert Shaw was not the centre of attention backstage. Mary's many friends flocked into her dressing room where she held court. Shaw roamed the corridors congratulating the other actors and chatting to the various people he knew. In her dressing room he gave a fair though brief performance as the proud husband. He'd go over to the restaurant and leave her to get ready, he told her. Taking Colin with him, he walked to Manzi's in Leicester Square where a table for 14 had been booked.

The management of the play had organised a first night party at Rags in Queen Street, but because Mary's family had come down from Scotland and she had other friends to entertain she had told Freddie Granville she would come on later, after her dinner. By the time Mary, leading her troupe across Leicester Square, got to the restaurant, Shaw was installed at the table behind a line of drinks. His mood had taken a distinct downward turn. He was certainly not prepared to play the role of proud husband again. He was morose and barely civil to Mary's friends and family. As Mary ordered drinks and

menus he told her he was tired and had to be up for a 5.00 a.m. call in
the morning – the last day's shooting on *Diamonds*. Mary ignored him
and tried to talk to her family about the play. Robert did not like to be
ignored. He decided he wanted to renew the arguments of the
previous night.

'Who's actually paying for all this?' he asked, making sure the whole
table could hear – not at all difficult for him.

'I am, Robert,' Mary replied smiling sweetly. 'From my own
personal money.'

'I didn't know you had any personal money.'

'I'm earning money from the play.'

It seemed there would be a rehearsal of everything that had gone
before, this time in front of Mary's family. The effort to maintain the
mask of affability, the delicate bone-china smile on her face, was
visible. But something stopped Shaw. Perhaps it was simply tiredness, he hadn't slept all night either and had been drinking Scotch
more or less continuously all day. He announced he was going back to
Curzon Street to sleep, to the obvious relief of many in the party, and
taking Colin with him, he got a cab back to the flat.

Mary's relief at avoiding another row was evident. She tried to
pretend there was nothing wrong, to play the perfect hostess, making
sure her guests had everything they wanted, telling stories that little
bit too loud, laughing at jokes that little bit too hard, and drinking a
great deal to drown her feelings, and, as her voice was still hoarse, to
ease her throat. Under the surface she was seething. Shaw had kept her
up all night, ruined her chance of giving a good performance on her
return to the West End; and now couldn't even be civil to her family.
Behind the face wreathed in smiles, behind the brittle laughter, was a
woman at the end of her emotional tether.

The dinner ended amicably enough and Mary's family, with the
exception of her brother Alan who lived in Guildford, were sent back
to their hotel. Mary, Noel Davies and her agent then got into a taxi to
go to the 'official' party at Rags. Mary had been used to the theatrical
parties of Binkie Beaumont (with whom she had been under
contract), sweeping into a crowded room to be greeted and fêted by all
and sundry, or swinging down to Harlem where the first night party
for *Look Back in Anger* on Broadway had been held. Spending five
minutes trying to convince the doorman, whose English was poor,
that she didn't need to be a member of the club but was an invited and
honoured guest was not what she had in mind. When finally she was
admitted, the room where the party was held was empty. No one, not
even the management of the play, remained.

For Mary it was the last straw. She railed at the man from Rags.

How could she be treated like this? She stood shaking, the white bone-china mask broken; she cried without tears. Noël Davies managed to calm her down by suggesting they go on somewhere, find a bottle of champagne and drink to the damnation of the management. But John French declined. He was going to New York the next day to try to sort out the position on *Love For Love*. He would call her in the morning he promised, before leaving for the airport, to discuss the reviews. Noël Davies and Mary walked off down Queen Street just around the corner from Mary's flat.

By the time they got into Curzon Street Mary's desire to 'go on' had evaporated. Noël walked her to her door and got her into the lift. She had had more than enough to drink.

Shaw was asleep when Mary burst in. He had taken a sleeping pill. Colin was asleep beside him on the double-bed. Mary literally dragged him into the living room. She hit him, screamed at him that he had humiliated her in front of her family, that they had come all the way down from Scotland to see her and he couldn't even spend 10 minutes being polite to them. She was screaming at the top of her voice again, her whole body trembling – the word 'cunt' becoming a sound with no meaning endlessly repeated like the cry of a wounded animal. Shaw hit her across the face. She slumped on to the sofa still trembling. But she said nothing. She watched him as he got her a glass of water and a bottle of sleeping pills. He put them on the table beside her. She took two pills, tucked her legs up on the sofa and rested her head on a cushion. Shaw went back to the bedroom.

In fact Shaw's call was not 5.00 a.m. that morning but 9.30 a.m. so when John French called at 9.00 he was surprised when Shaw answered the phone. But Shaw wanted to talk. He described what had happened when Mary got home. He was nervous and worried. 'I hit her,' he confessed. 'I had to. She was going mad.' Where was she now? Shaw put the phone down and went into the living room. After a moment he was back, 'She's asleep,' he said 'and she's been sick.'

At that moment the film car arrived to pick Shaw up for the morning shoot. He had to go. French said he would ring again from the airport. Considering what had happened, the reviews for Mary, though not for the play, were remarkably good. Shaw left the apartment leaving Colin, whose sleep had also been interrupted, to look after his mother. Colin was 13 years old.

As it happened Shaw's next shot for *Diamonds* was around the corner in Bond Street. The shot was relatively straight-forward and Shaw would be back in the flat by 11.00 a.m. while the next and final shot was set up for the afternoon.

Ringing again from the airport, the newspaper reviews in his hands,

French this time got Colin on the phone. He would go and see if his mother was awake yet. Coming back to the phone he said she was still sleeping. Zsuzsi Roboz called too. Once again Colin went into the living room. Once again, he told Roboz, his mother was asleep. His mother was dead.

When Shaw got back to the apartment he was met at the front door by his son. Colin was really worried about his mother. She had not moved and he couldn't wake her by shouting or shaking her. He'd closed her eyes too. 'And she's been sick Dad.' Shaw went into the living room and knew at once that Mary was dead. She had not moved from the position he had found her in earlier that morning. She was white and cold. Her head rested in a pool of dried vomit. He hurried Colin out of the room and called the police. What he had so accurately predicted the day before had occurred: his marriage was over.

The police arrived quickly. Shaw called his solicitor. He called his agent's secretary knowing his agent was already on a plane. He called the film production office. The latter was frantic. They had scheduled Shaw's last shot for that afternoon after which this film was finished. Now, how could they ask a man who had just lost his wife to work in two hours? They needn't have worried. Shaw went to work at 3.30 p.m. as scheduled. The shooting lasted an hour.

There would, of course, have to be a post-mortem and an inquest. For the time being the flat would have to be sealed. Annie Hester, John French's secretary, booked Shaw into the Savoy and fielded the telephone calls from the press. Shaw could go there as soon as he'd finished filming. She gave them a list of people who could be put through and arranged that everyone else should be told that 'we have no one of that name registered with us.' Shaw also asked Annie to do one other thing for him. Would she call Miss Jay in Ireland and tell her the news? It was an astonishing request to make of someone who was, apart from perfunctory telephone calls, a perfect stranger.

The press circus begun rapidly. Mary's death was big news. ('ACTRESS'S DEATH CASTS BIG SHADOW'). The fascination that the tabloids had displayed during Mary's marriage to John Osborne, and the subsequent divorce, was quickly revived. The fact that the play she was appearing in was called *The Exorcism* and that she died after the first night provided other angles: reporters were despatched to Freddie Granville who did nothing to point out that there was not the remotest connection between the plot of the play and the circumstances of Mary's death but took the opportunity to announce that he was going to have the theatre exorcised. This he thought, would make good copy.

And this was Shaw's main problem now – the press. He had called

Henry King and asked him how soon he would be allowed to go to
Ireland and did he think he need come back for the funeral? King was
shocked but of course he did not know of Miss Jay's pregnancy.
Presumably Shaw's rush to Ireland was motivated by the need to
discuss with her what they should do. The glare of publicity was
intense and a decision had to be made.

Shaw finished the filming on *Diamonds*. The crew around him
appeared to be more shocked than he was. He thanked them all
politely, shaking their hands and Ted Talmadge, who had driven
Robert and Mary for many years, drove him to the Savoy in the now
incongruous white Rolls Royce. Debbie arrived. Shaw ordered a
bottle of scotch and began calling friends on the phone. Later Harold
Pinter arrived with Antonia Fraser on his arm. Shaw had not met Lady
Antonia and was introduced while Pinter, who never drunk scotch,
ordered champagne from room service. The image of Harold Pinter
looking at Antonia Fraser like a love-sick schoolboy, Shaw was to tell
a friend the next day, was the first thing that had made him laugh all
day.

John French had heard the news on the way in from the airport in
New York and had turned around and flown back overnight. Ted
Talmadge had met him at the airport, the tabloid papers in the car
covered with headlines of Mary's death, and driven him to the Savoy.
Annie Hester had booked Shaw on the 11.20 a.m. flight to Shannon.

At the Savoy Shaw was awake and alert. Debbie had spent the night
with him and he seemed remarkably chipper. He dressed in a suit and
tie – unusually for him – and all three left for the airport again. There
were no reporters outside the Savoy but at the airport a vigilant
stringer – a reporter and cameraman are always on duty at the airport –
alerted the rest of the pack. Aer Lingus had no private lounge so Shaw
was left standing in the main concourse. A stranger came up to him
and asked him for his autograph, seemingly ignorant of the morning
news. Shaw gave it obligingly. Eventually British Airways were
persuaded to let him use their VIP suite.

Installed in the comparative privacy of the lounge, though by no
means on his own, Shaw decided he should call the other members of
the cast of the play. In an expansive mood and to the fascination of the
other occupants of the room he began a series of calls, his charm
oozing over the phone especially to Honor Blackman, as he received
their condolences and wished them luck for that night's performance.
He was persuaded not to call Mary's understudy, Margo Mayne.

By the time the flight was called the press corps were gathered
outside the VIP lounge entrance. To push through them to the gate
would have taken all Shaw's considerable rugby skills. But as the VIP

lounge had a back entrance straight on to the tarmac Shaw was spared the maul – rather to his chagrin – and taken to the plane on the back of an Aer Lingus luggage tractor. There were no new pictures of Shaw for next morning's editions.

Alan Ure, Mary's brother, who worked in London, took over the arrangements. The coroner told him that there could not be a funeral before the following Tuesday, 8 April, so he decided on 10 April at a crematorium in Guildford. Everyone in the family was keen to avoid the press horde so invitations were sent out with admonitions to secrecy. Alan was unsure as to whether to invite Osborne, whom he had met on more than one occasion. But Shaw told him he definitely should not be invited. Mary had left no will and all her money would go to Shaw.

The inquest was set for Tuesday 15 April. Dr Slattery was worried. The police had taken away 13 bottles of pills from the flat in Curzon Street; five were bottles of aspirin and paracetamol, the rest barbiturates prescribed by Dr Slattery.

John French was also worried. Shaw had told him on the phone that he had hit Mary before getting her the sleeping-pills. If that blow proved to be a factor in her death it would create a whole new set of problems. Communicating his concern to Henry King the two decided it would be wise to have Counsel present at the inquest.

On 10 April an Atzec two-engined aircraft landed at Blackbush, the nearest airfield to the crematorium near Guildford. Shaw and Miss Jay were met by John French and Ted Talmadge. All the arrangements were made. Ricardo Perez, the Shaws' driver from Madrid had flown in, Mary's family had arrived from Scotland, and friends had gathered, Harold Pinter and his wife Vivien Merchant among them. To fortify himself for the flight Shaw had had several drinks. In the car John French asked him what he had prepared to say or read, as it would undoubtedly be expected that he say something. The idea had not occurred to him. Bearing in mind Mary's Quaker beliefs, French suggested that the Quaker prayer, which Mary often mentioned, would be appropriate. He had got a copy from Judi Dench, who had also attended the Quaker Mount School in York. Shaw read it through once. Asking for a pen he cut some lines. He made no other comment and the car fell to silence. Miss Jay looked tired and drawn. As the Rolls Royce drove through Surrey a car pulled out in front. It was the Ford station wagon sold six months earlier. As it seemed to lead the way the occupants of the Rolls gazed in disbelief at the number plate URE 2. After 15 minutes the Ford turned off.

At the funeral Shaw's ability to perform under the most difficult circumstances was yet again put to the test. His reading of the Quaker prayer left few dry eyes:

Go placidly amid the noise and haste, and remember what peace there may be in silence. As far as possible without surrender be on good terms with all persons. Speak truth quietly and clearly – and listen to others, even the dull and ignorant; they too have their story. Especially do not feign affection. Neither be cynical about love – for in the face of all avidity and disenchantment it is perennial as the grass. Take kindly the counsel of the years . . . Beyond a wholesome discipline, be gentle with yourself. You are a child of the universe, no less than the trees and the stars . . . Therefore be at peace with God, whatever you conceive Him to be, and whatever your labour and aspirations in the noisy confusion of life, keep peace with your soul.

Mary had written, in one of her poems:

The sweet oblivion of nothing.
Death before age
That is what I want

And that is what she had got.

The secrecy surrounding the funeral had been effective. Not one photographer was present. After the reception at Alan Ure's house Shaw went to Blackbush and the Atzec took him back to Ireland. Miss Jay went into London with Ted Talmadge and John French, who later that evening drove her up to stay with a cousin in Gerrard's Cross. It had been decided that there was no option but for her to have an abortion.

On Monday 14 April Shaw arrived on a scheduled flight from Ireland and was taken to the Savoy. Arriving in the suite at lunchtime he was, for the first time since Mary's death, quite alone. At Drimbawn he had been surrounded by children. There was a never-ending stream of telephone calls from friends and relatives. There was continual bustle and activity. Now there was nothing to distract him.

He had a lot to think about. Not only had he sanctioned an abortion for the first time in his life, which, with his unbounded desire for procreativity, bore heavily on his mind, but the events surrounding Mary's death and his degree of responsibility for what had happened were difficult to escape. He began to brood.

He ordered a bottle of whisky from room service. Deciding to have a nap he took a sleeping pill. After a while he woke up. The Savoy had, for once, been unable to give him a riverside suite and he was in rooms overlooking the main entrance to the hotel and the Strand, which were comparatively noisy. He took another sleeping pill. The bottle of whisky was three-quarters empty.

Arriving at 4.30 p.m. after a meeting with counsel about the inquest the next day, John French could get no reply from Shaw's suite, though he knew Shaw was in. Going up to the door he banged and shouted. Shaw finally opened the door. His skin was grey, his eyes completely bloodshot. In front of the sofa were the bottle of whisky and a sprawl of sleeping-pills. He had no idea how many he'd taken, and now all he wanted to do was sleep. He collapsed back on to the sofa. French hauled him to his feet and began walking him round the room knowing enough about narcotic poisoning to realise that he had to keep him awake. After an hour he took him into the bathroom and put him under the shower. He held him while he peed. And then they walked around the room again.

By ten o'clock Shaw was asleep in the bedroom while French sat in the next room. He spent most of the night at the Savoy, getting a taxi home in the early morning to change for the inquest. It was a mistake. By the time he got back at 8.00 a.m. on Tuesday 15 April, Shaw had started drinking again. The task of getting him sobered up in time for court at 11.30 a.m. seemed impossible. The effects of the pills and the alcohol left in his blood from the previous day's drinking, combined with the latest consignment to make it impossible for him to stand up, let alone dress.

Ned Lynch arrived. There was nothing to do but to try to get him dressed in one of the Huntsmen suits Ned had commissioned and stuff him with coffee and food. Like the worst imitation of a drunk by a bad comedy actor, Shaw staggered about the suite, making a pantomime of the simplest of tasks and roaring with laughter at his own efforts. Sitting at the table provided by room service still in his pyjamas, he tried to get forkfuls of scrambled egg into his mouth, though frequently he found they would not stay in and dribbled down his chin. It was at this precise moment that Henry King arrived with Counsel to discuss proceedings. Shaw made no attempt to greet them but concentrated on his eggs, lowering his mouth to within inches of the plate. It was suggested that their conference should be delayed until the journey to court in the car.

Shaw's remarkable constitution came to the rescue, however. Once Ned Lynch hauled him into his Huntsman suit, the expensively tailored clothes seemed to have a sobering effect. By the time he was helped into the waiting white Rolls Royce Shaw was relatively sober. By the time he pushed his way through the cameramen outside the court he appeared perfectly normal. In court the police reported on the state of the flat, the number of bottles of pills, the time they had been called to the 'incident'. The pathologist reported his findings. Death was caused by the toxic effect of a mixture of alcohol and barbiturates which had resulted in vomiting and asphyxiation. Noël Davies was called to testify to her drinking that evening. Shaw was not called. His Counsel did not speak.

The first editions of the two (then) London evening papers both carried the story and pictures of Shaw arriving at the court. By later editions and in the morning papers the next day the story had been relegated to a small column on an inside page. More important events had overtaken it: 15 April was Budget Day.

Back at the Savoy Dr Slattery was in a mood to celebrate. The coroner had offered no criticism. Shaw joined him.

The following day the management of the apartment block called to ask for it to be cleared out. John French volunteered for the gruesome task and arrived at the Savoy with a taxi literally full of suitcases from the apartment – all Mary's things and some of Robert's. Philip Broadley had come over to see his friend and both men watched in horror as Shaw pounced on Mary's new cassette recorder which still contained the tape she had made to help herself learn her lines. Shaw began to play the tape. The voice of Mary Ure, dead for two weeks, echoed around the suite. Shaw played the tape over and over again.

On the following day Shaw and Miss Jay went back to Ireland together. Eleven months later Miss Jay would be pregnant again.

Chapter Fifteen

The apparent effect of Mary's death on her husband was a sense of relief. As he had said on the day of her death the marriage would have to end. But he was not to get off that lightly. Shaw was by nature a brooder. All his life he had brooded on the death of his father; now he had another death, far more real, close at hand, and in which he shared an actual, rather than imagined, responsibility. In a very real sense if Shaw wanted to blame himself for Mary's death, in the watches of the night when he hadn't taken enough sleeping-pills to knock himself unconscious, he could do so with a good deal of justification. The fact that it had conveniently solved a number of problems in his life made the associated guilt that much stronger.

The problem it had not solved was finance, which remained precarious. There was an urgent need for Shaw to do another film. During the past weeks he had been sent two scripts but neither were fully financed. Peter Snell was trying to set up *William the Conqueror* with Charlton Heston but when Shaw read the script his preference was for the part of Harold not William. However, he told Snell he would do the film if the money were found. The second script *Three Men Went to War*, written by David Newman (who co-wrote *Bonnie and Clyde*) and to be directed by John Sturgis, he found violent and unconvincing. Ben Arbeid had also called to say that he now had half the financing on *Bleak House* and offered Shaw the part of Grimes in *The Water Babies* which Shaw turned down as it was a part distinctly inferior to that of the other (animated) characters.

But a script had arrived which was more interesting. Dick Lester was to direct Sean Connery and Audrey Hepburn in a screenplay by William Goldman for Columbia Pictures, *The Death of Robin Hood* (which rapidly became *Robin and Marian*). Though it was not a prime example of Goldman's work (he wrote *Butch Cassidy and the Sundance Kid*, for example) it was at least an attractive proposition and, of course, the money was on the table: $100,000 to be precise for three weeks' work. Shaw had once said that he would never play the Sheriff of Nottingham; it was the sort of character part he despised. With nothing else on offer, and with Goldman's script giving the Sheriff some of the better scenes in the film, he changed his mind. But he was insistent the billing reflected the status of the part in the script, i.e. a leading role. If that were not the case he would not do the film no matter how much he needed the money. The first proposal Shaw rejected:

SEAN CONNERY

AUDREY HEPBURN

ROBERT SHAW

The second was better:

SEAN CONNERY

ROBERT SHAW

AUDREY HEPBURN

but the producers were not at all sure that Ms Hepburn would agree. She didn't.

Shaw flew to Munich, while the producers came up with a new formula, taking Miss Jay with him in first class, to do the looping of *The End of the Game*. Meantime a row had blown up on *Diamonds*. Shaw had paid for the wigs on *Diamonds* personally, since Stanley Hall, the owner of Wig Creations and probably the best maker of wigs in the industry, did not know Menachem Golan's company and would not give it credit. Shaw was due to be reimbursed for this amount. Golan, who let Shaw keep all the suits and clothes from the film, said that he had Shaw's agreement that this was a *quid pro quo* in exchange for the money due on the wigs. Shaw insisted it was no such thing. He wanted the £266. Golan, not without demur, finally gave it to him. It was uncharacteristic of Shaw. Golan never offered him another role.

The next proposal from *Robin and Marian* was:

SEAN
CONNERY

AUDREY   ROBERT
HEPBURN   SHAW

Shaw still wanted 'the ladder' (the second proposal) but agreed to look at the latest version on a mock-up of a poster. Holding a meeting at the Shelbourne Hotel in Dublin in relation to the outstanding matters on

Drimbawn, Shaw showed the poster to the assembled accountants, surveyors and lawyers. As they all agreed it was proper he accepted the film.

John Gaines had called from Los Angeles to tell Shaw *Jaws* was set to open on 17 June 1975. But Gaines had an ulterior motive for the call. He had been agitating for Shaw to leave Milton Goldman in New York, and now, with *Jaws* and Shaw poised on the brink of success, he thought the moment right to bring matters to a head. It was, he contended, anomalous for Shaw to be represented by one company in the States for films and another for the theatre. He would certainly expect to represent Shaw for West Coast theatre and APA had an agent who could do the job in New York. On the other hand there was no doubt that Milton was the most influential and likable agent on Broadway. In May, Gaines pushed the issue. Shaw liked creating dissent but he was bad at facing it himself. Had he told Gaines he was going to keep Milton that would be the end of it. Gaines was not going to turn round and tell him he was no longer prepared to represent him under such terms, not with what the whole of Hollywood were currently saying about *Jaws*. But Shaw acquiesced. Milton Goldman was abandoned.

Shaw's inability to say 'no' even extended to Tourmakeady. When John Walsh wanted his son to join him as a gardener at Drimbawn they had asked for him to earn the same as his father. Liam Flynn said this was patently ridiculous as the boy did not have his father's experience. But the Walshes went to see Shaw face to face. Having agreed wholeheartedly with Liam's view he now told the Walshes there had been a misunderstanding and of course Michael should get the same as his father. The same thing happened over a loan that Michael Walsh wanted for a car, an interest-free loan. Once again Liam Flynn demurred but this time when Michael Walsh asked for a personal interview it happened to coincide with a visit by his agent who had already been briefed by Liam. John French was given the job of telling Michael Walsh he could not have the loan. A few days later, however, Michael caught Shaw alone and the decision was reversed.

In any confrontation, so it seemed, Shaw, most unexpectedly for someone who was viewed by everyone who met him as a strong, forceful and unrelenting personality, would back down. With Elliot Kastner years before, with John Gaines, with John French when he asked him to sign an agency contract to combat Gaines' acquisitiveness, with the builders at Drimbawn and with his own staff, Shaw would always acquiesce in a face-to-face situation rather than risk a confrontation and argument. Confrontation, for him, was a spectator sport and not one he wished to play himself.

At the end of June, Jennifer Shaw called from Jamaica. Her new
Volvo had arrived in Kingston but £2984 in tax and duty was needed
to get it out of customs. Her step-father had had to arrange a loan to
prevent it being impounded for unpaid dues. In Jamaica at the time
prohibitive import duty was imposed on cars, of an engine size of
more than 1.5 litres, that were foreign and new. Jennifer's car qualified
on all three grounds. Naturally no one had bothered to check the
regulations *before* the car was ordered. And to make matters worse,
Jennifer complained, her alimony was continually late. Shaw's
brother also called to complain. Neither of the educational insurance
policy premiums had been paid (£400 and £900).

At the same time the attorney handling Mary's case against the
Phoenix Theatre Company called to say Hal Prince had offered $7,500
in settlement. Shaw accepted without demur.

Before setting out for America on a publicity tour for the opening of
Jaws, Shaw was offered a new John Williams musical – he had written
the music for *Jaws* and would later write the *Star Wars* themes – based
on the play *Becket*. The book, by Edward Anhalt, who though he had
written the book for *Elmer Gantry*, had more recently been responsible
for the despised version of *The Man in the Glass Booth*, was unlikely to
endear itself to Shaw. However, Shaw was clearly still a contender in
terms of Broadway musicals, largely due, no doubt, to Clive Barnes.

The difficulties of financing *The Lonely Passion of Judith Hearne* had
led to the replacement of Anne Bancroft with, yet again, Vanessa
Redgrave. But she had stated categorically to its producer that she
would only do the film if Robert Shaw played the male lead. The
attraction for her, it appeared, was Robert Shaw, not the script. Ted
Kotcheff (who had directed *Edna the Inebriate Woman* on television)
had now agreed to direct. There was naturally a billing problem and
Levin proposed:

ROBERT SHAW

VANESSA REDGRAVE

which seemed to satisfy all parties. The start date was to be 4 August
1975. The opportunities for Shaw to escape the tender clutches of
Vanessa Redgrave appeared to be narrowing but for various reasons
Levin could not as yet make the deal 'pay or play'. This was just as well
for an entirely different reason.

Shaw saw *Jaws* for the first time on 8 June in New York. He flew to
Philadelphia and did the *Mike Douglas Show* and then on to Los
Angeles for further interviews. He returned to Shannon on 14 June.
The word-of-mouth on *Jaws* prior to its opening was phenomenal.

Everyone who had seen the film came out raving about it, but though Universal opened it across America simultaneously, spending a huge amount of prints of the film and a large advertising budget, there were still residual doubts. Films had flopped before despite pre-opening hype. Once it did open however, the doubts vanished. It was the first picture to overtake *The Sound of Music* and *Gone with the Wind* in the Variety Top Grossers' Charts. In its first three days in America it took $7 million. Variety called it 'absolutely magnificent'. There were queues at every cinema. Within two weeks it was estimated that a third of the population of New York had seen it. Shark spotting became a new national craze. Several beaches across America reported panic as people fled from the water when someone thought they had spotted a fin. Within two months of its opening it had become the top grossing picture of all time. Even today, at the time of writing (1992), despite the ten times higher prices of cinema tickets, *Jaws* is still eighth top grossing picture at $129,800,000 (this is the figure for American earnings only not worldwide earnings).

The impact on Shaw's career was immediate. Sydney Sheinburg, the head of Universal Pictures, whose wife Lorraine Gray had been in *Jaws* with Shaw and greatly admired his work, decided to make an offer for a multi-picture deal. On 20 June, three days after *Jaws* opened, John Gaines called with an offer of two pictures at $250,000 with options for two further pictures at $300,000 and $350,000 and first position billing guaranteed. Shaw would not have script approval but the first script was being sent to him that day. The script, *The Scarlet Buccaneer* by Jeffrey Bloom, was to be directed by James Goldstone. *Jaws* was, at last, the breakthrough movie for Robert Shaw. There was a certain irony in the fact that it took him right back to playing a buccaneer.

The contract was complicated and the first script was poor. It was very much a standard pirate romp. For some years in Hollywood there had been a theory that the pirate movies would enjoy a resurgence of the success they had had in the '30s with Errol Flynn and Douglas Fairbanks. Now with the death of the Western there was a definite attempt to look for a winning 'genre' again. Whatever the limitations of this attempt, there was no question, from Shaw's point of view that it was the leading part, in every sense a romantic lead. On his way to Spain Shaw went to the Savoy to host a celebration dinner for his family before setting off to do *Robin and Marian*. From the Savoy he spoke to *The Scarlet Buccaneer* producer Jennings Lang, who told him they had hired James Earl Jones and Genevieve Bujold and would be sending a fencing master to Ireland as soon as he got back, and to John Gaines. Universal had added to the contract that there was a possibility of a sequel to *The Sting* for which his price would be $500,000. He would only have to commit to the movie if either Robert Redford or Paul Newman were involved.

Robin and Marian began shooting in Pamplona on schedule and Shaw joined the production on 23 June. It stayed on schedule. Shaw liked Dick Lester's no-nonsense rapid-shooting technique getting through more takes in a day than anyone Shaw had worked with Audrey Hepburn, who had come out of retirement for the picture, found it very difficult to cope, however. While she waited for second or third takes, to get her designer nun's habit perfectly displayed and her three-quarters profile lit, Lester had moved on to another set-up. There were no second takes for the sake of appearances.

There was another satisfaction for Shaw. His old friend and rival Sean Connery, who was playing the ageing Robin Hood, was having something of a dip in his career from the heady days of 1971 and record-breaking picture deals. He had made a series of unremarkable films that had found no popular appeal or critical acclaim and on the basis that a film star is only as good as his last film (usually films – in Connery's case *Zardoz, Ransom, The Wind and the Lion, The Man Who Would be King*) was no longer in any great demand.

The opinion of those in the business who had seen him as a very limited talent perfectly suited to Bond and little else appeared to be gaining credence again. Shaw, on the other hand, was in the ascendant. It looked as though he might even re-establish the position he had enjoyed relative to Sean when they had done his play *The Pets* for television in 1960. Shaw had suffered the humiliations since (as he saw them) stoically but that did not mean he had forgotten them. He was far more at ease with Sean now, expansive even, asking him questions about film deals, gross percentages and profits, even taking defeat on the golf course with equanimity.

While Shaw was in Spain, Alex Winitsky – the man who had set up *The End of the Game* – phoned to say he had a project which Sam Peckinpah had agreed to direct. It was a war story of a German soldier on the Russian front and his growing realisation of what the Nazi command was doing to Germany. Shaw had always been impressed with Peckinpah's work and was immediately interested in *Sergeant Steiner* (released as *Cross of Iron*). But Shaw's position had changed dramatically in the few weeks since the opening of *Jaws*. He could now be said to be 'bankable'. Having his name attached to a project (as was true of the other *Jaws* stars Scheider and Dreyfus) would attract finance. Winitsky did not have all the money for his film and Shaw's name attached to his package would make a great deal of difference. Naturally he was eager to cash in on their brief association. He would not be the only one.

Jack Levin was told that Shaw was no longer available for *The Lonely Passion of Judith Hearne* in August but if he could postpone Shaw would be happy to do it after *The Scarlet Buccaneer*. Levin could not as Redgrave had another commitment and, as Redgrave would not do it without Shaw, Levin had lost both his stars and was back to square one. The dalliance with Joe Cates was also ended. Television was definitely out.

Shaw finished on 14 July and hurried back to Ireland. The start date for *The Scarlet Buccaneer* was 14 September. Drimbawn remained a major problem and the situation with disputes over who was owed what and who should do remedial work was getting to the point of threats ('this is a strange country, and strange things can happen'). Fortunately for Shaw, there were more people in the village relying on the Golden Goose than had been upset by it and the threats never materalised. With his multi-picture contract money worries had vanished and Shaw responded with his usual extravagance. The plans for the swimming-pool and squash court did not seem so outlandish and one of the barns could be converted into an entirely separate guest-house. In addition the drive needed tarmac. The guest-house and the tarmac were sanctioned immediately at a cost of £23,000.

Shaw had announced to several newspapers on his arrival in Ireland that he was going to turn Drimbawn into a great garden, a garden he was going to open to the public and donate, eventually – though exactly when was not specified – to the nation, presumably the Irish nation. This idea had quickly succumbed, however, to a more menial desire to play golf in his own backyard. Instead of the tree planting and shrubbery collections, bulldozers were brought in to move earth and create tees from which he could drive to at least two or three greens. What was to have been a state garden became a six-hole golf course, the view down to the lough interrupted by the symmetrical flatness of a golf tee.

In Hollywood, as the saying goes, when you're hot you're hot. Shaw was hot, *Jaws* hot. His financial security was further enhanced by Paramount Pictures. Robert Evans, then head of Paramount, was planning a John Frankenheimer picture called *Black Sunday*. The lead in the film was an Israeli Mossad agent, a distinctly sour character, and Evans thought of Shaw after his portrayal of Quint in *Jaws*. A script was dispatched to Ireland while Shaw called Alan Bates to find out about Frankenheimer (Bates had done *The Fixer* with him). He thought Shaw would get on with him, after all they were both 'mad'. Frankenheimer, who had taken a year off from directing to go to France to learn to cook and whose caravan on location included a specially designed kitchen for him to prepare his own meals, was volatile but fair, Bates added.

Once again the script was very much a routine thriller, Palestinians using a brain-washed Vietnam veteran 'blimp' pilot (the airships that US TV sports coverage use for aerial shots of a game) to drop a bomb on the crowds at the Super Bowl. Naturally it is the Israeli agent who finally spots the bomb and foils the plot. But if Shaw had doubts about the script it was the money on offer that left his decision in no doubt – $500,000, double what he was getting for *The Scarlet Buccaneer* and the most he had ever been paid for a movie. The deal was confirmed at the end of August. Two months after the opening of *Jaws* the Jaws Effect was propelling Shaw to a new prominence with startling rapidity. Thirty-one days after its opening *Jaws* had taken $59 million. Shaw at least was going to earn more money then even he could spend.

On 12 September Shaw went to London staying at the Savoy and having dinner with Philip Broadley. Broadley was going through a bad patch and, he told his old friend, was flat broke. But he had a script that he thought Shaw would be interested in developing and which would provide a great role for him. He told Shaw the idea and it was greeted enthusiastically. Shaw would certainly buy it. 'We'll drink to it, boy'. It appeared Broadley's financial worries were over. In the morning Shaw told his agent that he thought he'd done something foolish last night. 'I think I did, had a bit to drink, you see, but I think I offered to buy that old bugger Broadley's script.' Broadley's agent was called. She had already been told of the deal by her client and that the price Shaw had agreed to pay was £10,000. This news dismayed Shaw. 'Can you get me out of it? Say I've no money in this country. Say it's a tax problem.' Broadley was told it was impossible for Shaw to buy his script as it would imperil his tax position. His oldest friend made no comment.

In Shaw's suite after dinner Broadley had skimmed through the script of *The Scarlet Buccaneer*. 'Why are you doing this shit?' he asked. 'For a million dollars, boy,' Shaw declared triumphantly. It was not true. But it was where Shaw had now placed the white tape he had to breast to cross the finishing line. The Million Dollar Movie was the trophy he now had to win.

Shaw arrived in Los Angeles by plane on 13 September, grandiose plans to sail through the Panama Canal having been abandoned in favour of confirming grandiose plans for the development of Drimbawn. On arrival Alex Winitsky arranged a meeting with Sam Peckinpah. Shaw was uncharacteristically nervous about the meeting but the two got on well over a bottle of scotch. Shaw was quite prepared to do *Sergeant Steiner* after *Black Sunday* but Winitsky would have to come up with a better offer than his current, pre-*Jaws* figure of $150,000. He suggested Winitsky gave the picture to Universal as a possibility for the second picture in his multi-picture deal. It was reminiscent of Elliot Kastner giving Fox *A Severed Head* seven years earlier and with the same result. Universal did not want the film.

But Shaw was having reservations about the script anyway and they were made worse by the discovery that the guaranteed deferment of $50,000 on *The End of the Game* had not been paid. The film was embroiled in a bitter dispute between various financing partners. Attempts to extract Shaw's deferment had failed and a letter to Alex Winitsky asking him for the money had brought a sharp response from his lawyers: 'Neither Alex Winitsky or Film Funding are parties to any agreement with your client.' At this point Shaw withdrew from *Sergeant Steiner* (James Coburn played the part eventually). *The End of the Game*, after much delay, was given a limited 'art house' release in America, was disliked by the few critics who saw it, and was never released in the UK. It has subsequently been seen on television.

Installed in a house on North Hillcrest Drive, Beverly Hills, Shaw went to work on the back lot at Universal Pictures. The multi-picture deal had caused a flurry of activity among the three sets of accountants and lawyers and tax schemes were being devised and revised by the moment. As usual the main problem with working in America was to avoid American withholding tax, which had been adequately dealt with in the past by employing Shaw from an Irish company, Moonstone Investments, which in turn was loaned his services from I.A.P. in Leichtenstein. However, in 1974, after *Jaws*, the American tax legislation had changed and in order for withholding tax to be avoided a US employment company had to be created. This would mean determining existing employment agreements and completely restructuring Shaw's tax arrangements.

Essentially a new scheme would only be worth instituting if Shaw was to become a US resident. John Gaines and Gerry Mehlmann, the American lawyer hired in 1974 to deal with the tax situation created at the time of *Jaws*, were keen that he should do just that. He was clearly going to be a major *American* star and a major client for both of them and dalliance with Europe would seem an unnecessary complication. In Gaines's case it would also be a means to get rid of John French whose role in Shaw's life he found particularly irksome. Shaw once again found it difficult to say 'no'. Despite all the schemes and dreams for Drimbawn, within weeks of his arrival in America he now found himself planning to be a resident in the US where, as Gaines and Mehlmann agreed, his career would undoubtedly lie.

On November 28 1975 a meeting was held in the North Hillcrest Drive House. John French flew in representing the Europeans: John Gaines, Gerald Mehlmann and Marvin Freedman, the American accountant, represented America. Shaw opened the meeting. He was heavily dissatisfied with the advice he was getting in Europe. For instance, The Will. The Will had been drawn up with John French and Henry King as executors. In it they could charge the estate fees for their services. He was not having that. The Will was to be re-drawn in America with Gerry Mehlmann as an executor and he was not going to charge for his services [or so he believed – it was not true]. And he had decided he was going to move to Los Angeles. It was the Americans who had recognised his talent and given him his chance, not the English. He owed England nothing. All the tax-planning should be based on that fact from now on, he wanted everyone to understand that. The Americans practically applauded Shaw's expression of confidence implicit in his statement.

The meeting reconvened in the afternoon. Shaw had been drinking in the morning and had more to drink over lunch. There was, however, something the Americans had not appreciated about Robert Shaw. He was not like other men. Robert Shaw did not pay tax. If Shaw was to become a US resident he, in common with the other citizens of that country would have to pay tax on his gross world earnings, a tax that at his level was currently 50%. There was no 'remittance basis' in America. If Shaw, as John French pointed out, wished to make his bed in the States, then he would have to lie in it at that cost. Was it true?, Shaw asked the Americans looking astonished. Of course, they responded. He would have to pay tax. Everyone had to pay tax. But apart from the tax River Enterprises had paid on his English films which had been off-set by company expenses (and the amounts for his novels and plays which had been small) Shaw had paid no tax to anyone since 1965. True, there was an outstanding tax case and the US would eventually claim $25,000 for the overrun days on *Jaws*, but generally speaking Shaw had lived tax-free, paying in Ireland only on the limited amounts he had 'remitted'.

The next day the meeting continued briefly. Shaw was now very drunk. He continued to insist his fortune was in America, but two weeks later the decision was reversed and Shaw dropped plans to buy a house in Los Angeles and become a US resident. An alternative way around US withholding tax was devised so that Shaw did not forego 30% of his fees.

Shaw's drunkenness at this meeting was symptomatic. The removal of financial problems had done nothing to ease his emotional problems, neither had the regularising of his relationship with Miss Jay. On 12 November she had written:

Mr Shaw is depressed and tired and thoroughly dispirited – so you know what that leads to. He seems happier this morning so perhaps he is pulling out of it.

He wasn't. The cause, or more accurately what he described as the cause, was the 'piece of shit' he was working on. Shaw was doing it for the money. *The Scarlet Buccaneer* contract was to be his escape route out of any further worries about money. Which made it no more palatable for him. The cycles of depression were getting longer, the 'highs' shorter. When he was not called in to work at the studio he would remain in his bedroom in underpants, socks and pyjamas watching sports programmes on television and drinking. He would change the socks and underpants compulsively three or four times a day.

He attended no more parties, did not go to restaurants or bars and lived a solitary life. The only people he would see were people at the studios. Norman Rossington, a friend who had worked with him on *Tiger at the Gate* and *The Changeling*, called at the house one day. Shaw refused to see him. 'Tell him I'm shooting.' He particularly wanted no reminders of the past.

His contempt for the quality of work he was doing was compounded by the knowledge and experience of the work he had done previously and therefore an understanding of his capabilities as an actor. After all, he had worked with some of the world's finest directors from Tyrone Guthrie and Glen Byam Shaw to Harold Pinter, Peter Hall, Fred Zinnemann, Lindsay Anderson, Tony Richardson and Joe Losey. The excitement he felt when the deals were being done, when the talk was of hundreds and thousands of dollars, when in two months deals for more than $1 million had been done, evaporated rapidly leaving him with the reality of running around on the Universal back lot trying to make a silly script credible.

But ultimately this was just an excuse. His unhappiness had become a part of his life, his depression, whatever the cause, an ingrained pattern. Three of the major causes had been removed in 1975: his marriage, money worries, and his inability to break through into the high earners in films. But the pattern remained and deepened. His affair with Miss Jay was an example of his complacency. He had established a relationship with her which did not require him to change. Another woman might have required him to do something about himself. Miss Jay, after 13 years of being his employee, would have found it impossible to assert a new agenda for his life. (Even after they were married she found it hard not to address him as *Mr* Shaw.) And he knew it. Shaw had no intention of straying outside his comfortable self-fulfilling and ultimately miserable psychological bind. Though three strands of the whip he used on himself had been removed there were still plenty left: his inability to write, his unresolved relationship with his father and to join them the spectre of Mary's death. He had spent no time grieving for Mary and it was catching up on him; the fact that the *Jaws* Effect had happened after her death made his sense of guilt that much worse.

Immediately *The Scarlet Buccaneer* finished, Shaw and some of the family flew to Miami, where the rest of the children were joining them for Christmas 1975, and Shaw began work with Martha Keller and Bruce Dern on *Black Sunday*. From London he heard he had won the Variety Club Award of Great Britain for Best Actor. Curiously it was the only award Shaw ever won for acting though he had been nominated for an Oscar (and he did win a prize at RADA). As he was unable to be present he sent John Mills a crate of champagne and asked him to pick it up for him and to read a telegram he was sending. The telegram read 'If Dickie why not Johnny?' (Richard Attenborough had just been knighted). At the televised awards lunch John Mills did not turn up, leaving two empty seats at the winner's table, perhaps too embarrassed by Shaw's cable. Mills never offered an explanation. Nor did he return the champagne.

The drinking was taking its toll on Shaw's ability to film now that he was leading the picture and required to do more than make up a few lines. Several days were lost or rescheduled. Days when Shaw was in any sense sober were becoming rare, the first drink of the morning topping up the previous day's blood-alcohol and making him instantly drunk. It was easier to film on him if he were sitting down, so scenes were restaged with hastily arranged chairs.

In February, Columbia, Shaw's most frequent employer, offered him the co-lead in Peter Benchley's second book *The Deep* which Peter Guber was producing with the English director Peter Yates on location in the British Virgin Islands and Bermuda. The deal, for $650,000 and 2½% of the gross over the first $15 million of receipts was, again, the most Shaw had ever received for a film and he accepted with no hesitation though the script of the film was another 'piece of shit' and even in commercial terms less satisfactory than *Black Sunday*. Shaw had accepted worse films for a great deal less money. There were no problems with billing either as the other lead was to be played by Nick Nolte, a new graduate to films from television's popular mini-series *Rich Man, Poor Man*. Television, as aforesaid, was not the same as film. Jacqueline Bisset was to play the almost purely decorative part of Nolte's girlfriend.

Under the deal with Universal the dates had to be cleared with them but as they appeared to have no idea what Shaw's second film under their contract would be, there was no hesitation in accepting the film that would make Shaw a millionaire in sterling as well as dollars. He was back in Los Angeles for studio work at the end of March to complete *Black Sunday*, and Columbia sent round a scuba diving expert to teach Shaw in the swimming-pool at the back of the house. The physical activity required broke the pattern of drinking for a while. Shaw splashed about happily learning the intricacies of scuba. But the interregnums did not last long and the scuba instructor was aware that they would have to be vary careful with Shaw on the shoot. Diving drunk is dangerous.

On 4 May 1976 Shaw returned to Drimbawn avoiding the 183 days residential qualification in the US. Miss Jay had visited an obstetrician and after amniocentesis was told she was going to have a healthy boy, whom Shaw promptly named Thomas (after his own father). The Irish countryside and the prospect of a new baby cheered Shaw up sufficiently for friends to be invited to Drimbawn once more. Shaw threw himself into plans for the house. The conversion of the barn into a guest-house had been completed on schedule and on budget and was a fine piece of building work. So now that Shaw had a reliable builder he could trust, the indoor swimming-pool and squash court could definitely go ahead. In America Shaw had been in a Jacuzzi for the first time and began investigations into how they could be imported to Ireland. On the family front, Dr Sandy Shaw proposed an agreement to cancel previous debts, scheduled new insurance policies at £600 a year and an endowment policy at £50 a month. Wendy, his sister, wanted to move house and have her brother's mortgage transferred to her new property but was not asking for any more money.

Shaw had agreed, as a gesture to Ireland, to open the Cork Film Festival, on the 4–5 June. He was in an expansive mood, tolerating approaches from the public, which he had come to dislike, and giving endless interviews on the subject of *Jaws*, which seemed to be the main topic of concern. He kissed the Blarney Stone while photographers scrambled for pictures. Driving back to Galway he conceived the rather strange idea that it would be nice to have a holiday home in the beautiful rolling hills of Kerry.

Film offers were now being received by the dozen. Of course, technically they were not offers, they were scripts from producers who wished to have Shaw's name attached to their projects in order to get it financed, or, at the very least, to bolster the package they already had with another name attractive to financiers ('Robert Shaw, you know, *Jaws*, top grosser of all time'). It was a new game for Shaw and not one he particularly enjoyed. The wheelers and dealers of this end of the industry, their briefcases bulging with scripts, their conversations dotted with dimunitive names for famed actors or directors, their minds filled with what name would deliver how much from which financier, were not the most attractive individuals in the business and would stop at nothing to get their script read by their target 'name' – and often wouldn't even bother themselves. Shaw's name was attached to dozens of scripts of which he had never heard.

Not that Stanley P. Walker fitted into the latter class, though he was keen to use Shaw's celebrity. Mr Walker had bought a terraced house in Leeds, which he intended to use as the centre of a multi-million dollar film industry to transform Leeds into 'the Hollywood of the North'. At Cannes in May he had hired Edward Dmytryk, the veteran director, who had inspected the terraced house in Leeds, advised him on his scripts and flown back to Hollywood as soon as the money ran out. In July Walker approached Shaw with two scripts. Christy Brown's *Down All the Days* (later *My Left Foot*) and Jack Higgins's *A Prayer for the Dying* (the latter being made with Bob Hoskins 11 years later just as Hoskins eventually played the part offered to Shaw in *The Lonely Passion of Judith Hearne*). The first project was little more than the novel typed out on plain paper – it was not, as advertised, a screenplay. But it was a fascinating piece of work and Shaw read it with enthusiasm. *A Prayer for the Dying* was less interesting, a violent thriller with IRA connections which Shaw felt would be too dangerous for him to get involved in. But misfortune must have befallen Mr Walker because after being told of Shaw's reaction to his scripts he was never heard from again.

Miss Jay and Shaw decided to get married in Bermuda, once filming had started on *The Deep*. It was in every sense a marriage of convenience. With Shaw's drinking getting increasingly out of control it was difficult for Miss Jay to feel any particular enthusiasm for becoming formally involved with a man she found it impossible to control. Pointing out the obvious benefits of his life, or the fact she was pregnant with his son, or his responsibility to nine other children (Charles Jansen had long since been instructed to call him 'dad'), apparently had no effect. Threatening to leave him would have done no good either, as he knew it was a threat it was impossible for her to carry out. Miss Jay was inextricably involved with Shaw, and with every aspect of his life. For the younger children she had been a surrogate mother, her son Charles treated like a brother. And now she was to have Shaw's own son. She simply had no choice, and Shaw knew it.

The marriage would change nothing. It would merely formalise her position and give her certain authority in relation to the outside world as Mrs Shaw. For Shaw it was the perfect solution: he would continue to receive everything Miss Jay had done for him and would, in return have to change not a thing. Her tearful appeals for him to 'stop killing' himself could go unheeded. She was a convenience not a threat. For Miss Jay the marriage was an insurance policy; at last in return for all the heartache and endless problems, she would have security and status.

The Will was changed again. Now Shaw was not going to be a US resident Gerry Mehlmann was no longer to be an executor and it was not to be probated in America. Henry King was brought back to draft yet another document, this time with Miss Jay and Dr Sandy Shaw as executors, with probate under English law.

On 11 July 1976 Shaw and Miss Jay flew to New York, connected with a flight to San Juan and then took a small plane to Beef Island. On 29 July they were married in Hamilton, Bermuda. Shaw had had three wives and married each in a different country.

The Deep was a long schedule, 20 weeks, and, with the amount of underwater work involved, arduous. Forty per cent of the film was shot underwater with Shaw's character, Treece, largely a reprise of Quint in *Jaws*. He had decided to use a Cornish accent for the part and managed to maintain it throughout the film. Shaw often used accents as his 'physical specific' for a character, the key to the way he would play it. Unfortunately he was not very good at sustaining them, nor did he bother with a dialogue coach. Often the accents were cobbled mixtures of trans-Atlantic American, Irish, as in *Jaws* and *The Sting*, with a veneer of something else – as in *Black Sunday*. Cornish was the other variant as in *The Scarlet Buccaneer* and *The Deep*. The problem was further complicated by the fact that he was an English actor working in America and would always have to decide whether he was going to play the part as an American, as in *Reflections of Fear*, or an Englishman, as in *The Taking of Pelham 1–2–3*. Sean Connery had very similar problems often with equally strange results.

Shaw got on well with Nick Nolte. The young actor was no threat to him. His sense of humour was like Shaw's. At the end of filming every day he would drop his trousers and announced 'Cock-tail time'. Shaw praised him lavishly telling the *New York Times* he was the most talented actor in America and adding perceptively:

> There is only one problem. He has it and I have it. It's a problem I had in my 30's and I had in my 40's. I didn't have it in my 20's because I couldn't afford it. It's certainly a problem I'm going to have in my 50's though. I drink too much. Will you tell me one great actor who doesn't drink?'

The Deep involved the largest underwater set ever built. With Shaw's unpredictability in terms of drink and the amount of diving required from the actors, it was soon realised that most of his contribution was going to have to be the work of a double inter-cut with close-ups from the underwater footage they did manage to achieve with him early on. It was too much of a risk on 140 foot dives with an inexperienced diver *and* a suspect blood-alcohol level.

While Shaw worked in Bermuda, life continued at Drimbawn. For some reason the Gandys had got into Shaw's bad books and were summarily dismissed from their position as principal keeper of the keys, and Campbell Ingram took over the post. The bulldozer working on the golf course cut the electricity supply to the house and a new trench for the power cable had to be dug. Stones in the lake were excavated to enable the use of a speed-boat and to make a breakwater. A powerful hi-fi – there were no neighbours to annoy – was brought in from England and special grass seed was ordered by Maurice Molly, a 'greens' expert who confidently predicted Shaw's greens would be playable by the spring. Golf clubs were ordered for Colin Shaw. Views also had to be canvassed as to where to send Charles Jansen to school now he was 13: Charterhouse, Epsom, Wellington and Sherbourne were considered but not Stowe, where Colin Shaw had been sent.

At the end of filming on *The Deep*, Shaw and Jay flew to New York where Jay gave birth to Thomas in December. Aside from the private medical facilities and the pioneering work done on ultra-sound, there was another reason for having the child in America. Shaw had been told that a child born in the States could sponsor other members of his family for citizenship. As Penny already wanted to make her home in Los Angeles, it seemed prudent to have an American citizen in the family.

Both *The Scarlet Buccaneer* (now called *The Swashbuckler*) and *Black Sunday* had opened in America and both had received poor notices and achieved little commercial impact. Judith Crist, a critic who had been as loyal in her support of Shaw in films as Harold Hobson had been in London theatre and Clive Barnes on Broadway, called *The Swashbuckler* a 'tacky pastepot job'. She was more enthusiastic about *Black Sunday* and was able to vent her usual admiration for Shaw, 'A sophistication beneath the ruthlessness, a pragmaticism to bolster the weariness, a dedication to withstand the sudden doubt about what 30 years of killing and murdering have achieved'. But though in general the notices for *Black Sunday* were better than for *The Swashbuckler*, that was not saying much. *Black Sunday* also had the misfortune to coincide with the release of a Charlton Heston film with virtually the same dénouement, *Four Minute Warning*. This time the luckless Super Bowl crowd were to be assailed by a mad gunman rather than a terrorist bomb. Both films were released within a month of each other. Both failed to find an audience.

Neither did *Robin and Marian*. Shaw's performance, in his last 'character' part, was witty and strong and much appreciated by the critics but Connery's inability to make Robin Hood's middle-aged dilemma real, or to establish a believable relationship with Hepburn, together with Dick Lester's quirky direction – always keen to pick up a visual gag often at the expense of consistency of emotion – made the picture peculiarly flat.

The *Jaws* Effect had elevated Shaw to a new and prominent status among the massed ranks of Hollywood stars. In that respect he had got exactly what he had wanted. But he had not been able to follow up its success with another. The matter was not entirely in his hands. It was a question of what he was offered; his only power in shaping his career was in what he accepted and what he rejected. Shaw did not attempt to use that power with any discernment. Though he was happy to read and consider the many interesting scripts he was offered outside the mainstream Hollywood production machine he never actually got round to doing any of them because, in the last analysis, his criteria for accepting a script was quite simple. It was not a question of being impressed by an interesting piece of writing, a good director, even a work which tackled important moral causes. Shaw had the opportunity to make films in all these areas. But by their nature these films could not provide him with the one criteria which governed his ultimate choice of what he did: money. Shaw was never able to resist the temptation to dash headlong into the next 'piece of shit' once a huge sum of money was on offer. In terms of fulfilling his talent for acting, Shaw's choice of material was appalling. It was a case of what might have been had he waited for better scripts. It is curious that 'what might have been' is a phrase that also aptly describes his application of his talent for writing, too.

Chapter Sixteen

Back at Drimbawn for Christmas with the new baby, however, it looked as though his next picture would break this dismal pattern. With Anne Bancroft cast as Lady Deadlock and Anthony Harvey set to direct (his picture *Dutchman* had proved an immense critical success), Ben Arbeid and Peter Shaw (no relation) had found a third financial partner to join Rank Films and Twentieth Century Fox to finance *Bleak House*. In order to accommodate Shaw's tax problems in England, Dickensian London was going to be reconstructed in nineteenth-century quarters of Cork.

There was also another project, far removed from the commercial work he so despised. The Mexican Government ran a huge film industry from studios in Mexico City, making 80 or 90 Spanish language films for the huge cinema audiences of South America. One of their producers, Bertha Navarro, had bought the rights to Malcolm Lowry's *Under the Volcano* which he had written in Cuernavaca in the shadow of, or more accurately, with a view of, Popocatepetl. It was an ambition of Ms Navarro's to film the book where it was written as a Mexican film with a Mexican crew, to be their first really international film, as opposed to the many American films shot in Mexico with American crews. She had approached various European actors – including Dirk Bogarde – before settling on Shaw.

Shaw knew the book and was fascinated by the idea of playing a drunk. Whether he should play it while he was in fact drunk, or he should play it sober, acting drunk, was a matter for eager debate. It was, he said, 'a very tough part'. It would challenge him in a way he had not been challenged as an actor in a film for a very long time. And he was prepared to put his money where his mouth was, he told Navarro, and take less than his current market price, as long as they were to meet all his expenses. The major problem Navarro had, however, was that she wanted the film to be directed by Paul le Duke, a young Mexican director whose previous experience included making excellent documentaries on the corruption of Mexican society (poor peasants deprived of their land by unscrupulous businessmen offering them money to pay for the funerals of their children, which they regarded as vital and were frequent in a country with 37% infant mortality; oil workers in the new oil industry in the Gulf of Mexico duped of their earnings by being plied with tequila and whores on pay-day) but did not include a feature film. This was a distinct financing problem.

Another attraction of the film for Shaw was that it had been scripted by Gabriel Garcia Marquez, whose novel *One Hundred Years of Solitude* was high on his list of great books. Though the screenplay was by no means perfect Shaw found the idea of working with Marquez fascinating. He speculated to a friend that meeting and talking with Marquez was exactly what he needed to get him back to writing. In fact Marquez (later to win a Nobel Prize) had given up the novel as an outlet for his talent and had decided he must use his skill to more political ends, faced with the turmoil besetting Mexico and the whole of South and Central America. He was now working as a journalist having recently returned from Cuba where he had described their involvement with the conflict in Angola.

It was planned that the film would be shot on location in and around Cuernavaca itself, largely untouched by the ravages of American tourism save for Coca-Cola advertisements and motor cars. Houses for Shaw to stay in were investigated including the one used later by the Shah of Iran on his flight into exile. The vast mansion was equipped with a huge swimming-pool and came with its own private zoo. Shaw opted for something a little less opulent. Paul le Duke arrived for a stay at Drimbawn and impressed Shaw. All was set but for the money. In fact it was a change of government policy that ended the project; the Mexican government had decided they were spending too much on the film industry, the money for the option on the book was not forthcoming and the project was cancelled. The book was later filmed by John Huston with Albert Finney in the lead.

Nor was *Bleak House* to be made. John Briley and Ben Arbeid had trooped over to Drimbawn for script discussions in January 1977 with a proposed start date of 1 March. By the end of the month the script changes had answered all Shaw's criticism in relation to the end of the film which he had thought, rightly, to be confused. But a week before the financiers were to commit and Shaw's employment would have become 'pay or play', Rank Films decided they were going to pull out of film production altogether and withdrew their backing. Neither of the other two partners was prepared to up their ante to make up the difference left by Rank, and though, for a moment it looked as if Peter Shaw would persuade Paramount to pick up the film with the substitution of Vanessa Redgrave for Anne Bancroft, it was not to be. John Briley's excellent screenplay was never made.

Sixteen

John Gaines in Hollywood was not at all happy with Shaw's dalliance with what he regarded as 'art house' movies. Shaw, he felt, should be going all out for commercial films and 'big bucks'. But as Gaines was not able to come up with any 'big bucks', hard as he might try, there was not much he could do about it, at least for the time being. Gaines's attitude was not only a question of what Shaw should or should not do to fit the image of a Hollywood star. He had another item on his private agenda. Having successfully got Shaw to abandon Milton Goldman he now wanted Shaw to do the same with John French. But the spring of 1977, with most of Shaw's interest concentrated in Europe, was not a good time to push the point. He would have to wait for his moment. Shaw's dalliance with 'art' continued.

The spring saw three distinguished directors make the long trek to Drimbawn. And it was a long trek. There were only two flights a day from London to Shannon and from Shannon it was a two-hour drive to Tourmakeady, often longer when visitors got lost on the tortuous Irish roads or confused by the twin language English/Gaelic signposts which were, at best, erratic. John Boorman, a director of the Irish film studios at Ardmore visited Shaw about his interest in joining the board of the studios which publicly – especially in the *Irish Times* – was great and privately was nil, and Roman Polanski came with a view to Shaw being in his French production *The Tenant*. Polanski and Shaw did not hit it off especially as the visit coincided with one of Shaw's bouts of uncontrollable drinking and Jay (for the sake of simplicity she will not be renamed Mrs Shaw) had to find a number of excuses for her husband's illness!

Michelangelo Antonioni's visit was more successful. The great 'maestro', as his producer Robert de Vecchi referred to him, arrived with a 25-page script of a movie that was, according to Shaw, exactly the same plot as the movie he had directed in America with Jack Nicholson, *Vanishing Point*, except that the hero's vanishing point was now on a large luxury motor-boat moored off Miami. Shaw was in better form for the maestro's visit, however, and had prepared a rabbit stew – one of his favourite dishes but on this occasion, he felt, rather under-flavoured. Sitting around the massive table in the cellar-like kitchen his guests were given generous portions. Shaw was unaware that Antonioni had a twitch. It started, when it started, in the eye but almost immediately worked its way down into his left cheek. From the cheek the muscles of the neck took up the spasm and communicated it on to the shoulder. The shoulder raised the arm and the hand inexorably. Shaw, having no idea what was going on, merely thought his visitor wanted the salt, and thrust it into Antonioni's outstretched and twitching hand.

253

Between these visits, Harold Pinter and Antonia Fraser arrived for their first trip to Ireland, Antonia Fraser waxing lyrical about being in the middle of Yeats country. They were given a guided tour of the estate and then, after dinner down in the kitchen retired to the sitting room where a huge log-fire burned. Lady Antonia got out her well-thumbed copy of Yeats and began to read aloud, so thrilled to have the opportunity to read Yeats in his own *mise en scène*. Robert Shaw was not so thrilled, however, made an excuse and left the room during *The Lake Isle of Innisfree*. Had Shaw been invited to read it might have been different.

It had been two years since Pinter had seen Shaw and he was shocked at the amount Shaw was drinking. On Saturday night they had a long discussion about life and booze. Pinter told him frankly that he was drinking too much. 'You drink too much too,' Shaw retorted. 'I drink for pleasure,' Pinter replied. A long argument ensued, the result of which was that Pinter got Shaw to swear that he would not have a drink at all on Sunday. 'That's fine with me, boy. We'll play tennis.' But by the time Pinter came down to the kitchen for breakfast Shaw was already sitting up at the kitchen table, quite drunk. Pinter was disgusted. Shaw, he said, had given him his word that he would not drink.

The Pinters (accurately Harold Pinter and Lady Antonia Fraser as they were not yet married) cut their visit short and left Drimbawn first thing Monday morning.

Between these various visits, Shaw's activities were largely conditioned by the amount of booze he consumed. That is not to say he did not drink every day but some days less than others, so he was able to play golf or walk to the nearest pub – no more than a wattle-and-daub barn half-a-mile down the road where three clods of peat burnt perpetually in a tiny grate and its smell pervaded everything and everybody. On a bad day he would not get dressed, staying in his pyjamas all day, listening to music blasting out on the stereo and picking the hard skin off his feet and eating it.

On the good days his appetite demanded more than dried skin. He had always been a voracious eater when the mood took him – which it did less and less because of the drink. His favourite food was anything with bones he could suck on, rabbit, hare and game. He loved to fish in the stewpot and suck every last piece of meat off every last bone. He had a taste for smoked salmon which was particularly good in Ireland, but liked it in slices, not wafer-thin, but thick, like a steak. A friend on a visit to Drimbawn was asked to bring a large supply of game, as he was driving over, and kippers which Shaw loved and had had shipped all over the world. Unfortunately the weather turned unseasonably hot and by the time the friend arrived the *poussin* he had brought as well as the game, had gone off and smelt high. He hadn't the heart to tell Shaw the truth after Shaw had greeted the high smell rapturously. 'That's how I like it, boy, well hung.' On nights when 'high' chicken was on the menu the family generally ate little.

Shaw was capable of showing great affection to his children and would play many a childish game when he was in the mood. The depressing sight of their father lying in a drunken heap at Drimbawn, unable to pull on his clothes or walk upstairs, was balanced by his ingenuous sense of fun. With Ian Shaw, for instance, over breakfast at the enormous kitchen table he had invented a game. Whenever he said 'Good morning, Ian', the young boy had to kiss him on the cheek. Ian would dutifully oblige and then resume his seat at the table, which because of its size took some time, as well as having to climb on to an adult-sized chair. As soon as Ian was seated again Shaw would repeat 'Good morning, Ian.' The child would look resigned, get down from his chair, and trudge heavy-footed to his father kissing him on the proffered cheek. As soon as Ian got back into his chair once again Shaw would repeat 'Good morning, Ian' and the whole performance would be renewed, except that Ian's look of resignation and exasperation would be ever more pronounced, his walk more heavy-footed, and his sigh of resignation more profound. Sometimes the game would last for half-an-hour, Shaw almost crying with delight at his son's pantomimed reactions.

Shaw made little attempt to write now, and occupied himself, when not drinking, like a cliché of an out-of-work actor, waiting for the phone to ring, sitting on the steps outside the French window of his study on fine days. At Tourmakeady all calls went through the local village switchboard so often the whole village would know if the Golden Goose was about to lay another egg. If a caller did not know the situation and behaved as though the phone system was normal, the village would quickly get to know all the financial details too. There were few people in Tourmakeady who did not have a pretty good idea of what Robert Shaw earned.

The phone system was even more peculiar at night which, of course, was the time calls came from America. In order to save power the Irish phone company reduced the voltage on telephone lines from 7.00 p.m. This had no effect on voice reproduction but meant that the bell on the phone merely tinkled. Unless somebody was standing right by the phone the chances of hearing an incoming call were virtually nil. To make matters worse the Tourmakeady exchange was shut down at night and services transferred to Westport. There were frequently callers begging and pleading with Irish operators to keep trying knowing, having spoken to Shaw moments earlier from the house, that he was definitely in. The Irish operators were not inclined to patience.

Every visitor was given a long list of items desperately needed from England. Pre-recorded cassettes for the new hi-fi were high on the list. Janis Joplin – who had committed suicide – Randy Newman, and Carly Simon, whom Shaw had met in Martha's Vineyard, were all requested. He had also heard the work of Janis Ian and was particularly fascinated by one of her songs 'Goodbye to Morning':

> And I think I found the answer
> where you left it on the shelf
> but it's too late to wonder
> if I left it there myself
> And the room begins to rock
> The walls begin to steam
> and the clock won't stop
> and I'm living in between
> So I wave goodbye to morning
> and stake my life on dreams.

All her cassettes were brought over to Drimbawn but none of her other songs held his interest like this one. She was, he maintained, singing about suicide.

Golf balls were another essential as Shaw was losing so many from his new tees and he ordered dozens of coloured Penfolds which he thought would be easier to find. He would pay the children for any ball they found but even their fervent efforts could not make up the deficit. The Phillips salesroom catalogue was also brought over as Drimbawn was quite sparsely furnished and Shaw had decided to buy antiques. In the playroom Shaw had bought a new Philips video recorder and tapes of the Five Nations Championships, recorded in England (only the Irish matches were shown on Irish television) were sent over to be watched over and over again. But the most frequent item requested from England was sleeping pills and Dr Slattery was bombarded with demands for prescriptions. Shaw had heard that a new pill call Dalmane was particularly strong and immediately ordered one hundred from Slattery who could be relied upon not to demure.

Shaw had had trouble sleeping since the middle '60's. Neither Mary nor Robert had slept without pills for years. But Shaw's lack of sleep was becoming chronic. Whatever pill he took it did not seem to matter, he still woke in the middle of the night, soaked in sweat from his nightmares. He dreamed of his father. He dreamed his father came into his room and woke him up and kissed him goodbye. He stood on a chair to see out of the high window in his room as his father walked down to a long beach out into the sea. He looked back to see his son at the window then walked out until the sea engulfed him. Some time later this dream became the story of his father's death. Shaw was afraid to sleep because he was afraid to dream. Time to go to bed was a time to panic. He searched for a pill that would bring him a night of oblivion and never found one.

Shaw pursued the idea of a holiday home in Kerry which he had conceived at the Cork Film Festival. He took Jay and Thomas to stay at the Tower Hotel, Glenbridge in Kerry, and driving around in the Mercedes 450 SL visited various sites including a beautiful position in Waterville Bay where a derelict school afforded a site for a new home. Returning to Drimbawn he asked Liam Flynn to make an offer on the property. But word had spread that the prospective buyer was Robert Shaw and the asking price had gone from £5,000 to £15,000. The other plots in the area had also magically increased in value since the green Mercedes was spotted nosing around. The idea was abandoned.

Ireland was a small country and Shaw's residency well known. Not only did people know what sort of car he drove, there were few in the country's telecommunications who did not know his home telephone number. It was quite sufficient, in most cases, to tell the Irish overseas operator that you wished to be connected with Robert Shaw to get straight through to Tourmakeady and hence to Drimbawn. One American woman who had conceived a passion for Shaw discovered this state of affairs and was put through to the house where Jay answered the phone. She rang off and called again and again until on the third attempt she got Shaw personally. She immediately launched into a long description of what she wanted to do to him sexually. A moment later her husband came on the line. He'd heard everything she'd told Shaw and he was prepared to pay her fare over. 'She's not going to give me any peace till she's fucked you, Robert,' he said. Shaw let Jay answer the phone for the next few weeks.

In July Shaw was offered the chance to play in a Pro-Am golf tournament organised by Sean Connery and Sir Iain Stewart, the man who ran the charity set up from the proceeds of his *Diamonds Are Forever* fee. It was a tournament to be televised by the BBC and held at Gleneagles. Shaw agreed to appear and planned to take Colin and Jay to the Orkneys after the match, the third wife he would have taken back to Stromness. But over the next weeks he agonised about the decision. He would love to be seen winning a round on television, but what if he lost? In August he cancelled telling the producer and Sean

Connery he had another commitment – he did not. He cancelled the trip to the Orkneys too.

In September 1977 Shaw flew to America for the opening of *The Deep*. Benchley's book had sold 200,000 copies in hardback and made $3 million in paperback. Riding on the success of *Jaws*, it was almost a sequel, a sequel without the shark. Columbia had made a massive attempt to launch the film. They did deals with Revlon cosmetics and Rolex watches and any other sort of commercial tie-up they could think of; The boat seen in the movie was paraded at the New York Boat Fair. Displays of cosmetics and watches with underwater gear accompanied the opening of the film in every major department store and shop across America. Shaw, Nolte and Jacqueline Bisset were prevailed upon to attend openings and talk shows. But it was to no avail. The publicity could not disguise the fact it was a poor script sloppily directed. Shaw himself had made some efforts to tighten the dialogue but the problem of the script was in the development of the story. In effect the climax of the film came in the middle, when the drugs are recovered from the sunken ship, and after this the end itself seems something of an anti-climax. The four films Shaw had made since *Jaws* had all flopped.

An issue arose on the *Mike Douglas Show*, however, that made the trip to America more than the usual round of interviews. A lady called Anita Bryant in California was trying to get that State to pass an ordinance banning homosexuals from teaching children. The first stage in this process had just been through the legislature and Mike Douglas had asked what Shaw thought, as something of a professional father. Shaw, quietly and with no bombast, told the audience that he had ten children and would have no hesitation whatsoever in having them taught by a man or a woman who happened to be homosexual. He had known and respected homosexuals all his life, they had produced great works of art, great films and great books and were kind and sensitive and, in his opinion ideally suited to dealing with young children. The idea that a homosexual would corrupt or deprave a child was simply nonsense: in some senses it was much more likely that heterosexuals would sexually corrupt children. It was an impassioned performance and letters of support and abuse poured in.

Shaw attend the Royal Première of *The Deep* in October at the Empire Leicester Square, at which Prince Charles was the main guest. In the receiving line for the first time Shaw stepped away from the neat rank of nervous participants to greet Larry Ellis, a photographer on the *Daily Express* whom Shaw had known since *A Man for all Seasons*. He chatted to him about the old days much to Ellis's embarrassment as the Prince approached getting closer to the empty place where Shaw should have been standing. Just in time he was persuaded to step back into the line. Later he declared the prince a delightful man and had told him he was welcome to come to Drimbawn whenever he was in Ireland. Earl Mountbatten, Charles's uncle, was murdered only a few miles from Shaw's home five years later.

The *Jaws* Effect had receded. John Gaines worked to come up with another commercial offer while John French was fielding the 'art house' pictures, or so it appeared. In 1976 Benny Fisz had enquired whether Shaw would like to play Guy Burgess in a picture he was making on the subject of *Philby* with Michael Caine in the leading role. Now in the summer of 1977 he sent Shaw the Arthur Hopcraft script with an offer to play Philby himself. Shaw was immediately fascinated and declared the script 'superb'. He sent for every book he could get on the subject. Benny could not make his offer 'pay or play' yet and could not offer Shaw more than $500,000 but, bearing in mind that some of the picture was to made in England where Shaw would have to pay tax, he was prepared to split the fee so half the money was for writing a – completely fictitious – screenplay. Eventually with much bargaining the fee was increased with Shaw to receive $500,000 for writing the 'screenplay' and $150,000 for acting. The $500,000 would attract no tax in Ireland as it was derived from writing, and writers lived tax-free.

The latter part of the offer was particularly attractive to Shaw as it would help to regularise his tax position – however untruthfully – in Ireland. The Irish Revenue, according to Liam Flynn his accountant, were out to 'get' Shaw. The series of interviews he had given suggesting that he was making his home in Ireland ('before I settled here in 1969,' 'my children will live in this house as long as I keep it. It is their home', and 'Ireland is my spiritual home') had not helped. If Ireland was his home then he would have to pay income tax there on his worldwide income. In order to prove it was not he bought a grave-site in Truro which, in the arcane world of tax law, was a way of signalling that he had no intention of *dying* in Ireland and was therefore not domiciled there. A large writing fee, albeit tax-free, would at least show Shaw was earning money in Ireland and not just there for tax avoidance. It would also mean he would have a huge sum of money available in Ireland, tax-free, to spend.

In August Shaw also had another offer that fascinated him. The producer of the BBC Shakespeare series called to ask him to play *King Lear*. They were gradually working through every Shakespeare play and at some point in 1978, at Shaw's discretion, would like him to do Lear. Though Shaw was clearly too young the power and presence he would have bought to the role would undoubtedly have made it a fascinating performance. He accepted at once though he knew financially the BBC would come nowhere near his film fees. He could not, however, commit to a date.

Shaw's concerns over money had disappeared but on 20 August his bank balances were to receive yet another infusion of funds, this time for doing nothing. The multi-picture deal with Universal had stated that his second picture for them would commence nine months after the end of the first. As no picture was planned, and there was nothing even remotely right for Shaw, Universal acknowledged their option on his services had lapsed and sent him a cheque for $250,000 as agreed. Universal seemed to have lost interest in making Robert Shaw a star, and, judging from the complete lack of concrete offers, since the end of filming on *The Deep*, so had everyone else.

In November 1976 Oliver Unger had approached John French to find out whether Shaw would be available for the supposed 'sequel' to *The Guns of Navarone*, another Alastair MacLean book featuring the same characters – *Force Ten from Navarone*. It had been intended to make the film in the spring of 1977. But difficulties over financing had delayed the production until the autumn and as the money was now mostly American it was John Gaines who received the next approach in August 1977, for a start date on or about 19 September. As Benny Fisz was not yet in a position to give Shaw a commitment on *Philby* and despite the script of *Force Ten* being extremely weak, Shaw accepted the $750,000 on offer, $50,000 of which would be paid for screen writing services as a gesture to the Irish Revenue. At first it was thought that the picture would involve two weeks work in England but later this became five weeks so $125,000 had to be allotted for this on which English tax would be paid. Billing was straightforward with Robert Shaw in the first position above the title. None of the other stars, Barbara Bach, Edward Fox, Franco Nero and Harrison Ford (as yet not subject to the *Star Wars* Effect or the *Indiana Jones* Effect) had grounds for argument. The film was to be directed by Guy Hamilton.

The payment for screen writing was in theory anything but fictitious. Without the skill of Carl Foreman, who had died the previous year, to give the screenplay a shape, it was a hopeless mess. The mission that the commando team are collected together to undertake evaporates 30 minutes into the film and the rest of the time the commandos racket around looking for something to do. Since it is also made clear that the war is almost won anyway the tremendous urgency and drive attached to the mission in *The Guns of Navarone* is entirely dissipated in *Force Ten*, and no one really seems to care what they do.

Shaw sent the script to various friends and collected suggestions. He wrote to the producers with the best of these but the major problems of the script were never solved and Shaw made no further attempt to earn his fee in this respect. It was yet another 'piece of shit'.

Before setting off for Yugoslavia, where the bulk of filming was to be done, Shaw ordered a white Range Rover with power steering, the absence of which on the old model was giving everyone who drove it well-developed arm muscles. His mother had been commissioned, after a five-day visit to Drimbawn in the summer, to buy some antiques for the house and went about the chore with a passion. Wing-chairs, dining room chairs and turn-leg tables were found and purchased with more to come. In addition it had occurred to Shaw that perhaps Jay should have a car of her own. Nothing extravagant of course. A Renault Estate car was practical and would be good for transporting the children but he finally settled on a new small Volvo. The car was duly ordered and arrived in London in time for the English filming on *Force Ten*. Jay was delighted. She was less delighted when two months later Shaw was promising the use of the car to Rachel while she was in England.

On 24 September, Jay, Thomas and Shaw flew to Venice and were then driven to Opatija. It was ten months since Shaw had last worked. In Opatija, part of Yugoslavia that had once belonged to Italy, a magnificent villa had been rented for the Shaws, overlooking a spectacular and rocky bay. The villa had been built for a famous Italian diva of the 1890s and most of the interior construction including a tiny minstrel's gallery, was in the finest marble. Shaw very quickly settled down into a routine of work. His Yugoslavian driver would pick him up and drive him to work. Shaw would tip him $50 and he would hand over a brown paper bag containing a bottle of Polish vodka. On the way to location Shaw would consume most of the bottle. If there was time he would get his driver to stop at a village bar en route where Shaw would down further vodkas before arriving at location where the faithful Ned Lynch would try and get him in condition to face the cameras. On his way home he would finish the rest of the bottle in the brown paper bag, tip the driver another $50 or $100 because he couldn't remember whether he'd done it already (and if asked the driver would shake his head) and then fall asleep in the back of the car, only to spend the night once home, roaming the house trying to avoid the demons that waited for him in his nightmares.

It is perhaps a tribute to his remarkable constitution that his body was able to absorb this kind of treatment day after day, and appear relatively upright and coherent for the camera. Alastair MacLean's constitution was clearly not so robust. On his visit to the location, though he was perfectly able to talk at length while drinking and smoking with equal rapidity, he had to be carried everywhere he went. He was simply too drunk ever to stand, let alone walk.

In November it was proposed that the unit take a break in Venice before moving to a new location. Jay hoped this might be an opportunity to sober Shaw up. It was not to be. When the news came through that the insurers had agreed to the break – there had been a spate of kidnapping in Italy and it was necessary to get permission from the completion guarantors in case they felt it was too risky – a suite was booked at the Gritti Palace for the weekend.

As it happened John French had come over for the weekend so the Shaws prepared to drive to Venice in his hired Mercedes. When Jay had been unable to fit his suit and a pair of slacks and a jacket into the already packed suitcase – the Shaws, as we have seen, never travelled light – to the great amusement of son Ian, Shaw decided he would wear all his clothes at the same time. He was already wearing a pair of slacks and a golfing sweater when he climbed into his Huntsmen suit and then, over that put on the other pair of slacks and another jacket. Looking now like the Pirelli man he climbed into the Mercedes.

Already drunk before the car journey began, and with the extra clothes hampering his movement, Shaw nearly managed to plunge into the Grand Canal on arrival in Venice before lurching abroad the vaporetto. At the Gritti Palace, as there was some delay over the rooms, Shaw staggered into the bar to tell all and sundry that he was going to get Jay pregnant again whether she liked it or not – and that he already had nine children and Richard Burton might get one million dollars a picture but he'd never done *that*. As he had been unable to do up the zip on the last pair of trousers, his overall appearance was far from debonnaire. Upstairs in the suite he pulled off his many layers of clothing, pulled on his pyjamas and asked Jay to sleep with the children. He wanted to be undisturbed. He ordered steak tartare from room service then took two sleeping-pills.

In the morning Jay discovered he was awake but still in his pyjamas. The minibar in the room had been raided and he had consumed its entire contents with the exception of the half-bottle of champagne – which he hated because he said it gave him heartburn – and a bottle of Coca Cola. Miniature bottles (a double measure) of gin, whisky, brandy, vodka, Campari, Dubonnet, sweet Martini, dry Martini, Chartreuse and sherry littered the room. The steak tartare had become embroiled in the sheets at the bottom of the bed. 'Looks like I've had a menstruating tart up here,' he said picking the bits of meat from the sheets.

With much effort he was dressed and reservations made at La Colomba, a fish restaurant around the corner. Arriving at the restaurant Shaw appeared suddenly lucid and normal. He ordered four double scotches and a stick of celery. No one knew the Italian for celery so a variety of vegetables were brought until the right one was found. Shaw drank the scotches, ordered four more – 'if you order four at a time you don't have to wait between drinks you see, boy. Very logical' – and ate the entire head of celery from root to leaf. Then he rested his head on the table and slept.

Back in the hotel, while Jay took the children out and tried to persuade the hotel management not to refill the minibar, Shaw sat with John French in the suite. Shaw had drawn all the curtains in the corner suite and the room was dismal and dark. For a while he was lucid as he lay flat out on the bed having changed again into pyjamas. French had asked him why he was drinking so much. 'Because I need it. I need it. I shouldn't be doing this shit.' It was not long before he was in tears. He was wasting his life, he was 'doing this shit' when he should be writing. He had so much to write but he had to work to survive and he couldn't work like this and write. He had so many children to support. But really he wanted to write. Then, with tears streaming down his face he started to talk of his father. Finally he said 'I just wish he hadn't left me alone.' Shaw was 50 years old.

When, in the morning, his agent had suggested to him that he had enough money already to live comfortable and do no more 'pieces of shit', the idea was greeted with great excitement as though it had never occurred to him and over lunch in the hotel he told the assembled masses, including the producer of the film John Sloane and Barbara Bach that this was to be his last picture, and that they were lucky because they could use his retirement in their publicity. But by 4.00 p.m. he was talking of 'one big one, just one more big one' and by the time it came to leave the next morning the idea was forgotten. On Shaw's agenda, the next objective was the $1 million film. He might hate himself for wanting it but that was what he wanted. He would never retire to write. The pattern was set. There was only one means of escape.

The drinking was much worse than it had ever been, whatever the cause. In December he came to England for the studio work at Shepperton. Ted Talmadge met him off the plane. Shaw was so drunk he could not speak and was having trouble standing. He was wheeled to the car on a luggage trolley. Now that his non-residence had been firmly established it was felt he could rent a house and one had been found near Shepperton appropriately called Black Lake Farm. The family were installed for Christmas. But Shaw wanted nothing to do with Christmas. It was almost impossible to shoot on him and day after day was lost. In addition it was decided to change the end of the film – which would make the whole endeavour no less coherent – and deals were done for Shaw's engagement to be extended due to his 'illness'.

On Christmas Day Shaw did not emerge from his room. On Boxing Day he fell through the 'glass' door between his bedroom – he was sleeping on the ground floor for safety reasons and the fact he couldn't climb the stairs – and the living room. The 'glass' turned out to be Persplex but he was cut and bruised nevertheless.

Shaw returned to Drimbawn on 25 January 1978. Benny Fisz had confirmed that he had all the money in place for *Philby* which would start in the first week of March with Mike Hodges directing. Shaw had heard through a journalist on the *Daily Express* that Philby had approved of the casting of the 'socialist' Shaw. Shaw elaborated on this by telling another journalist that he had spoken to Philby in Moscow on the phone, that Philby had not only advised him how to play the role but had invited him to Moscow on a visit. None of this, of course, was true.

But when at the end of January John Gaines received an offer of $750,000 for Shaw to star in *Avalanche Express* with Lee Marvin, Gaines saw his opportunity to finally wipe out these European dalliances and, killing two birds with one stone, to remove John French as his agent. Gaines wanted to sole charge on his new international star. By suggesting to Shaw that Fisz would not be able to come up with the money for *Philby*, despite the fact that contracts had been issued, that French was a fool to believe that he would and that it was far more important for Shaw to be in American films, where the real money was, he gradually got Shaw to renege on his agreement with Fisz and accept *Avalanche Express.*

There was no question that Shaw felt *Avalanche Express* was another 'piece of shit' and that Philby was an interesting role in an extremely well-written script. The money differential was hardly substantial especially considering his 'writing' fee of $500,000 could go to Ireland and be spent with no tax consequences, money he needed to continue the work on Drimbawn. Fisz provided him with every possible financial guarantee to counter Gaines's dire warnings, and Shaw knew perfectly well he had the money. His decision to take *Avalanche Express* was therefore surprising. It was easily explained, however. John Gaines and Hollywood were now in the driving seat of his life. The road to the $1 million picture was in Los Angeles not London.

Fisz threatened to sue. Shaw's withdrawal meant the end of his financing. Shaw knew perfectly well that Fisz would not sue. Reneging on his deal with Fisz, Shaw justified to himself and friends by memories of how little Fisz had paid him for *A Town Called*

Bastard, and how he'd never got his deferment. Since the deferment was from profits and there had never been any profits the latter was only to be expected. But the decision was made and it was necessary for Shaw to justify behaving badly to someone who had always been fair to him and had supported him in films since 1962.

Firing John French was also done at John Gaines' behest and for the same reason he had abandoned *Philby*. What Gaines wanted Gaines got. It was also a decision to turn his back on Europe. John Gaines in American could deliver the fabled $1 million film, John French in Europe could not. If Gaines was no longer prepared to tolerate John French, as he had been no longer prepared to tolerate Milton Goldman two years earlier, he would have to go. At one point Shaw had encouraged, and enjoyed the conflict between the two men. But now he was too tired to cope with Gaines's continual harrassment on the subject, and French had to go. He could not bare to call him personally however. A letter was despatched from Marvin Freedman the US accountant.

Shaw's relationship with Gaines was exactly the same relationship he had had with Phil Yordan in the '60s. He respected neither man intellectually and indeed was not keen to be seen in public with Gaines – he didn't want to take him to the meeting with Sam Peckinpah for instance. Gaines's literary education, as he freely admitted, was nil. But, as with Yordan, none of this counted. Both men had treated him like a star. Gaines had fêted and flattered him when he got to Hollywood, Yordan had paid him huge salaries. Both men had *delivered*. That, above everything else, was what mattered, and what counted. The fact that he understood and appreciated that things were rarely that simple was a part of his intelligence he kept well compartmentalised.

In March 1978 it looked as though the English tax case would at last be settled though at the higher end of estimates. The British Revenue was not taking a sympathetic attitude to Shaw's case. Henry King now reckoned that the case would not be settled for less than £120,000. In 1977 he had instructed Counsel to look at the possibility of suing Goddard's for negligence in their handling of Shaw's tax affairs and had been given an opinion that Shaw had good grounds for such a case but that it was now too late to sue since the Statute of Limitations prevents cases being brought after six years of any tort. Shaw was faced with paying the money, or, as he now had no assets in England, not paying and never setting foot in England again. As usual his reaction was aggressive, but in the end he would not want to cut himself off from England entirely.

The two months since arriving back at Drimbawn had seen Shaw once again gain a slim hold on his ability not to drink. The new Range Rover had arrived and Shaw drove it over the estate a couple of times. But strangely it did not revive his enthusiasm for buying expensive cars. Now that he could actually buy almost any car at any price his interest in doing so seemed to have disappeared, as had his interest in writing. At the end of 1977 Shaw had hired, at long last, a secretary to replace Jay. There were many unanswered letters to catch up on but transcripts from the red spiral exercise books were few and far between. *The Ice Floe* was firmly blocked.

Mark Robson, the director of *Avalanche Express*, at 65, had directed some notable movies *(Inn of the Sixth Happiness, Peyton Place, Valley of the Dolls)* and in fact had considered Shaw when he was first in Hollywood in 1971 for *Happy Birthday Wanda June*. Robson was, like Guy Hamilton, a jobbing director, concerned only to shoot the script on time and budget. Worries about content were not for him. Which was probably just as well. *Avalanche Express* was a script born in the ravages of the Cold War and had little cinematic surprise or genuine psychological motivation though the whole film relied on character to make its dénouement credible: equally the preposterous idea that a defecting Russian officer would actually get on a train to flee the KGB strained credibility from the start.

Shaw viewed the prospect of working with Lee Marvin, one of the legendary Hollywood drinkers, with alarm. Perhaps it was his competitive instincts again, fearing he would get into a drinking match with Marvin that he would not be able to win. He needn't have worried. Marvin was not interested in being sociable. He had brought along a retinue of his own, including a bodyguard, and had no interest in Shaw. Maximilian Schell, who had also been cast in the film, for obvious reasons, was not going to be disturbing the plans Shaw had made to try to keep himself out of trouble during the film. But after an initial bout of control the drinking returned, though not as badly as on *Force Ten*. His contempt for the script was marked and he made no secret of it.

While in Munich Shaw completed the looping on *Force Ten from Navarone*. Ten days before the end of filming Shaw got a call in his hotel room. Mark Robson had been taken to hospital and tomorrow's shooting was postponed. It was not a surprise. From the start of shooting it had been clear that Robson was a sick man. As the filming progressed his ability to stay on set was becoming less and less and Monte Hellman, a director who had learnt his trade largely on the American equivalent to 'B' movies (in America called 'cheapies'), had been brought in as a precaution. On 6 June Robson was dead.

Back at Drimbawn by the beginning of July Shaw's mood

improved again. Peter Barkworth had said he thought Shaw was a 'country boy' and there was no doubt the countryside and rural peace had a calming effect. He had a new competitive experience to deal with: a prospective son-in-law. Evzen Kolar, an assistant director, who had worked on *Avalanche Express*, was brought to Drimbawn by Debbie for a ritual initiation into manhood rights. Shaw beat him at tennis and boule but suddenly lost interest in proving that he could 'best' a 25-year younger man.

Shaw was out of work again. The flood of offers that had followed the *Jaws* Effect had ebbed to a dribble and speculative projects from Europe were of no interest to John Gaines who wanted only deals that were 'pay or play'. Costa Gavros wanted to talk to Shaw about a European movie with Dominique Sandor and Columbia, the studio that had employed Shaw consistently since *A Man for All Seasons* in 1966, making eight films with him in all, had a movie in development, Gaines was told, that had a part for Shaw.

Neither *Force Ten from Navarone* or *Avalanche Express* would have any commercial success, and their critical reception was appalling. In truth they were scripts that should never have been made, examples of the inability of Hollywood to actually know what it is doing. It was the scatter-gun approach. If you shot enough pellets one will bring the bird down. There was no apparent script control, no analysis of what an audience might want, and, ultimately no real appreciation of what a good film was. The six films Shaw had made since *Jaws* were all failures, if not disasters.

His tax planning had been a success, however. Since and including *Jaws* Shaw had earnt $3.6 million dollars. If the English tax case were settled at £120,000, as looked likely, on his entire income since 1965 he would have paid little more than 15% in tax, mostly on the pictures he had made in England which were the lowest fees in any event. Had the tax planning in 1965 not been so awry this would have been reduced to 10%.

On 28 August 1978, a Bank Holiday in England but not in Ireland, Shaw was with Jay driving the new white Range Rover on a road between Tourmakeady and Westport. Shaw suddenly winced with pain and clutched his chest. It was clear from his face that this was not one of his bouts of hypochondria. Jay immediately stopped the car and Shaw got out. He stood resting against the bonnet for a moment and then cried out in pain and fell into the low hedging at the edge of the road. Jay ran round to his side. 'What's happening to me?' he said trying to struggle to his feet but only falling back further into the hedge. 'I'm frightened,' he said.

There were few passing cars. Trying to stay at her husband's side

Jay managed to flag down two men in a car who promised to get to a phone and call an ambulance – the nearest house was at least a mile away and not all houses had phones. Jay was not at all sure that the two men would do as they had promised and flagged down another car. It was 45 minutes before an ambulance arrived. The ambulancemen led Jay away as they got her husband on to a stretcher. He was already dead. He had turned 51 a few weeks earlier on 9th of August.

If Shaw had had a presentment of an early death it had come true. In fact it was a self-fulfilling prophecy. Shaw's main objective in life, it seemed, had been to re-create an image of his father. He had succeeded in re-creating his flamboyance, his philoprogenitiveness, his sportsmanship and now finally his suicide. Shaw had killed himself just as surely as his father had with poison. Shaw had used his poison, alcohol, to drink himself to death – a long-drawn-out chronic suicide.

What would have happened to Shaw's acting career can only be a matter of conjecture, but the fact that he had not followed up the success of *Jaws* did not mean his career was necessarily on a downward track. Sean Connery survived a period of equally uninspiring films and in terms of acting Shaw had a great deal more to offer. It is unlikely Connery would ever have been offered the chance to play *King Lear*. What would have happened in terms of his writing is another matter: would or could he have written his 'one lasting book?' At one point in his life acting and writing had gone very much hand-in-hand, particularly around the period of *The Sun Doctor* in 1961. More recently it had proved simply impossible for Shaw to write *and* act. In *Omnibus* he had speculated on leaving his writing for *ten* years and then retiring to write again. 'It will always be there.' He did not live to find out whether that was true.

Shaw wrote, in *The Sun Doctor*, the book most involved with his feelings for his father and his father's early death:

> On my hundredth birthday I would like my great-grandchildren to bring in a cake with a hundred candles on it and I'd blow them all out and sit alone in the darkness that evening able at last to see my life laid out understandably.

Doctor Halliday never got his wish. Neither did Robert Shaw.

Index

Index

271

Index

Index

Made in the USA
Monee, IL
01 November 2022

16910431R10162